George S Bradley

The Star Corps

George S Bradley

The Star Corps

ISBN/EAN: 9783337036874

Printed in Europe, USA, Canada, Australia, Japan

Cover: Foto ©ninafisch / pixelio.de

More available books at **www.hansebooks.com**

THE STAR CORPS:

NOTES OF AN ARMY CHAPLAIN,

DURING SHERMAN'S FAMOUS

"MARCH TO THE SEA."

REV. G. S. BRADLEY,
CHAPLAIN 22D WISCONSIN.

MILWAUKEE:
JERMAIN & BRIGHTMAN, BOOK & JOB PRINTERS, SENTINEL BUILDINGS.
1865.

TO THE

WIVES, WIDOWS, PARENTS, BROTHERS, SISTERS, CHILDREN AND

FRIENDS OF THE BRAVE BOYS WHO PATRIOTICALLY

LEFT THE ENDEARMENTS OF HOME AND LOVED ONES

FOR THE TENTED FIELD, THE WEARY MARCH,

THE FEARFUL CHARGE, THE BATTLE

ROAR, A SOLDIER'S GRAVE, THIS

VOLUME IS RESPECTFULLY

DEDICATED, BY

The Author.

PREFACE.

In presenting this volume to the public, we expect the *critics* will find plenty of fault, but we would say at once that we have not written anything for them. We lay no claim to literary merit, but wish simply to present a plain, unvarnished story of our "tramp" through Georgia and the Carolinas.

We propose to use "our journal and published letters," freely, and shall copy them for the most part as they first appeared in the public newspapers of the time.

Much of the matter in the following pages was written by the roadside while on the march, or amid the noise and bustle of camp. Frequently while writing, we listened to the booming of cannon and rattle of musketry, and again we wrote amid the dead and dying in hospital, or on the battlefield.

We write for the friends at home, who have watched "Sherman's March to the Sea" with such intense interest, and we trust they will find something of interest here.

Our purpose is to present a history of "Coburn's Brigade"—the 2d Brigade, 3d Division, 20th A. C.

Perhaps many will look over these pages and lay down the book with disappointment, owing to the fact, that some things of interest are omitted, or touched upon with a passing remark, while others of comparatively no importance stand out prominently.

If the 22d Wisconsin appears more frequently than any other of the Brigade, it is owing to the fact that we know more of that—being with it—than of any other one,—and not that it contains better men, braver commanders, or has performed harder work, or made longer marches.

While we rejoice that so many of your loved ones have been permitted to return home, we remember that many, very many, sleep far away in the Southland.

> " And perhaps it is well, for some one must fall
>   For this bleeding country's sake,
> And our old flag be saved though our brave boys die,
>   And mothers' hearts should break.
> Our starry flag waves in triumph to-day,
>   For the victory at last is won,
> Though many bright homes are filled with grief
>   For a noble fallen son.
>
> " And the cries of the stricken-hearted
>   Are still borne on the balmy air;
> For scarcely a home in our sorrowing land
>   That has not a vacant chair.
> But, thank God ! no more weeping Rachels
>   Shall mourn for a brave fallen son;
> But, O God ! help those who are mourning
>   To say, ' Thy will be done !'

"There are homes to-day bright and happy,
  And mothers' hearts filled with joy,
As they wait on their own pleasant thresholds
  To welcome their long absent boy.
O, there'll be many a happy fireside,
  When the gallant boys come home,
But ours will still be desolate,
  For MY BOY will never come."

G. S. BRADLEY.

Racine, Wis., July 3d, 1865.

INTRODUCTORY.

In order to have a clear conception of things at the time the 2d Brigade entered the field, it will be necessary to review matters somewhat.

On the 25th of May, 1862, Gen. Banks' forces retreated from Winchester to Martinsburg, Va., fighting all the way.

On the 31st, occurred the battle of Fair Oaks, in which the Union forces were driven back with great loss.

The next day our side gained some advantage.

June 9th, occurred the battle of Port Republic, Va., between Shields and Jackson's forces, where after a severe fight, the federals were forced to retire, with the loss of two guns, and a large number of killed and wounded.

On the 14th, there was very heavy fighting on James' Island, S. C., about five miles from Charleston, in which the Union forces were repulsed with heavy loss.

On the 26th, the battle of Mechanicsville, Va., was fought. The rebels, 60,000, under Jackson, succeeded in getting to the rear of McClellan's right wing, and the Union forces were compelled to fall back.

The battle was renewed the next day—the fighting terrible—the union forces falling back to Gaines' Mill.

During the night our right wing fell back across the Chickahominy.

On the 28th, eighteen loyal states petitioned the President to call out additional troops to suppress the rebellion, for everything was at this time looking very bad.

On this day, also the 29th and 30th, there was hard fighting, our forces in the meantime having fallen back to James River.

On the 12th of July, the battle of Malvern Hill took place, the last of the seven day's fighting before Richmond. After very severe fighting, the rebels were repulsed, but our loss was severe; McClellan was in no condition to follow up any advantage secured. His great Peninsular Campaign had proved a failure.

About this time, Gen. Pope was assigned to the command of the Army of Virginia.

On the same day that the rear of McClellan's army crossed the Chickahominy, Pope's retreat commenced, and the rebels pressed him back towards Washington in the most hurried manner.

On the 26th, a large rebel force had appeared almost within cannon shot of Washington.

On the 30th, Pope, after severe fighting on the old battle ground of Bull Run, was compelled, with heavy loss, to fall back to Centerville.

On the same day also, occurred the battle of Richmond, Ky., in which the Federal forces under Gen. Nelson were overpowered and forced to retreat—the rebel forces numbering 15,000, under Gen. Kirby Smith. Our forces had to fall back to Lexington.

On the first of September, the Legislature of Kentucky, from fear of rebel raids, adjourned from Frankfort to Louisville.

Kirby Smith was now supposed to be advancing upon Cincinnati, and there was a terrible excitement all along the border. About this time, a large portion of the rebel army crossed into Maryland, and things were certainly looking very gloomy. Perhaps at no period of the war had affairs seemed more discouraging.

Meetings were held all over the North, and men were called upon to enlist. It was felt that the critical moment had arrived when every one who could go *must* go.

Under this state of affairs, the Second Brigade entered the field; with the exception of the 33d Indiana, that had already seen hard service near Cumberland Gap.

Without speaking further of matters in general, let us trace the history of the several regiments separately, till we find them in Lookout Valley, preparatory to entering on the Atlanta Campaign.

For the history of the 33d Indiana, I am indebted to Joseph R. Shelton, and that of the 85th, to Lt. Col. J. E. Brant.

Capt. Henry A. Ford furnished me with a part of that of the 19th Michigan.

THE STAR CORPS.

THE THIRTY-THIRD INDIANA.

The 33d Indiana was organized at Indianapolis, Ind., Sept. 16th, 1861, by Col. John Coburn. Left Indianapolis on the the 29th of September. Passed over the Jeffersonville R. R. to Louisville, Ky., the same day, and arrived there at night.

Next day (30th) the regiment lay in the city, and on the 1st of October took the cars for Lexington, Ky., arriving there in the evening—staid there all night, and next morning started for Nicholassville, where the regiment staid that night.

On the 3d, marched 17 miles to Camp Dick Robinson. Lay ten days at this place. An incident occurred here which may be related: Our regiment was encircled by a strong guard line, some 10 men on a relief—and on the 6th, the guards were satisfied that the enemy were aiming to get into our camp and poison our stock. The guards were ordered to load their guns and be very vigilant. At a late hour of the night, two of the guards heard a noise which they imagined might come from some one trying to enter the guard line. They whispered together as they met at the end of their beat, and determined if they heard any more noise to fire. In a few minutes the noise was heard again, and the crack of the sentinel's musket was heard, arousing the whole camp, when lo! it was nothing but a *loose horse* that had caused all the excitement.

On the 13th, the regiment marched for Dick's River, where we went into camp at Crab Orchard. Next day at noon, went into camp 3 miles south-east of this place.— Called the place Camp Coburn. Lay here 3 days, then marched to Wild Cat—distant 25 miles—to meet the invading army of Zollicoffer. Arrived there on the 20th and found only one regiment, Col. Garrard's 3d Ky., waiting to dispute the progress of Zollicoffer. The next morning, we were roused by the "long roll," and in a few minutes all were ready for the coming battle, which commenced at 8 o'clock. Four companies of the regiment were marched hastily to the top of Hosier Hill, and four were sent on the right to guard a pass on Rock Castle River hill. We were soon engaged in a desperate struggle with the enemy, which resulted in driving the invader. We lost in this engagement 2 killed and 11 wounded.

Marched to London in pursuit of the flying rebels. Lay at this place till the 13th of October, when we marched to Crab Orchard in order to meet the enemy at Mill Springs.

Went into camp at Crab Orchard on the 17th. Here began a scene of suffering which cannot be described.— Many times there were scarcely enough men in health to get wood for the camp, and nearly every house in the town was used as a hospital. All that the citizens could do for us was done, but 45 men died in a few weeks, and altogether we here lost some 70 men from sickness.

On the 7th of January, the 33d left their encampment for the city of Lexington, where they arrived on the 10th. Went into camp 3 miles north of the City. Here the regiment enjoyed good health and quiet for the rest of the winter. At Lexington, the regiment enjoyed the full confidence of the citizens, and they would here record their gratitude to them, and especially for their uniform kindness. The Ladies' Soldiers' Aid Society deserves especial mention, as it was the means of restoring many of our brave men to health.

On the 11th of April, we left Lexington for Cumberland Ford by way of Crab Orchard. After 13 days march, we went into camp at the Ford with the army of Gen. George W. Morgan.

After lying at the Ford for over a month, we marched for the Gap by way of Roger's Gap. After marching and counter-marching several times in the mountains, we proceeded up the Valley to the Gap, which was evacuated the day before, (June 18, 1862). Six guns were captured, together with some other valuables.

We lay here in a quiet manner for a few weeks, and then participated in the fight at Tazewell.

The regiment with the balance of the command was soon cut off by Bragg's invading Kentucky. We lived very poorly till the evacuation of the Gap, which took place Sept. 18th. After we were surrounded, we were immediately put on half rations, which were afterwards reduced to one-fourth rations, and the only chance then to live was by trading with the citizens, who came as near the Gap as our pickets would allow.

We skirmished with the enemy every day, and sent out foraging parties, which sometimes foraged in the same field with the rebels—we on one side and they on the other.

When the Gap was evacuated, our regiment marched out in advance of the column.

On the 20th, we encamped at Goose Creek Saltworks, near Manchester.

On the 22d, the regiment and the whole army moved north through the hills towards Boonville. Passed this place and Proctor the same day, and lay on the rocks of the river bed at night close to the town. Water was quite an object, and some days there was none to be had. The regiment rested one day at West Liberty, where Marshall had just left. Here we had plenty of water and all enjoyed it very much.

On the 29th, occurred the skirmish of Crocker's Neck, in which, the rebels were driven away in confusion.

After 17 days of severe suffering for want of water and supplies, as well as from hard marching, we arrived at ———, Ky., (Oct. 3d), and were pleased with a place to rest. Here we crossed the Ohio River—some wading the stream, while others went over in boats. We moved down the river on the Ohio side to Sciotaville. As we passed the town of Wheelersburg, we were met with an excellent dinner by the citizens of the place, for which we were very grateful.

From Sciotaville, we took the train for Portland, and from this place we marched to Oak Hill—distant 3 miles.

Lay here till the 14th, when we took the train for Cincinnati.

On the 15th, we passed through the city and went into camp at Covington, Ky.

During our first campaign, including the marching and fighting to London, and back to Mill Springs, we were under the command of Brig. Gen. Scheopff.

The second campaign from Lexington to the Ford, Gap, and the retreat, we were under the command of Col. Coburn and Brig. Gen. Baird, as Brigade Commanders.

At Covington we got an outfit and prepared for another campaign.

At this place we were put into a brigade of new troops, the 14th and 19th Ky. being separated from us and put into other brigades. Col. Coburn took command of the brigade, now composed of the 33d Ind., 85th Ind., 19th Mich. and 22d Wis.

Left Covington on the 26th of October, and arrived at Georgetown Nov. 1st.

On the 12th marched to Nicholassville, where we arrived on the 15th and went into camp. Lay here till Dec. —, when we marched for Danville, where we arrived on the 12th, went into camp and remained a short time.

Here we commenced, as a brigade, to run after John Morgan, which was our regular business for the winter.

Left Danville on the 26th of January, and arrived at Lonisville on the 30th. Left Louisville, on transports, on the 2d of Feb. for Nashville, where we arrived Feb. 9th. Lay in camp at this place till Feb 21st. Then marched to Brentwood, distant 12 miles. Lay at this place till the 2d of March, when we went to Franklin. On the 4th we were ordered out to Spring Hill, where the desperate battle of Thompson's Station occurred.

On the 4th we met the rebels, and after fighting for a

short time they fell back. We pressed them for a short distance and then went into camp for the night. The Col. commanding found that the rebels were too strong for us, and so reported, but his orders were *positive* and he must obey.

The following is a copy:

"SPECIAL ORDER, }
No. 15.   }   (Extract)

VI.... Col. Coburn, with his Brigade and Battery, with 600 Cavalry, will, to-morrow, at 8 o'clock, proceed along the Columbia Pike as far as Spring Hill, and send out a party from there on toward Columbia, and on through to Raleigh Springs on the Lewisburg Pike, where a cavalry force from Murfreesboro will communicate with it on the ensuing day.

VII.... Col. Campbell will be furnished from the three regiments. Col. Payne of the 124th Ohio Vols. will report to Col. Coburn to accompany this command.

Four (4) days rations will be taken; 2 in the haversack and 2 in the wagons. A forage train of 80 wagons will accompany the expedition. Only 4 wagons to the regiment and 2 to the battery will be allowed.

By order of
BRIG. GEN. C. C. GILBERT.
GEORGE R. SPEED, Lt. and A. A. A. G."

Col. Coburn moved out at the time appointed in the above order, and proceeded about four miles, when we met and dispersed the rebels, they losing 11 men killed, while we had only one wounded.

On the morning of the 5th at 7 o'clock, the brigade moved out, and at 8 the skirmishing began. At 9 we were in line of battle and offered the enemy fight. We did not wait long but sent out a skirmish line to the R. R., and soon found plenty of the enemy.

We fell back to the hill we first occupied as a main line, and soon the thunder of artillery and musketry told us that the whole line was engaged. The fight lasted for six (6) hours, and, being surrounded by four lines of battle it was easy to see our doom.

When the brigade surrendered, there was not an average of one round of ammunition to the man.

Our loss was quite heavy.

The regiment, after a hard day's fight, had to witness the humiliating sight of the old flag, they so much loved, trailed in the dust.

Our captors did not jeer us, but when told our number, they said they had lost more men than our whole number in the fight. We surrendered at 4 o'clock, and had fought nearly all day in hearing of a force which could have relieved us, if they had been sent forward.

After the surrender, we were marched to Columbia—a distance of 12 miles. A few of our wounded men were with us and suffered severely. We lay in the Court House at Columbia part of the night which was not spent in marching.

We were marched from Columbia to Shelbyville, and from there to Tullahoma, where we were put on board the cars for Richmond.

Our sufferings were great from the time of capture to the time of release, which with some was only 30, with others 60 days. The weather was very inclement, and we lay out of doors nearly all of the time, which caused a great many to be sick.

At Tullahoma our rubber blankets and overcoats were taken from us by order of Gen. Bragg.

All the way we were very much crowded in the cars. We were 7 days on the cars. We left Tullahoma on the 12th, passing through Stevenson, Bridgeport, Chattanooga, Knoxville, Bristol, and Lynchburg.

The 33d was released from Libby the 1st and 3d of of April, 1863. Arrived at Annapolis on the 2d and 5th. From there we were taken to Camp Chase, Ohio, thence to Indianapolis. After one month, the officers came up and the regiment was reorganized.

The regiment was received with great honors by the citizens of Indianapolis. The boys were all furloughed home for a few days, and on the 12th of June, the regiment started again to the field, and on the 18th rejoined the portion of the regiment that was not captured.

The regiment thus completely reorganized, we prepared to march.

June 23d, the regiment marched from Nashville to Murfreesboro, where we arrived on the 27th. Here we lay two days, then marched to Guy's Gap, where we remained till the 18th of July. Then we returned to Murfreesboro. During our stay at the Gap, we did very heavy picket duty. At Murfreesboro we went into regular camp with constant drilling. We lay here till the 6th of September, when we were deployed on the R. R. from Tullahoma to Dechard.

The several companies had frequent skirmishing with the enemy.

At Dechard, Capt. Burton was in command of the post.

On the 5th of November, the regiment was consolidated at Christiana, where we remained till Feb. 25th, 1864, when we marched to Nashville, having re-enlisted at Christiana as veterans. We were kept at Nashville on guard duty till the 25th of March, when we were furloughed home for 30 days.

After a pleasant visit among home friends, we once more started for the field of strife.

The regiment as rapidly as possible marched to Lookout Valley, crossing a spur of the famous Lookout Mountain, and then on towards Buzzard's Roost, where Sherman's mighty hosts were concentrating.

THE TWENTY-SECOND WISCONSIN.

The companies comprising the 22d Wisconsin, recruited almost entirely in the counties of Rock, Racine, Green and Walworth, were ordered into camp on the 25th of August, 1862. The organization was effected at Racine during the latter part of the month, and the regiment was mustered into service on the 2d of September.

But a short time was allowed them in camp. They left Racine on the 16th for Cincinnati, having been ordered to that place in anticipation of the threatening movements of the rebels under Kirby Smith.

On the 22d, they crossed the Ohio river on the pontoon bridge, and marching into Kentucky, encamped four miles south of Covington at "Camp Bloodgood."

Broke camp on the 7th of October, and marching on the Lexington pike, arrived at "Camp Smith" on the evening of the next day.

On the 13th, marched to "Camp Gilmore," where they remained three days camping on Eagle Creek.

On the 19th marched to Big Eagle Creek, and resuming march on the the 21st encamped at Georgetown.

On the 24th, they moved to Lexington, where they remained six days, marching to Sandersville on the 30th.

Nov. 13th, marched to Nicholassville, where they remained performing provost guard duty, until the 12th of December, when they started for Danville, arriving next day.

From Danville they moved in various directions through the surrounding country, to meet and foil the movements of the enemy—particularly Morgan.

At Danville and Nicholassville, the regiment suffered terribly from sickness. At times there were scarcely well ones enough to take care of the sick. The water was not fit to drink.

A few extracts may perhaps be interesting here:

"The new year has dawned again upon us. The gallant 22d are yet in existence, and are not gobbled up by Morgan as it has been reported, although they have been nearer John Morgan's forces than a great many of the boys dreamed of. Last Monday morning the 22d and 33d Indiana, were ordered to be on the Pike and ready to march, destination unknown. Just as we got outside the city, we found that we were to go to Lebanon to reinforce troops there and baffle John Morgan, as he was advancing on Lebanon. That day we marched 16 miles. Tuesday morning again on the road towards Lebanon. When we had reached within five miles of Lebanon we were ordered back to Danville, and we reached the old camping ground of Monday night, tired and wet. We have since learned that a force of rebels planted a battery a few miles from us along a group of hills, to rake us in the morning as we should go to Lebanon, but as fortune would have it, we were to go to Danville. The 33d Indiana is an old regiment and is the best in the Division, the largest and most powerful. They told us Wednesday morning that they intended to tire us out, but they failed. Faster and faster the 33d marched, but close upon their heels followed the 22d. After getting to Danville, they acknowledged that no regiment had kept so close to them as the 22d.

Sunday, the long coveted green-backs were distributed to the boys. They have stood long in need of them, and to-day each one smiles like a basket of chips. Sickness is on the decrease I think in the regiment.

*　　*　　*　　*　　*　　*　　*

Occasionally, yours,
GLENDOWER."

Under date of January 2d, 1863, Chaplain Pillsbury writes as follows:

"On arriving at Danville, I learned that death had been doing his work there as well as at Nicholsville. Hugh Stuart, who left the latter place well, so far as I knew, and of whose sickness I had learned nothing, had fallen and his remains were on their way to the grief smitten home. Thirty of the regiment have now fought their last battle.

But a small portion of the desolations of war are seen upon the battle-field. Were leading military men required to write letters of condolence to bereaved friends, instead of issuing orders to brigades and divisions, perhaps they would become more anxious to strike a settling blow. Put all the generals, on both sides, into the ranks and let them take the chances and fare as privates, and the war will be brought to a close in less than three months.

Sickness in the regiment, I am happy to say, is at the present time abating, both as regards the number sick and the severity of prevailing diseases.

Our regiment has recently 'marched up the hill and marched down again,' and repeated the march. By order of the commanding General, two brigades, then in this place, marched for Lebanon a distance of twenty-eight miles, on Friday morning of last week. It rained in torrents a large part of the day, and we camped for the night wet and cold, after marching fourteen miles. During the night orders came for us to return to Danville; and on Saturday we marched back to our old camping ground.

Early on Monday morning, agreeably to orders, the 22d Wis. and 33d Ind., marched again for Lebanon. When within five miles of that place, on the next day, orders came for us to return to Danville. So we returned to the camping ground left in the morning. During the night orders came for the regiments to hasten to Lebanon. But before getting under way, orders were countermanded, and we still again sought our camping grounds in Danville. The boys begin to think it a difficult thing to find the way to Lebanon, having marched seventy-two miles and finding themselves where they started. This is military life, and these are the incidents of war. It is simply our business to obey orders and ask no questions. It is now said that Morgan with 5,000 of his cavalry camped within three miles of the 22d Wis. and 33d Ind. on Tuesday night, and that we should have been attacked, had he not supposed that we had reinforcements at hand. As to the correctness of the report, it is difficult to determine—the country is full of rumors and much excitement prevails at times. That Morgan is somewhere in the vicinity of Lebanon there can be no doubt—some of his men have been captured and brought into this town. His presence also gives Kentucky guerrillas an excellent opportunity to pillage the country, claiming to be Morgan's men, and thus giving him and his banditti credit for much of which they are not guilty. That this game is practiced quite extensively is undoubtedly true."

On the 26th of January, 1863, the regiment left Danville for the last time, arriving at Louisville on the 30th. Here they went on board of transports for Nashville. The following letter will be read with interest:

"NASHVILLE, Tenn., Feb. 8, 1863.

The fleet of some forty steamers, containing the command of Gen. Baird, accompanied by five gunboats, anchored in the Cumberland river, against Nashville, last evening. It being too late to disembark and go into camp, all remained on board during the night. Our passage on the whole, a distance of some 600 miles from Louisville to Nashville, was pleasant; no serious accident occurring, except the loss of one man from the *Champion*, Jacob Wachter, of Company B, who fell overboard and was drowned.

It is now Sunday at home; but who can tell the day of the week here? All is commotion—men, horses, mules, carriages, guns, hard bread, bacon, corn, hay, and thousands of unnamed articles, moving hurriedly and in apparent confusion. The quiet church is forgotten, and all are rushing forward to some field of strife. We embarked on the Sabbath, and now we disembark on the Sabbath. War, perhaps consistent with itself, knows no Sabbath, and in the army he does well, who does not forget when that quiet day returns to smile upon his distant, peaceful home.

On leaving Louisville, the fleet was ordered to rendezvous at Fort Donelson. Above that point, it was considered unsafe for steamers to pass unless protected by gunboats, several having been fired on but a few days before, and a large body of rebel cavalry being reported on their way to take possession of the river. We arrived at the place of rendezvous on the evening of the third day from Louisville, which proved to be really a small place called Dover, about one mile above Fort Donelson. Here we anchored and remained till the second morning, waiting for portions of the fleet which had fallen behind to come up.

The day before we arrived, the 83d Ill. Infantry, quartered at Dover, for the holding of Fort Donelson, were attacked by some 4,000 of Morgan's cavalry, under the command of the noted Forrest. The object of the movement was evidently to get possession of the fort, and beat back or destroy the fleet. The rebels anticipated easy work, and came in almost rejoicing over their victory. The 83d numbered on the morning of the attack, 580 men fit for duty. Besides their rifles, they had one heavy gun and six light pieces of artillery.

The Colonel commanding the 83d—I regret that I cannot give his name—saw that to bring out his men in line of battle to meet such an overwhelming force, must result in the destruction of his regiment. Dividing them into squads, under commanders down to corporals, he sent them out to fight in their own way, choosing their own positions. As the enemy came charging up the ravine, a deadly fire was poured into them from different points, and men and horses fell into confusion. Three times, and from three different directions, the rebel hordes charged upon them and were nobly repulsed. At the time we left, 210 of the enemy's dead had been buried, and others were still supposed to be undiscovered. Many of their wounded have been brought in, and the dwellings of citizens for several miles are said to be filled with them. The most daring recklessness in some instances characterized the movement of the rebels. In one case, a Colonel rode up hastily within twelve feet of the mouth of the large gun and demanded its surrender. And a noble horse, whose rider had been shot, kept in his position and accompanied the Colonel in his dashing movement. A soldier standing behind the gun replied, 'I think we'll fire once more first," applied the match, and the two horses and the dashing Colonel lay in one heap of death. Our loss was ten killed and twenty wounded, two of the latter dying on the following day.

After retreating to the timber, the rebels were forming for another attack in the night, and they probably would have succeeded in taking the little band of brave boys, had not a few shells from gunboats, whose timely arrival seemed providential, caused them to seek safety in the distance. The 13th Wis. regiment, commanded by Col. Lyon, stationed at Fort Henry, 12 miles distant, came over, but too late to render any assistance. Several of the dead were unburied when we arrived, and the wounded were to be found in almost every house. It was my first visit to any thing like a battle-field retaining fresh marks of the struggle. Dead horses lay scattered over the entire ground, and blood, still fresh, crimsoning spots of snow which fell during the night, told where the unfortunate soldiers lay down to die. The funeral dirge echoing along the hills, and over the waters, announced the business of armies the day succeeding a battle. The loyal soldier, pale from the loss of blood sprinkled upon the altar of his country, and the unconscious rebel with a minnie ball resting in his brain, and blood running down his cheeks, lay almost side by side. Just there lies the brave but deluded child of the South, maimed for life, and near by the loyal son of the North, whose mangled limbs demand the surgeon's knife. Not far distant, the brave captain, who yesterday led forth his noble band to hurl back his country's foe or die in the attempt, with unyielding fortitude almost forgets that the flesh was torn from his bones while traveling the road to victory. A slight waving of the hand beckons me to a pale face upon the opposite side of the room. Putting my ear close to his lips, he whispered: 'My brother and I stood side by side yesterday, and both fell at the same time. My brother died this morning, and I must soon follow him!' A rebel ball had passed entirely through his chest, and his clogged lungs told full well that his work was done. But I can still hear distinctly the broken whisper: 'My brother and I will soon meet where there is no war!' Noble sons of Illinois! over your graves shall float your country's honors, while rest is yours above the storm. But enough of such scenes as these; may they soon be numbered among the things that were.

Marks of the desolating hand of war were seen at almost every point as we ascended the river, but we saw no indications of the presence of armed rebels. We passed the wrecks of several boats which had been destroyed but a short time before.

Nashville has suffered severely. There are but few inhabitants remaining in the city. A very large majority of them have been driven back into the country for means of subsistence. I think there is but one public house open, and that would be considered unworthy of patronage in almost any other place I have seen. A breakfast which it required a resolute appetite to conquer, cost one dollar. The Capitol presents a fine appearance, and there are some noble residences, but on the whole the city is rather an insignificant affair. The streets are narrow, and now almost unendurably filthy. There is hardly any appearance of business except what is done through the Government.

The ruins of the once noble suspension bridge across the Cumberland remain, a monument of Southern recklessness. In it, their own Zollicoffer had invested $25,000, embracing all which he left two orphan daughters. After he had fallen in defense of their own cause, and contrary to the earnestly expressed wishes of the citizens, the rebel army applied the match, and stripped the orphan children of their own Zollicoffer of their last dollar.

This evening the regiment marched about three miles out of the city and pitched their tents for the night. We are anticipating a march to Murfreesboro in a few days.

Yours, truly,
C. D. PILLSBURY.

The regiment went into camp a few miles from the city on the Franklin Pike, remaining and performing the ordinary rounds of military duty, till Feb. 21st, when tents were struck, and the regiment marched to Brentwood Station, some ten miles South of Nashville. Remained here doing picket and R. R. guard duty till the 2d of March, when orders came to move on further towards Franklin, for the purpose of reinforcing Gen. Gilbert. Two days after, 263 men of the regiment, under command of Col. Utley, joined an expedition, consisting of four other regiments and a battery, the whole under command of Col. Coburn, of the 33d Indiana, which was ordered to proceed to Spring Hill, where a sanguinary engagement took place, resulting in the capture of almost the entire Brigade.

Col. Utley, at the commencement of the engagement, turned his command over to Lieut. Col. Bloodgood, who succeeded in saving a portion of the regiment, by falling back to Franklin.

In the battle of Spring Hill, the 22d lost 12 commissioned officers and 142 men, in killed, wounded and prisoners.

On the 8th, the forces under Col. Bloodgood were ordered to Brentwood. Here they were attacked on the 25th by a large force under Gen. Forrest. After a sharp skirmish, during which they lost three men wounded, they were completely overpowered by numbers, and compelled to surrender. All were sent to Richmond. Soon officers and men were exchanged and sent to St. Louis, where a reorganization was effected, and on the 12th of June the regiment was ordered to Nashville, where it arrived on the 15th. Here it remained a week, marching on the 22d to Franklin. On the 3d of July the regiment was ordered to Murfreesboro, where it remained till Feb. 24, 1864. During their stay at this place, their military duties being very light, the boys employed their time in making "shell-work," some of which was very fine.

Feb. 24th they were ordered back to Nashville, where they remained until the 19th of April, when they set out for Lookout Valley, making the journey in about 10 days.

THE NINETEENTH MICHIGAN.

This regiment was mustered into service Sept. 5th, '62, and left for the field Sept. 14th. Arrived at Cincinnati on the 16th. The rebel forces under Gens. Kirby Smith and Heath were falling back from the front of Covington.

We were assigned to guard duty at Gravel Hill Station, the Ohio being quite shallow here. We were to defend this point against the passage of Morgan and others.— Here John Morgan was said to have been in our camp one day, in the guise of an old man, peddling stationary. He was meditating an attack on our lines, and took this method to find out about matters. The attack was averted— as generally believed since—by change of camp next day to a more defensible position. Oct. 14th we were transferred to Covington, where, soon after, we were brigaded with the 33d and 85th Indiana, and 22d Wisconsin, in Gen. Gordon Granger's "Army of Kentucky."

On the 1st of January, 1863, we were stationed at Danville. The "Army of Kentucky" having been transferred to the "Department of the Cumberland," a "Reserve Corps," the 19th, moved with its brigade to Nashville, where it arrived Feb. 7th, proceeding thence to Franklin.

On the 4th of March, with 600 cavalry and 200 additional infantry, it took part with its Brigade in a reconoisance in force. After a march of four miles, skirmishing commenced with the enemy's scouts and advanced pickets, but the rebels retiring, the Brigade encamped, the 19th having lost in the skirmish one wounded.

The march having been resumed on the following day, the enemy were met in force at Thompson Station, 9 miles from Franklin. After an engagement of some six hours, their ammunition became exhausted, and the entire force surrendered to the enemy, excepting a few who succeeded in making their escape.

The rebel force proved to be an entire cavalry division, 18,000 strong, under Gen. Van Dorn. The 19th went into action with 512 officers and men, of which 113 were killed and wounded. Those of the regiment who had escaped, and those who had remained in camp at Franklin, were sent to Brentwood, organized with the remaining fragments of the Brigade, and placed under an officer belonging to another regiment. This force was shortly afterwards captured by Gen. Forrest and sent to Richmond.

The enlisted men of the regiment were soon paroled and sent North.

The commissioned officers were exchanged May 25th. The regiment was reorganized at Camp Chase, Ohio, and on the 8th of June left Columbus, arriving at Nashville in season to take part in the advance on Tullahoma. On the 23d day of July, the 19th was ordered to Murfreesboro, where we went upon garrison duty on the fortifications. Company D, numbering 50 men, having been stationed at a stockade on the Nashville and Chattanooga R. R. at Stone River, was attacked on the 5th of October by a large number of rebel cavalry and artillery, under General Wheeler, and after a short and hopeless resistance, having lost 6 wounded, the company surrendered, but after having been plundered all were released.

On the 25th of October, the regiment was ordered to McMinnville, where it remained till April 1864, when it once more joined its brigade to participate in the Atlanta campaign.

THE EIGHTY-FIFTH INDIANA.

The 85th Ind. Vol. Infantry was organized in Terre Haute, Ind, and mustered into the service September 2, 1862—and thence went to Indianapolis, Ind., September 3d—was there armed and partially equipped.

Thence was sent to Covington Heights, Ky., via Cincinnati, where in constant bivouac it did heavy guard, picket and fatigue duty, on the Licking River, and in the vicinity of Fort Mitchell and Latonia Springs. October 8th and 9th, marched to Falmouth, Ky., where it remained until Oct. 26th, building railroad bridges, doing provost and picket duty. Thence marched, via Cynthiana, to Paris—thence, October 28th, to Lexington Ky.—thence, Nov. 14th, Nicholasville. Here the regiment suffered very much from sickness, not being yet hardened to the severities of camp life. December 10th and 11th the regiment marched, via "Camp Dick Robinson," to Danville, Ky.

Made a reconnoisance on the Lebanon Pike with brigade and division, on the 26th and 27th of December, for the purpose of heading off John Morgan and his forces, then on a raid through the State. Returned to Danville on the 27th, where it remained until January 26th, 1863, furnishing heavy details for picket and guard duty, and detachments to protect the Kentucky and Dix River bridges. Thence marched to Louisville, via Harrodsburg and Shelbyville—distance 85 miles—arriving at Louisville on the 31st of January. Thence on steamboats, the Harrison and Fort Wayne, constituting a part of the fleet carrying General Granger's forces, moved via Ohio and Cumberland Rivers, to Nashville, Tenn., arriving on the 7th of February; thence marched to Brentwood; thence to Franklin, Tenn. On the 4th of March moved out with brigade on the Columbia Pike, and on the 5th of March was engaged in the battle of Thompson's Station, where after 6 hours fighting, and the loss in killed and wounded of about 60 men, the regiment with brigade was compelled to surrender to the rebel forces, commanded by Generals Van Dorn, Forrest and Wheeler.

In this engagement the regiment lost in killed, Captain Floyd of Co. "A", of whom it can be said truly, no nobler and braver man ever drew a sword.

Here also fell other good and noble men, such as Sergt. Shepherd, Corporals Lusk, Conaway and Liston.

In this disastrous battle the regiment changed front 7 times, and fought as bravely as men ever fought, but to no purpose. Surrounded and cut off from any hope of reenforcements, the surrender was inevitable, and as the flag was lowered and the men lay down their arms, many wept bitter tears of disappointment.

The terror of the march to Tullahoma, Tenn., under guard, and the ride from thence, via Chattanooga, Knoxville and Lynchburg, to Richmond, Va., and the horrors of Libby Prison, are, and ever will be vivid to the minds of those who shared in them.

The enlisted men were released on the 1st of April, and the officers on the 5th of May, after which they were sent to Indianapolis, Ind.; thence to Franklin, Tenn., arriving on the 13th of June 1863, where that part of the regiment not captured were stationed.

At Covington, Ky., the regiment was brigaded with the 33d Ind., 19th Mich., and 22d Wis., under command of Col. John Coburn, 33d Ind., afterwards known as "Coburn's Brigade." The history of the regiment from this time is a part of the history of the brigade, serving in it through the Battle of Thompson's Station, and in the imprisonment. Afterwards, in Middle Tennessee, the regiments were separated, the 58th Ind. being stationed for a while at Murfreesboro; thence moved to Wartrace, Tenn., where regimental headquarters were established, companies being stationed along the road from Christiana to Duck River bridge.

On the 5th of October the regiment was concentrated at Duck River bridge, excepting Company E, which was captured by Wheeler's force at Christiana, on the 5th day of October.

In the month of November the regiment moved to Fosterville, Tenn., where it remained until Feb. 28th, 1864; thence marched, via Murfreesboro, Tenn., back to Lavergne, Tenn., where it was re-equipped and prepared for the summer campaign. On the 20th of April started for Chattanooga, and on the way the regiments composing the brigade were re-united. Arrived in Lookout Valley on the 2d of May, and from that time forward through the "Atlanta Campaign," the regiment shared in every battle where the "tri color" of Col. Coburn's Brigade was seen waving. Entered Atlanta on the 2d of September.

From thence with brigade, on the 15th of Nov., 1864, started with "Sherman to the sea." Arrived at Savannah on the 21st of December.

On the 31st of December crossed the Savannah River with the brigade into South Carolina; thence to Purysburg and Robertsville, where with the army again it bid adieu to all lines of communication. Marched through South Carolina, and with the brigade was engaged in the battle of Averysboro, North Carolina, on the 16th of March, 1865. Arrived at Goldsboro on the 24th of March.

Thence on the 10th of April, started for Raleigh, N. C., where we arrived on the 14th of April.

From thence on the 29th, started for *Home* via Richmond and Washington.

Participated in the Grand Review of "Sherman's Army," on the 24th of May, at the Nation's Capital.

The regiment was mustered out of service on the 12th of June, 1865, and started for home on the day following, where it arrived in safety amid the congratulations of many anxious friends.

BATTLE OF SPRING HILL.

Col. Coburn's brigade, consisting of the 33d and 85th Indiana, the 19th Michigan, and the 22d Wisconsin, accompanied by the 124th Ohio, the 18th battery and 500 or 600 cavalry, marched out of Franklin on the 4th inst. on a reconnoitering and foraging expedition. The cavalry took the lead of the column, followed by the 33d Indiana, the battery, 124th Ohio, 19th Michigan, and the 22d Wisconsin in the order given. The 85th Indiana was guard to the train in the rear. On the 2d day, the 85th Indiana and 124th Ohio changed positions.

After proceeding some four miles, the cavalry being deployed as skirmishers to the right and left, the enemy were discovered with a battery planted upon a hill about one-half mile in advance, supported by infantry drawn up in line of battle, amounting, in all, perhaps to 1,000 men. About this time, the enemy announced his presence by a messenger which went whizzing over our column and lighting upon the ground, about 60 feet from our boys. This messenger was acknowledged by a general dodging of heads.

The 33d Indiana and the 22d Wisconsin filed to the right, and the battery took a position on a hill to the left, supported by the 124th Ohio and the 19th Mich. Our battery then opened upon the enemy, and quite a brisk fire was kept up between the batteries for an hour and a half, when the rebels fell back. Our battery fired about 60 rounds. The infantry took no active part in this engagement. Our forces followed the retreating foe over the hills they had occupied, and through a succeeding valley, then returned to the hills and took dinner. They then advanced about a mile and a half, and camped for the night. The enemy lost several killed and wounded—one with the name of J. H. Harden written upon his coat, lay beside the pike when our troops passed. In this first day's skirmish, we had two men wounded, one of the battery, and one of the 19th Michigan.

During the night, we had strong pickets posted in every direction from the camp, with positive orders to shoot any person who should approach from the outside.

Early in the morning, a reconnoisance was made three miles to the front and upon the hills upon both flanks, and no enemy reported in sight. About eight o'clock the column advanced, the 22d Wisconsin taking the lead of the infantry, the cavalry in the front, next two guns of the the artillery, then the infantry. The column felt its way along slowly and carefully, skirmishers being thrown well out on the front and flanks. Soon they began to pass picket fires which had evidently been left by rebel pickets early in the morning. About the houses of farmers and planters along and near the pike, an ominous silence reigned. On the retreat, it was learned from the negroes, that nearly all the citizens in the vicinity were with the rebel army during the battle. As the brigade came to the foot of a range of hills which crosses the pike, and through a depression in which it passes, a shell from a rebel battery, stationed at the other side of the valley beyond and nearly one mile distant, fell in the midst of the cavalry, but, fortunately, it did not explode. The cavalry immediately fell back; the infantry deployed on both sides of the pike, the 85th and 33d Indiana to the right, and the 19th Michigan, and the 22d Wisconsin to the left, and advanced up the hills. Three guns of the batteries took position on a hill to the left of the pike, and two on a prominent position to the right. The battery immediately opened upon the enemy, bringing a response of shot and shell from three different positions.

Thompson's Station is situated in a valley, nearly semi-circular in form, both ends of which open into the country on the flanks of the range of hills, on which our brigade was stationed, and in the rear of our position. On the south side of this valley, near the centre, and on the right and left, about one-half mile apart, the rebel guns were stationed. On that side of the valley, throughout its whole length, from where the guns were stationed southward, is heavy timber. In this timber, but out of sight, the whole rebel fore was drawn up in line of battle. After the artillery had been engaged some time, the rebel battery on their right and our left, moved still further to the right; and men could be seen nearly one mile distant, on our left, in trees, signaling to the battery, indicating a position which would bear directly on our infantry. Soon the battery opened with grape and canister, which came so close that the 19th Michigan was obliged to change its position.

In the mean time, Col. Coburn had advanced the 85th and 33d Indiana regiments on our right down into the valley, and they had made a charge upon the battery situated near the left of the enemy's position. As they approached the battery, two regiments, hid behind a stone wall in front of their battery, rose up and poured volley after volley into their ranks; and immediately the whole rebel line emerged from the woods. At the point opposite the 22d Wisconsin and the 19th Michigan, they were in column of battalions. The Indiana regiments were soon compelled to fall back across the valley, which they did in good order, fighting as they went, until they arrived at their position on the hill. That position they maintained until they were surrounded, and their ranks decimated by a heavy fire from both sides of the hill, when they surrendered.

The 19th Michigan and 22d Wisconsin sustained the attack on the left with unflinching courage. Their fire was so severe and well directed, that, until they were ordered from their position, the rebel line did not advance one inch from where they first engaged it. But to their left, the rebels were advancing unobstructed across the open country, infantry in line, supported by artillery, for the purpose of capturing our train and cutting off our retreat.

Soon after the engagement became general, Col. Coburn finding himself severely pressed, ordered the 19th Michigan to his assistance, thus leaving the 22d Wisconsin unsupported to contend against a force, probably, ten times as great in point of numbers as its own. Such an unequal contest could not long be maintained, nevertheless, the regiment held its ground until Col. Coburn became alarmed for the safety of his rear, and ordered it to fall back and engage that portion of the rebel line on our left, which was rapidly closing on the pike. This order was delivered to the Lieut. Colonel, who notified the Colonel, but he seems not to have understood it. Lt. Col. Bloodgood, in command of the right, gave the order to move by the left flank down the pike. About one-half the regiment followed the Lieut. Colonel, and engaged the right flank of the enemy, until they were outflanked, when they fell back, fighting as they went, and with the battery arrived safe in camp. The Colonel was soon driven from his position, and retreated upon the hills to the right and rear of the position occupied by Lieut. Col. Bloodgood, a little more than one mile from the battle field, where he was captured, and all who remained with him.

The rebels had, before this, closed in upon the three regiments upon the right, and compelled them to surrender. They fought, however, with such desperation, that, although they were surrounded, the rebel general found it necessary to bring a battery around, with grape and canister, into position so as command them entirely, and was about to open upon them, when Col. Coburn surrendered.

Our boys were said to have fought cooly, deliberately and bravely. Several instances of bravery were mentioned, amounting almost to rashness, and it was with evident reluctance that they left the field, though ordered to do so, and almost surrounded by an overwhelming force.

It should be stated, that Col. Coburn, becoming satisfied that he was to meet an overwhelming force, either in the evening of the first day, or early in the morning of the second, sent an orderly to Gen. Gilbert asking re-inforcements. To this request, Gen. Gilbert said, "Col. Coburn must be scared," and returned the following order, "Your force is sufficient; advance."

The causes of the sacrifice of this brigade are, as we understand them, as follows:

1st. Gen. Gilbert, after being duly advised that they were in force at Spring Hill, ought not to have precipitated a single brigade upon them without adequate support.

2. When Colonel Coburn saw the strength of the rebel

line, after he had drawn his two regiments back across the bottom, he ought not to have permitted a general engagement; but at once reversing his train, placed the battery in a good position in the rear, and with his brigade in a defensive attitude, retreated toward Franklin, until the other brigade could have been sent to his assistance. But instead of this, he permitted the brigade to become engaged in a position, where the more desperately it fought, the more certain it was that every man would be captured. The only reason why any portion of the 22d Wisconsin escaped, was that their position on the left was not so far in advance as the regiments on the right, and being left alone, the odds against them were greater, and they were overpowered a few minutes before the rebels closed in on their rear. If the rebels had not pressed quite so hard in the front, in all probability nearly every man connected with the brigade would have been captured.

These are my views of this military movement, which resulted so disastrously to our brigade. Perhaps no one is chargeable with intentional wrong, much less with treachery; but it is, I think, somewhat difficult to justify the order of Gen. Gilbert, and his neglect to send out his brigade to Col. Coburn's assistance, though all the time reminded by the incessant roar of battle within his hearing, that a severe and doubtful contest was going on.

BATTLE OF BRENTWOOD.

After the battle of Thompson's Station, in which many of the 22d were captured, the balance of the regiment was stationed at a point on the railroad, running from Nashville to Franklin, for the purpose of protecting the road from the depredations of guerrillas. We were about 9 miles from either place. We numbered about 540 men, including officers, teamsters, and the sick. The number fit for duty must have been less than 400 men.

About two miles south of us, the remnant of the 19th Michigan Infantry, numbering in all 230 men, was stationed to guard the railroad bridge across the "Big Harpeth." A small stockade had been built here for protection against the attack of infantry. We had neither cavalry or artillery at either of the two points. The loyal forces were quite strong at both Franklin and Nashville.

Lieut. Col. Bloodgood was in command of the 22d at Brentwood Station, and when notified of the state of affairs at the bridge, on the morning of the 25th, so many of his men, as it was thought prudent to take out of camp, were started immediately to the aid of the 19th Michigan. But when they had reached the height of a small elevation, not more than one-fourth of a mile from the camp, and were enabled to look down the opposite side, a large number of rebel mounted infantry were in full view not more than half a mile distant, forming in line of battle on either side of the street. Our advance force was then quickly deployed to the right and left, in the timber as skirmishers.

Next, a flag of truce was discovered approaching us

from the enemy. Major Smith was sent out in advance to meet it. We received a communication, stating that we were entirely surrounded by Gen. Forrest's command, demanding an immediate and an unconditional surrender, and declaring that we should be cut to pieces otherwise. "Come and take us" was the answer returned.

Upon the return of the flag of truce, the enemy commenced moving toward our lines as infantry, a portion of them having dismounted for that purpose. When sufficiently near, they were fired upon by our skirmishers, and quite a smart firing was kept up on both sides for about ten minutes. At this point, a piece of artillery was discovered in position to shell our camp, and horsemen were rushing down the hill upon every side. Next a flag of truce approached the enemy from our lines, the firing ceased, and a surrender of our feeble force followed. We had three wounded, and one accidentally wounded himself after the surrender, and subsequently died. I saw one of the enemy's officers dead upon the field, and they had five severely wounded with them in an ambulance on their return.

The rebel force consisted of three brigades under the commands of Generals Forrest, Armstrong and Stearns, and a battalion of independent scouts, under the command of Major Sanders of Nicaragua notoriety, numbering in all not less than 5,000 men.

Perhaps some men might have contended longer, but, in my judgment, it would have been but a reckless sacrifice of life to no purpose. Certain strictures upon the conduct of Col. Bloodgood, and insinuations of cowardice which have appeared in the Chicago Tribune, and one or two other papers, are but the cowardly attacks of some one entirely ignorant of the facts in the case. The 230 men guarding the bridge, and represented as having been surrendered without resistance, were a remnant of the 19th Michigan Infantry, two miles south of us, and with whose surrender, Col. Bloodgood had nothing to do.

This movement was characteristic of Forrest's command, as all well knew. To place such a feeble force in such a position, with neither cavalry nor artillery, was to place them in the hands of the enemy. Every family in the neighborhood answered the purpose of pickets for the enemy, informing them fully of our position and circumstances.— With two pieces of artillery, our position might have been maintained till the arrival of reinforcements, and a very different result might have followed.

On the ninth day after our capture, all, officers and privates, were paroled and sent by way of Richmond to be returned through our lines.

Under the drilling of the "Confederates," our "boys" learned that they could do some very smart marching, and that upon very light rations. The rebels fared but very little better than we did.

We were captured inside of our own lines, the enemy having made a forced march of thirty miles, flanking our forces at Franklin during the night, and it required dispatch and rapid movements to avoid an attack in returning. We marched not less than 75 miles, seemingly, through all the forests of Tennessee, to reach Columbia, a place 28 miles from where we started. But had our positions been reversed, and the circumstances the same, we should have marched them as they marched us, and had the Big Harpeth crossed our path, in the absence of other means of crossing, they would have been required to ford it, as were our boys, though the water came near their arms. War is war, and in passing judgment upon treatment received, that fact should be borne in mind.

NOTE.—The Author would here acknowledge his indebtedness to Chaplain Pillsbury, of the 22d Wisconsin, for reports of the above battles.

"COULD WE ONLY KNOW!"

PARTING WORDS OF ELDER DUNN'S MOTHER.

As the dear ones leave the hearthstone,
   Murmuring farewells soft and low,
How the heart, in wild uprisings,
   Crieth "could we only know."
Know that this our dearest treasure,
   Tended by our strictest care,
Would but list when evils gather
   For the mother's voiceless prayer.

Prayer, perchance, that in life's morning
   All unheeded was, but now,
In the hour of manhood's trial,
   May it not the spirit bow?
Voice of pleading heard in childhood,
   Far adown the walks of life,
Sounding louder and yet clearer,
   Serves to strengthen for the strife.

Memory paints with golden pencil
    All the tracery of the past;
Touching lightly—leaving sunshine
    Where but shadows should be cast.
But beyond this gilded picture,
    And from out this "long ago,"
Come their voices in their wildness,
    Crying, "Could we only know."

And in our momentous present,
    Never more despairing cry
Was upraised to the All-Father,
    E'en though knowing we must die.
All the wealth and all the pleasures,
    Earth can give, or Fame bestow,
Freely, *Gladly* would we give them,
    "Could we, could we only know."

Only know if slain or dying,
    Wounded, sick, or captive taken,
Know the hearts best idol was not
    Bound by sin's most galling chain;
Only know that by the camp-fires,
    Brother, son, or husband dear,
Kept the incense burning, ever,
    On the altar, bright and clear.

Upward then, our soul-gaze turning,
    Rising out of self, beholds
Hearts all crushed, and torn, and bleeding,
    By the woes the war unfolds,
Looking anxiously for starlight,
    When there gleams no single ray,
Giving token that the midnight
    Will be followed by the day.

In this night of pitchy darkness,
    Stands our nation, filled with gloom,
Scarcely having faith sufficient
    To avert its dreaded doom,—

Longing so to know the future,—
　See the end of all this woe,—
Dumb it is with very anguish,
　But the soul cries, "only know."

Still in this eventful present,
　We would see a Father's hand,
Feel that day from out of darkness
　Yet must break upon our land ;
How or when we may not question ;
　Trust and pray the whole night through,—
If 'tis best, our God will give us
　Full and clear the end to view.

　　　　　　　　　　MRS. G. S. BRADLEY.
COLLEGE HILL, HILLSDALE, MICH.

PRISONERS OF WAR.

After the surrender at Spring Hill and Brentwood, our men were started for Richmond. The following, which has been kindly furnished by R. L. Adams, will serve to give some idea of the journey to that place.

He says: "But as prisoners of war we were hurried away by our captors—Forrest and his command—on an uncertain and tedious march through back ways, by muddy lanes, through fields, over fences, through streams, large and small, and over, in fact, the roughest and most disagreeable route possible. We were led in a roundabout way to avoid being recaptured by our forces which were on the track. We marched three or four miles to gain one.

March 28th, 1863, found us at the old Court House in Columbia, Tenn.—arrived during the night, completely jaded out, having marched a day with little or nothing to eat. We were quartered in the Court House, which had the appearance of having been used for this purpose a long time, and was none the more comfortable for its abundant supply of filth and vermin.

Here we received a very meager ration of hoe cake and meat. Received here also a written " parole of honor."

March 29th—Marched nine miles this P. M. over a road too rough to be tolerable even for a footman. Camped for the night upon a rocky hillside.

March 20th—Marched again this morning on our journey towards Richmond. Passed through cedar swamps and woods for quite a portion of the day. About 5 P. M. we stopped at a little town called Farmington, known as a *Union* town. But few people were here except women and children, who were outspoken in their *Union* sentiment, in spite of the presence of rebel officers.

They were not wanting in their expressions of kindness, both in word and deed. One good lady, who with her little ones lived in a log house, will ever be remembered. She made us welcome to everything she had, even to rails from her fence, which enclosed her little garden. May God's choicest blessings be bestowed upon this truly loyal and noble hearted woman!

We spent the night as comfortable as could be expected under the circumstances—corn meal being dealt out to us, with a little bacon to use as best we could to satisfy hunger. But the night was too cold to sleep.

March 31st—Started on our march again this morning. Reached Shelbyville about 3 P. M., distance 15 miles, but passed beyond some three miles, when we stopped for the night in a cedar thicket, which shielded us from the wind, and where we had plenty of wood, so that we spent the most comfortable night here we have since being taken prisoners.

April 1st—Marched for Tullahoma to-day, arriving about 3 P. M.

Found "butternut" soldiers as thick here as bees—this place being Bragg's headquarters. We were quartered in the highest part of the town within some earthworks, but so low as to be no protection from the wind. We found it very difficult to keep warm, having only a very small allowance of wood.

Some of the boys spent most of the night walking about to keep warm. We had one consolation—we were not to walk any further. Up to this time, most of those having charge of us were human, and kind, but some, including some of the officers, were harsh and even brutal. There were two officers in particular—Capt. Forrest and Lieut. Coffee, who should be held in execration. Most of the privates seemed to cherish an affection for the old flag still. It was evident that many of them would leave the rebel service at the first opportunity.

April 2d—Marched at sunrise out of our cold camp to the depot. To our surprise, we were compelled to leave all our overcoats, blankets and canteens before going aboard the train. We were crowded into box cars—60 in each, so that the ride was tedious enough.

Arrived at Chattanooga about 9 o'clock in the evening. But little wood was furnished us, and, with no blankets, sleep was out of the question. The night, being so cold, seemed intolerably long.

April 3d—This morning dawned on our poor boys sleepless and cold. At 3 P. M. we were ordered on board a train for Richmond.

The country through here is rough and mountainous. All the little towns along the route have a forsaken, dilapidated and uninviting appearance. The fields are growing up to weeds, and very seldom did we see any farming, except some little garden spots. The inhabitants are mostly women, children and negroes.

April 4th—Reached Knoxville about 6 P. M. It appeared to have been once quite a flourishing little city, but the effects of war were plainly visible here. About noon we changed cars and moved on. The general appearance of the country is rather mountainous.

April 5th—Arrived in Bristol during the night. The weather being cold, we suffered for want of our blankets. Having to wait over one day for want of transportation, we were marched a little out of town near a piece of woods, where we found wood plenty, and so made ourselves quite comfortable. Slept some during the day, but during the night it was too cold to sleep.

The hours seemed long and tedious. We were impatient to be hurried through as fast as possible. Bristol is about on the line between Tennessee and Virginia.

April 6th—Left Bristol this morning at 4 o'clock. The country appeared rougher than any we have seen—passed through several tunnels. The scenery was romantic and grand.

Pine and cedar prevail mostly.

April 7th—Arrived at Lynchburg at 10 A. M. This

seemed to be a city of considerable importance, situated on the James River.

Here we changed cars for Richmond.

April 8th—Arrived in Richmond at 9 A. M., and were marched over to Libby, where, after being searched, we were furnished with our quarters under strong guard."

In addition to the above, read the following:

U. S. GENERAL HOSPITAL,
ANNAPOLIS, MARYLAND, May 13, 1863.

"Free! Free! Thank God we are free once more," was the glad shout that went up from the lips of our party of two hundred and fifty Union officers, who had been held in "durance vile" for many long weeks and months by the bars, bolts, and bayonets of Jeff. Davis' rebel horde of minions, as with countenances beaming with joy, and eyes moist with tears, we stepped aboard the good steamer State of Maine at her mooring at City Point, on the morning of the 5th inst., whither we had been sent fom Libby Prison, Richmond, for exchange. Never were men more thankful to the Divine Ruler for the blessing of freedom, or more grateful to a government for the efforts made to bring about their liberation. 'Tis true, that at times, when the prospects looked dark, and we were desponding and sickening with hope deferred, fearing that we should be held and treated as felons and criminals, all through the sickly months of summer, we would complain somewhat at the seeming indifference of the government, to the suffering and indignities inflicted upon us by the traitor mob. But the indifference was only seeming, and we now rejoice that our excellent commissioner (Col. Ludlow) did not accede to the compromising terms demanded by the traitor Ould, as to the conditions of our exchange. Better to end our career in rebel dungeons, than that the government should yield to the dictates of those, who held us in their power. Our sufferings and imprisonment have only made our faith stronger in our cause, and increased our confidence in the integrity of our government and its administration, causing us to strengthen our resolution to suffer and endure even more, if it were possible, and then *die* for its *honorable maintenance*. I wish, Mr. Editor, that it were possible to compel that class of people at the North, known as "copperheads" to make the trip as we did through rebeldom. They would perhaps receive better treatment than we from their friends, the *more honest traitors* in arms; but the journey would effectually cure them of the insane idea of our establishing a peace with treason, with anything but the sword. For us, who have gone through the fire, there is no such thing as *peace* until the flames of treason are smothered by our rain of leaden hail, or quenched with our life's blood. Every officer and man is anxious to get back to the field again, and I hear more complaining at the delay here, than when we were shut in behind the iron-barred windows of Libby prison.

You have been apprised, by a far more able pen than mine, of the particulars of that terrible fight and its results, as well as the sufferings endured by us all while on the march from there to Richmond prisons; in fact, no human power can tell all we suffered. Robbed of everything, stripped of our clothing and blankets, exposed to the severest weather, compelled to ford streams, where the water came up to our armpits, and forced to lie in the mud. I only wonder that any lived to tell the tale. Men died with praises to the Most High, that He in His mercy ended their sufferings; others prayed for death, which did not come until they had reached the shelter of the old flag, then nature, which had born so much, gave way, and the soldiers' cemetery at Annapolis is their last resting place. Yours truly,

WM. BONES.

PRISON LIFE.

"To those who have entertained the opinion that the people of the South were a superior race, and possessed of a much higher order of civilization than the North, the facts recently brought to light of the wholesale starving and inhuman treatment of our prisoners, must be not a little instructive. We would expect such treatment and such barbarities from North American Indians, but who could have believed it of any of the American people? Jeff. Davis, Lee, Stephens and others, can never be excused for the horrible treatment of these poor men. They were crowded within the Libby prison, dying from disease and want, or they were left on Belle Island exposed to every inclemency of the weather, or they were cooped up in the pens of Andersonville, Millen, and other places, dying by tens of thousands, wet, cold, hungry, and abused. No wood was allowed them, when forests covered the hills; no meat or good bread, when the unused gifts of the North were rotting at the doors of their prisons; weak, despairing, heart-broken, a great throng of the unhappy and helpless victims of the rebellion. And yet in all these years, with the sad report of these cruelties ringing through the world, when he must have known of them, Gen. Lee never issued an order, nor made an effort to stop them. He had but to say the word, and the Federal prisoners would have been treated like ordinary prisoners of war. But no such word ever came from the chief captain of the rebellion. On him must rest the damning stain of these great wrongs and cruelties. He is responsible for the starved and murdered young men of the North. Along with the memory of his first great crime of treason, will always endure that of these horrible brutalities to the prisoners of the North. They should never be forgotten. They are wrongs against civilization itself. General Lee is said to have been a harsh and cruel slaveholder; he preserved his character with the prisoners he captured. He has committed crimes, and scattered woes and griefs, which he can never atone for, and which we should never forgive, till he himself, at least, has avowed his penitence."

The following account of a private in the 82d N. Y. regiment, is but one of the many tales of suffering that might be related. After speaking of his capture, and his journey to Andersonville, during which, "all blankets, haversacks, canteens, money, valuables of every kind, extra clothing, and in some cases the last shirt and drawers, had been previously taken from him and his companions," he says:

"On reaching the Stockade Prison, we found it crowded with twenty-eight thousand of our fellow soldiers. By crowded, I mean that it was difficult to move in any direction without jostling or being jostled. The prison is on an open space, sloping on both sides, originally seventeen acres, now twenty-five acres, in the shape of a parallelogram, without trees or shelter of any kind. The soil is sand over a bottom of clay. The fence is made of upright trunks of trees, about twenty feet high, near the top of which are small platforms, where the guard are stationed. Twenty feet inside, and parallel to the fence, is a light railing, forming the "deadline," beyond which, the projection of a foot or finger is sure to bring the deadly bullet of the sentinel.

Through the grounds, at nearly right angles with the longer sides, runs, or rather creeps, a stream through an artificial channel, varying from five to six feet in width, the water about ankle deep, and about the middle of the enclosure, spreading out into a swamp of about six acres, filled with refuse wood, stumps, and debris of the camp. Before entering the enclosure, the stream, or more properly sewer, passes through the camp of the guards, receiving from this source, and others farther up, a large amount of the vilest material, even the contents of the sink. The water is of a dark color, and an ordinary glass would collect a thick sediment. This was our only *cooking and drinking water.* It was our custom to filter it as best we could, through our remnants of haversacks, shirts and blouses. Wells had been dug, but the water either proved so productive of diarrhœa, or so limited in quantity, that they were of no general use. The cook house was situated on the stream just outside the stockade, and the refuse of decaying offal was thrown into the water, a greasy coating covering much of the surface. To these, was added daily, a large amount of base matter from the camp itself.

There was a system of policing, but the means were so limited, and so large a number of the men were rendered irresolute and depressed by imprisonment, that the work was very imperfectly done. One side of the swamp was naturally used as a sink, the men usually going out some distance into the water. Under the summer sun, this place early became corruption too vile for description, the men breeding disgusting life, so that the surface of the water moved as with a gentle breeze.

The new comers, on hearing this, would exclaim, "Is this *hell?*", yet they soon would become callous, and enter unmoved the horrible rottenness. The rebel authorities never removed any filth. There was seldom any visitations by the officers in charge. The surgeons were at one time sent by President Davis to inspect the camp, but a walk through a small section gave them all the information they desired, and we never saw them again.

The guards usually numbered about sixty-four—eight at each end, and twenty-four on a side. On the outside, within three hundred yards, were fortifications on high ground, overlooking and perfectly commanding us, mounting twenty-four twelve pound Napoleon Parrotts. We were never permitted to go outside, except at times in small squads to gather fire wood. During the building of the cook house, a few, who were carpenters, were ordered out to assist.

Our only shelter from the sun and rain, and night dews, was what we could make by stretching over us, our coats or scraps of blankets, which a few had, but generally there was no attempt by day or night to protect ourselves.

Our rations consisted of eight ounces of corn bread,

(the cob being ground with the kernel,) and generally sour, two ounces of condemned pork, offensive in appearance and smell. Occasionally, about twice a week, two table-spoonfuls of rice, and in place of the pork, the same amount (two table-spoonfuls) of molasses were given us about twice a month. This ration was brought into camp about 4 o'clock, P. M., and thrown from the wagons to the ground, the men being arranged in divisions of two hundred and seventy, subdivided into squads of nineties and thirties. It was the custom to consume the whole ration at once, rather than save any for the next day.

Letters from home very seldom reached us, and few had any means of writing. In the early summer, a large batch of letters—five thousand we were told—arrived, having been accumulating somewhere for many months. They were brought into camp by an officer, under orders to collect ten cents on each—of course, most were returned, and we heard no more of them. One of my companions saw among them three from his parents, but he was unable to pay the charge. According to the rules of transmission of letters over the lines, these letters must have already paid ten cents to the rebel government."

A correspondent of the Philadelphia *Press*, in an account of a visit to the returned prisoners at Annapolis, gives the following fearful description of the condition of the men:

"All the men were filthy, ragged, or naked, and swarming with vermin. They came to 'God's country' with scarcely enough strength to articulate their joy. Their limbs were palsied and stiffened with a scurvy, which marked them everywhere; their bodies were smeared all over with the excrement of their diarrhœa, in which they were compelled from sheer weakness to lie; their hair was matted with filth of the same character; some, with their limbs and bodies filthy as they were, were swollen by dropsy, to such enormous tension, as to suggest the idea of bursting to the pitying eyes that were bent upon them. Lice of great size swarmed over them—ravenous, torturing—living in burrows in the flesh, honey-combing it all over with their dwelling places. They were almost the bulk and shape of grains of wheat. Their bites were keen—their combined attacks excruciating. Others were, in addition to these ills, afflicted with 'ground-sores.' Their bones pierced through the tightly drawn flesh, reduced by starvation; and at the hips, shoulder-blades, and other projecting portions of the body, these sores were formed and peopled with hideous, slimy maggots, whose very motion was untold agony to the unhappy sufferer, who had neither the means, the strength, nor, perhaps, in the stupor of suffering the will to remove them.

There were but few of these, however, though, as the soldiers tell us, on their oaths, such sights were quite common at 'Anderson.' But the poor victims died too fast for any large number to accumulate at one time. They might be seen at all points, gasping under their horrid pains, the maggots, disporting, eating, piercing nearer, nearer, every day, to the vitals. In some instances, they formed lines of communication between one sore and another, by eating little conduits for some distance under the skin. Through these ways, they traveled in lines, the living arcade over them heaving up and down as they moved! No care was taken of these martyrs, no medicines given, no facilities for even a very moderate attempt at cleanliness, and they died by scores, to be buried like brutes, in great heaps, in unmarked graves. Our friends of the Commission will soon present these facts, and others far more horrible, in a detailed way."

Such is Southern chivalry, in its great attempt to enter upon a career of independence. Such are some of its credentials for entering the great family of nations. Is it any wonder that the South failed? Their whole system was one of fraud and inhumanity. They seemed to delight in starving and torturing Yankee prisoners, and were never so happy as when they laid away thousands in their last resting place.

God surely could not smile upon such a nation, and their destruction has been swift and terrible.

Do you say the North was too lenient toward such fiends? Perhaps so, but after all it is better to be thus, than act the part of such inhuman monsters. We shall stand better before God and before the world in the exercise of mercy. But there should be no mercy toward Davis, Lee, and their tools. *Hang them!*

CAPTIVITY OF COBURN'S BRIGADE.

Written on old envelopes, in " Libby Prison," by EDWIN R. F. HART, Co. C, 22d Regiment.

 A tale I will tell of what lately befell
  Some Northwestern boys, sir;
 A thousand or more, a number of score,
  All stripped of their joys, sir.

THE STAR CORPS. 61

'Tis held in derision to live in a prison,
    As if we were felons, sir ;
But the fortunes of war, have brought us thus far,
    And not stealing melons, sir.

It was a bright day, we met in the fray,
    The host of Van Dorn, sir ;
We shall never forget the trap that was set,
    As true as I'm born, sir.
Though ten to one, we wished not to run,
    But fought them for five hours, sir ;
We made a great slaughter, but had to back water,
    Because overpowered, sir.

Our cavalry fled, artillery sped,
    Things began to look blue, sir ;
Our General, Gilbert, proved not worth a filbert,
    And yet we stood true, sir.
The great C. S. A. then came in our way,
    We don't think it great, sir ;
As prisoners of war they starved us—I'll aver
    We had little to eat, sir.

One ration for three, did not quite agree,
    With stomachs like ours, sir ;
When we meet Rebs. again we'll pay them like men,
    We will by the powers, sir ;
We stood in the mire, in the rain, without fire,
    It seemed very hard, sir ;
We forded cold streams, and had no sleep and no dreams,
    It killed eight of *their* guard, sir.

When we reached Tullahoma, all will allow me,
    That Bragg had his say, sir ;
We stood all aweary, the wet night dreary,
    Our strength giving way, sir.
Gathering brush for our fire, we grouped in the mire,
    And then wrung our socks, sir ;
In giving us meal, the Rebs. seemed to feel
    As humane as hard blocks, sir.

Our overcoats blue, and blankets quite new,
    They took from the Yanks, sir ;
They scorn Northern foes, but not our fine clothes,
    Which they took without thanks, sir.
'Twas a cold frosty morn when thus we were shorn,
    They stripped officers, too, sir ;
Rebs. to the dickens, they'll watch their own chickens,
    With that we are through, sir.

The cars were so old we shivered with cold,
    Some were minus a door, sir ;
Too dirty for hogs, fit for old Egypt's frogs,
    Was the filth on the floor, sir.
We sat bolt upright, rogues never pinned so tight,
    Or lay several deep, sir ;
With aches in our bones, with curses and groans,
    We hardly could sleep, sir.

Days to weeks hurried on, we were famished and gone,
    Ere to Richmond we came, sir,
To find the bad air and eat the bad fare
    Of old Libby prison of fame, sir.
Ourselves on the brink of the grave, we'll think,
    Those dead in the battle well off, sir ;
Deprived of our canteens, our coat and our blankets,
    And every one hoarse with a cough, sir.

Like beasts in a den, these long famished men
    Can scarcely wait for meat, sir ;
But from morning to night, they talk with delight
    Of dainties to eat, sir,
The soup is not sweet from such horrid meat ;
    For life we do desperate things, sir ;
We eat the stuff up, drink soup from a cup,
    And whittle the bones into rings, sir.

But we're ready to shout, rebellion's played out,
    Through sheer want it wanes, sir ;
Their money's vile stuff, with food not enough,
    The right soon will gain, sir.

And as April is come, we are on the way home,
Hurrah for the stripes and the stars, sir;
Look boys, there they be, on an arm of the sea,
Farewell to the cursed flag of *bars*.

THE "KENTUCKY POLICY."

This work would not be complete, did we omit some incidents that transpired during the Kentucky campaign.

When the 22d was about to leave "Camp Wells," an order was received from General Gilmore, to leave behind all contrabands who might be within our lines. The Colonel did not feel himself called upon to guard the negro property of slaveholders, nor did he lead a regiment of soldiers from Wisconsin, to be employed in sending back fugitives to their rebel masters.

The consequence was, that several fresh volunteers entered the ranks just as we were leaving the premises of a noted "secesh," on whose grounds we had been encamped.

The following is the order referred to above:

"Head Qrs. Division, Army of Kentucky,
  North Williamstown, Ky., Oct. 15th.
General Order
  No. 5.

All contrabands, except officers' servants, will be left behind, when the Division moves forward to-morrow morning. Public transportation will in no case be furnished to officers' servants. Commanders of regiments and detachments will see this order promptly enforced.

By command of

BRIG.-GEN. Q. A. GILMORE.

W. L. M. BURGER, Capt. and A. A. G.

P. B. PARSONS, Lieut. and A. A. A. G., 2d Brigade."

After pitching our tents at "Camp Jones," the following came:

Oct. 18, 1862.

COLONEL:—You will at once send to my headquarters the four contrabands, John, Abe, George and Dick; known to belong to good loyal citizens. They are in your regiment, or were this morning.

Your obed't servant,

Q. A. GILMORE, Brig.-Gen.

To COLONEL WM. L. UTLEY, Commanding 22d Reg. Wis. Vols.

REPLY.

HEAD QRS. 22d REG. WIS. VOLS.,
Oct. 18, 1862.

GEN. Q. A. GILMORE—*Dear Sir :* I have just received your order to deliver up certain contrabands said to be in my regiment.

Permit me to say, that I recognize your authority to command me in all military matters pertaining to the military movements of the army. I do not look upon this as belonging to that department. I recognize no authority on the subject of delivering up contrabands, save that of the President of the United States.

You are no doubt conversant with that proclamation,

dated Sept. 22d, 1862, and the law of Congress on the subject. In conclusion, I will say that I have had nothing to do with their coming into camp, and shall have nothing to do with sending them out.

Very respectfully, your obed't servant,
WM. L. UTLEY,
Col. Commanding 22d Reg. Wis. Vols.

The Colonel was immediately called upon to report himself at headquarters. This order he complied with. The interview was short and somewhat spicy. Said the General, "I sent you an order this evening."

The Colonel replied, "Yes, sir, and I refused to obey it."

The General thought he must be obeyed, and said he "should dispose of the matter at once." The Colonel thought it would not be settled in a remarkably summary manner. The General finally said that he should repeat the order in the morning. To this the Colonel replied, "General, to save you the trouble and folly of such a course, let me say, I shall refuse to comply in the same positive manner."

The morning came, but the order was not received. Instead of an arrest, the Colonel was put in command of the Brigade, with orders to protect the supply trains, while marching to Georgetown.

Shortly after the above, the Colonel called on the General, and was informed that the Act of Congress and the Proclamation of the President had been more carefully examined since the affair at Camp Jones, and that a different policy would be instituted. No more "niggers" would be returned, but that those coming into our lines would be organized into a brigade by themselves for appropriate services.

The 19th Michigan fully sustained the position taken by the 22d.

The affair at the time created a good deal of discussion both in Kentucky and the North, and we trust some good to the blackman has resulted therefrom.

As a Michigan regiment was marching through Georgetown, almost in the immediate vicinity of General Gilmore, some 40 persons with drawn pistols rushed into the ranks, and forcibly took out every contraband.

Before leaving that place, General Gilmore himself was seen to get off his horse, and accompany a slave catcher to a passing regiment, and assist him in taking a flying fugitive from the ranks, and he was heard to threaten the trembling transgressor of Southern rule with death, should he again attempt to transform himself from a slave into a man.

Honourable work for a Commanding General in the loyal army of the United States!

Is it any wonder that for two long years, the North gained little or nothing by the war? Shame on those men who attempted to prop up the vile system, and a deeper shame on the viler *copperheads* of the North, who applauded the efforts of such men.

With such a policy in carrying on the war, God could not give us the victory. Consequently our enemies were allowed to triumph again and again, and not until the government was willing to acknowledge the rights of the black man, did the rebellion begin to wane. And you, fathers and mothers, have lost many a dear one, before this lesson was fairly learned.

May God save us from any such folly in the future.

Rumor said the 22d would never march through Georgetown, without having the contrabands taken out of our ranks.

The other regiments of the Brigade marched to Lexington a few days before us, leaving Wisconsin to look out for herself.

Some imagined that the *brave* General anticipated trouble, and thought it advisable to keep at a safe distance. The Governor and several other gentlemen witnessed the dress parade the evening before we were to leave, and after they had expressed their admiration of the regiment in general, and the Band in particular, the Governor declared the dress parade a very fine affair.

Significant allusion was made to the never-to-be-forgotten "nigger" question. The gentlemen were informed by the Colonel, that any forcible attempt to take contrabands from his regiment might not prove a profitable business, and also requested them to say to the citizens, that if such an attempt was to be made, he wished them to remove the women and children from the town, as he should march through with loaded muskets and fixed bayonets, and if a single shot was fired, he would sweep the streets and close the history of Georgetown.

The next morning the regiment, with loaded muskets, marched through the place unmolested.

General Gilmore more than once played into the hands of slaveholders.

Under date of Nov. 17, 1862, Chaplain Pillsbury, from whom I have gathered the preceding facts, writes as follows:

"Probably slavery exists in Kentucky in its mildest

form, but the removing of the veil of rebellion exposes some startling facts.

In my judgment, ten dollars per year will furnish the rags which hang upon many a poor slave, particularly those of the female sex.

When we left Lexington, we comforted ourselves with the hope that the slavery question, which had proved a constant and grievous annoyance from the time we entered the State, would trouble us no more, but in this we have been sadly disappointed. The slave catchers follow us day and night, and seem determined to crush us if in their power to do so. It is not, however, so much the desire for the "nigger" himself, which drives them to desperation, as the necessity of breaking down the principle upon which we stand.

The Negro is a personal and comparatively trifling matter, and, probably, we have a smaller number of them than any other regiment in Kentucky, but the *principle* involves the position of the State. On the very day after arriving at this place—Nicholasville—the Colonel was informed that a gentleman, outside the lines, wished to see him.

The Colonel remarked, "Another negro catcher, I presume."

On approaching the lines, a large, portly old gentleman appeared, lying back in an elegant carriage, with a negro servant for driver in front. He informed the Colonel that he was in pursuit of a boy, who was in his regiment, at the same time presenting an order from the General, directing that he be permitted to enter the lines and get the boy.

The Colonel coolly informed him that such orders were not current in his regiment.

The old gentleman then went on to say that he too was

opposed to slavery; that he was the only survivor among the *Honorables* who voted for the famous Missouri Compromise, and that he had written an essay against slavery, and in favor of emancipation, which was eagerly sought after by the President at the present time.

Said the Colonel, "If you had done these things honestly, and from principle, it would certainly have been very commendable; but, sir, your mission here to-day gives the lie to all of these professions. I do not permit nigger hunters to ransack my regiment. If you will drive back into town, and return at 3 o'clock P. M., I will look through the regiment, and, if I find such a boy, and he is willing to go with you, I pledge you my honor that you shall have him."

He reluctantly consented, and turned his horse towards the village.

After he left, the Colonel found the boy, who frankly acknowleged that he belonged to the old gentleman. The little fellow then gave us a tale of sorrow, and that with such an air of truthfulness and intelligence, as astonished those who listened to it.

And when at last, he drew up his diminutive little figure, called upon us to see what beating and starving had done for him, and cried, "See me; I am almost 19 years old—what *am* I? and now they beat me because I am no larger, and can do no more," moisture was seen to gather in the Colonel's eyes, and he left the tent with a significant determination on his brow.

Before reaching his tent, he met the old slave hunter returning long before the appointed time, so eager was he for his prey.

"Have you found the boy?" were the first words to tremble on the old man's anxious lip.

"Sir," said the Colonel, fixing his "wicked look" upon him, "I have found a little yellow boy who says he belongs to a man in Lexington, who hired him out to a brutal Irishman for $50 per year. The Irishman never having seen him, was dissatisfied, he being much smaller than anticipated for a boy of 19, and as his master would not take him back, he declared, with an oath, that he would lick it out of him—that the man beat him for anything and for nothing—that he had been to his master many times, and told him that he could not stand it. His master would say, "Go back, you dog."

He also says he showed his master his neck, with the skin torn off, where the Irishman had tied a rope around it, and dragged him about. And yet his master would give him no protection—had commenced hiring him out when only five years of age, and had left him there ever since, taking all his wages.

He says that he has been beaten, and worked and starved, till there was nothing left of him, and that he was then beaten for not being bigger. He also says that he endured it till he could no longer, and fled.

He lived on black walnuts till the snow came, and he was obliged to seek shelter somewhere. He sought protection from several regiments, but could gain no admission till he came to this.

Now, sir, is that your boy? Are you the fiend of a master of whom he speaks? *You*, who came to me boasting of your wonderful works in the cause of the oppressed? I say, sir, is that your boy? Are *you* that master?

These declarations fell with terrible force upon the old

gentleman's trembling nerves. It was some time before he could answer, but finally faintly replied, "It is my nigger, but niggers will lie."

The Colonel then told him that they would go and see the boy. When we arrived at the quarters, the little fellow, instead of shrinking away from his presence, walked out with a firm step, and meekly but boldly said, "How do you do, Massa?"

The Colonel said to him, "This man claims you as his property, and says you ran away and left him."

"Yes, sah," said the little fellow, and then he proceeded to rehearse the whole story in a calm, respectful, but decided manner. The master struggled in vain to resist the force of the simple tale. The following questions and answers passed between the master and the slave:

"Have not I always treated you well?"

"No, massa, you have not."

"How so, sir?"

"When I went to you for protection from those who beat me, you refused to give it, and drove me back like a dog."

"But did I not tell you that I would take you away?"

"Yes, massa, but you never did it."

Ah! it was a beautiful sight to see that little abused slave confront so nobly that proud, bloated, aristocratic slaveholder. The Lord was with the weak, and gave him power to confound the mighty.

The Colonel then asked the boy if he was willing to go home with his master.

He replied, "No, sir," and that "*No, sir,*" went to the heart of every loyal man who heard it.

There he stood, that boy who came into our lines cold,

barefoot, ragged and hungry, amidst a dreary snowstorm, asking food and shelter, and raiment, after having spent days and nights in the woods, living upon black walnuts. Was he to be returned to slavery?

Turning to Judge Robertson, the Colonel said, "I don't think you can get that boy. If you think you can, there he is, try it. I shall have nothing to do with it."

This gentleman slave hunter is no less a person than the Chief Justice of the State, and is said to be the most learned jurist in Kentucky.

He will be likely to remember the scathing which he received from a Wisconsin Colonel for some time. I regret that the whole North could not have heard it.

The Colonel was threatened with Kentucky laws, but he thought it might be profitable to his country and the cause in which he was engaged, were he even sacrificed, did that rend the delusive veil and permit the nation to look in upon Kentucky as she is.

The Colonel intimated to the Judge that he preferred that he should leave the camp, lest an excitement should be occasioned among the "boys."

The idea of leaving without his nigger was evidently a painful one, and he was inclined to argue the case.

State subjects were dropped, and the conversation became at once rich and animating. To an intimation from the Judge that we were a set of "nigger stealers," the Colonel replied. "*You* talk about nigger stealing! *You*, who riot in idleness, and who live on the sweat and blood of such little creatures as that! *you*, whose costly mansions, and churches, even, are built out of the earnings of women and children, beaten out of them by brutal overseers! *You*, who hire out little children to brutes, who beat and starve them, stealing from their backs and mouths their small earnings! *You*, who clothe them in rags, and when, at last, they can stand it no longer, and flee from that protection which you denied them, you hunt them down like a ravenous beast, to drag them back to their chains, toils and sufferings, that you may eke out a few more pennies from this last life drop! *You* talk about *our stealing*, when all the crime which we have committed was to feed, clothe, and shelter that poor, half starved, suffering little boy! Sir, I would rather stand in the place of that slave to-day, than in that of his proud oppressor. It will be more tolerable for him in the day of judgment than for you."

Said the Judge, "If that is the way you talk and feel, the Union can never be saved. You must give up our property."

The Colonel replied, "If the perpetuity or restoration of the Union depends upon my delivering to you with my own hands that poor little overworked creature, dwarfed by your own avarice, the Union may be cast into hell, with all the nations that forget God."

He then told him in his own peculiar scathing style, what kind of "*Union men*" he had found in Kentucky. Said he, "I have not seen a half-dozen who did not damn the President. You may put all the pure *Unionism* in Kentucky into one scale, and a ten pound nigger baby in the other, and the *Unionism* will kick the beam."

Before leaving, the old jurist condemned the President's Proclamation; declared that it had no bearing upon Kentucky, and that it was the policy of Generals commanding our armies to ignore both the action of Congress and the Proclamation.

From our lines the old gentleman drew a very straight line to the "General's Headquarters," and to this place the Colonel was soon summoned, where he enjoyed another interview with the persevering Judge and several other Kentucky gentlemen.

Colonel Coburn, now in command of this Brigade, arose and stated in a very gentlemanly manner the policy of commanding Generals in Kentucky, which is simply this: To look at a slave in an encampment as in the same condition precisely that he would be were there no regiment there—that any person has a right to enter the encampment and take out a fugitive at his pleasure.

The Judge corroborated the statement, and added, "The Proclamation of the President is to have no consideration in Kentucky.

The Colonel commenced by saying that he regretted to be under the necessity of differing from his commanding officer. Said he, "I reverse the Kentucky policy, and hold that the regiment stands precisely as though there was no slavery in Kentucky. We came here as freemen from a free State, to defend and support a free government.

We have nothing to do with slavery, and we will never be made nigger catchers. We came at the call of the President, and still recognize his authority.

It is useless to think of stating all that was said, but you may be assured the old slave-catching Felix trembled as he listened to such bold declarations upon the Union-neutral soil of Kentucky.

But he could not leave without making one more effort to obtain the dwarfed human property now in danger of being transformed into a man. And turning to the Colonel he said, "Are you willing that I should go and get my boy?"

"Yes Sir," said the Colonel, "you may go, and I will remain here."

"Do you think I shall be permitted to take him?"

"I think not, but I cannot tell."

"Will you send him into some other regiment?"

"*No Sir!* said the Colonel, "I would see you in hell first."

The Colonel has since been indicted by a Kentucky court at Lexington for *man-stealing; but he has not yet been arrested.* It will be remembered that there is now a little spat from Wisconsin down here in the center of Kentucky. How long a more serious collision with the insulting and heaven daring slave power can be avoided, it is difficult to calculate. It is my clear conviction that Judge Robertson's principles correctly and fairly represent the Unionism of the State.

With the loyalists here, the Government is worthless without slavery, and loyal soldiers from the Free States are expected to employ their arms, and to spill their blood, if necessary, in defence of that heaven-daring, God-insulting institution. The struggle has not yet terminated."

Under date of Feb. 2, 1863, he writes as follows:

"On the subject of slavery, the people are very nearly united—almost to a unit. The leading men of the State and the most influential classes of the people are resolutely, almost madly determined to sustain the institution at all hazards. They are ready to peril anything and everything in its support. The Governor and the Legisture, openly, and in an insulting manner, denounce the

President, Congress, and all others who suggest the offering of slavery to save the Union. With Kentuckians slavery is the first object, and I really believe the State would join herself to the Southern Confederacy at once, had she no hope of a pro-slavery triumph in the North, and were she not to closely watched by the loyal armies.

The 22d maintained her position, unwaveringly, till she left the State. No contraband was taken from our ranks, nor given up at the demand of the slave-catcher. We were incessantly harrassed by the slave powers from the time we entered the State till we left. All seemed to understand our position, and to keep themselves posted respecting our movements. They had their plans made to obtain our contrabands at Louisville surely. The pretended owner of the three once ordered to General Gilmore's headquarters, and which order Colonel Utley refused to obey, followed us to the wharf and made every possible effort to obtain them. Many others from Danville, and, indeed, from nearly every place of any consequence through which we had passed in the State, were there. Many more slave catchers hung about the regiment than there were contrabands connected with it. No other regiment had withstood their brow-beating. All others they had conquered, and taken fugitives from their ranks. The 22d had become noted for its firm adherence to Northern principles, and they could not bear the idea that she should leave the State without bowing to the God of the South. Word had been given out that no regiment should take contrabands on board of boats. Orders were issued to all other regiments to leave them. The 22d was left in camp till all others had gone on board the transports, and nearly all had moved down the river. The order came for the 22d to move to the wharf. A citizen friend approached the Colonel and told him that he would have trouble in going through the city, and said to him: "Don't fire the first gun." "Fix bayonets!" sounded along the line, and the order was promptly and cheerfully obeyed. Reckoning myself more of a *civil* than a military man, I was somewhat in advance of the regiment. While making my way through the crowd, in front of the Gault House, in which General Nelson fell, a gentleman stopped me, and asked, "Has the 22d passed? I replied that it had not, but it was coming down the street. "Then," said he, "you had better stop, there will be music when it passes here." "Why?" I responded. He replied. "They took every nigger from the regiments which have passed, and they declared that they would die rather than let the 22d Wisconsin leave the State with a nigger among them." Said I, "I hope there will be no forcible attempts to take one from the ranks, for if there is *there will be music*. By this, the regiment was in sight. The unexpected swamp of bristling bayonets evidently had a tendency to cool the over-heated Southern blood. But the tempting bait appeared, and several chivalrous champions of Southern rights approached the ranks, one rushing in between two companies and laying hands upon a fugitive. "Snap" went a cap! Fortunate for Mr. Slave-catcher that the pistol in the hands of the fugitive missed fire. A dozen bayonets converged to the spot where the slave-hunter stood, some of which evidently penetrated his clothes, and he came from the ranks at a greater velocity than he entered them. This bold charge and hasty retreat terminated this mode of warfare. A terrible shaking of southern fists and threats in unstinted measures succeeded. Amid the excitement, Col. Coburn and two of his Aids came up—the Colonel walking upon the sidewalk, and the Aids riding upon horses between the sidewalk and the ranks. Pointing to a contraband, one of the Aids said to the raging, defeated hero, "Is that your nigger?" "Yes," was the emphatic reply. "Then why don't you step in and get him?" "I mean to.". "You dare not," and this short dialogue ended. Colonel Coburn seemed very much pleased at the turn which things had taken, and said to his Aid, "Keep your eye on those fellows." There can be no doubt, from circumstances, that the 22d was left to march through Louisville alone, that she might settle the question with Kentuckians in her own way. It is a significant fact, that orders were issued to every other regiment, by General Granger, to take no colored persons on board the boats, who had not free papers. In referring to this order, Colonel Utley said to General Baird, "Ours have no free papers, but all have declared their intentions."

An attempt was made to prevent the Commercial from leaving with contrabands on board; and the Captain—a Kentuckian—declared, that he should be responsible for all negroes who left in the boat. The Colonel informed him that the boat was under the control of the Government, and that, as commander of the troops on board, he had command of the boat, and ordered him to steam up, and make all necessary arrangements to move down the river. This order terminated the second charge of the day.

But the defeat was not to be acknowledged yet; and next and finally came the Sheriff of Jefferson County, to serve writs upon Col. Utly, in favor of one Hogan, who, report says, introduced secession resolutions at the democratic caucus in Frankfort a few days since, and to whom General Gilmore had once afforded important services, for three negroes, "Abraham, George and John," valued at $800 each. The Colonel received the papers with becoming dignity, and though informed by the Sheriff that all actions would be withdrawn upon conditions of giving up the fugitives, and instructing him as to his danger of being held responsible in any and every State, should an execution be issued against him, he gave the order, and the Commercial, with all on board, contrabands not excepted, moved down the river as calmly and quietly as though nothing had happened.

The independence of the Colonel and the regiment, has made a most favorable impression on the judgments of the people, notwithstanding their refusal to bow to the yoke of the South. Even amidst the excitement in Louisville, some of the most enraged were heard to say, that it was a "bully regiment." And citizens of standing in the community are known to have said, that the regiment honored itself by standing firmly and boldly by its principles. General Baird and his officers are highly gratified with the results, prize the regiment highly, and seem fully determined to sustain the Colonel in the position he has taken.

We come out of Kentucky unsoiled by her slavery principles."

In closing this chapter, I will do so by giving an extract from one of the public papers. We are not at all surprised at the revelation.

"KENTUCKY LOYALTY.——One year ago to-day, we

published, by request of the speaker, the remarks of Judge ROBERTSON, of Lexington, Ky., at a public meeting held in that city, to denounce the 22d Wisconsin Vol. Infantry, because its officers and men would not obey the laws of Kentucky, instead of those passed by Congress.

At the time we were assured that Judge ROBERTSON's son was in the rebel army, and with his father's approval at that. The following paragraph from the telegraph news from New York, is a fitting final to the Judge's *conditional* patriotism.

NEW YORK, Dec. 31.

Yesterday P. M. ten prominent rebels, recently captured by our forces in Kentucky, arrived by the express train from Washington, in Jersey City, and were transferred to Fort LaFayette by order of the Government. Two of them, named Redgar and Bowen, resided in Jersey City, but left for the South on the breaking out of the war, where they remained until the time of their capture. Another of the party is a son of Judge ROBERTSON, of Ky., who has, during the past six months, been engaged in guerrilla warfare."

Surely, you brave men, who stood so firm at that time, as you read these pages, will rejoice in view of the fact, that you did thus stand so firm. You did well. The slave is now free.

IN MEMORIAM.

Inscribed to the mother of Geo. McHuren, one of the 22d Wis. Vol., who died of disease contracted by exposure on that memorable march performed by the 22d Wis., after being taken prisoners near Franklin, Tenn.

Mournfully murmering rain-drops,
    Come to my window pane,
Bringing me thoughts of the spring time,
    Ne'er to be mine again.
Nature must surely be weeping,
    Tears I so long have repressed;
Calm be the swelling of anguish,
    Rising within my breast.

Sighing and moaning, the wind-harps
    Breathe but a saddening tune;
Seeming almost with the Nation's
    Bleeding heart to commune.
Grieving that loved ones to save her
    Nobly have fought and have bled;
Wailing an anthem of glory,
    Over the patriot dead.

Lonely and wearied and saddened,
    Sit I in dreams to-night;
Tracing the earlier life-path,
    Bordered with flowers so bright.
Gone is their fragrance and beauty,
    Moistened now only by tears;
Memory fails to recall them,
    Fresh as in earlier years.

Dimly that golden hued future,
    Comes to my soul once again;
Trooping, a thousand wild fancies
    Take up abode in my brain.

Breathings of love's first devotion,
   Swell high the heart as of yore;
Instantly real-life whispers
   Joys to be felt never more.

Dreaming am I of the morn, when,
   Led to the altar a bride,
Pledged I to cherish and honor,
   Whatever on earth might betide.
Tremblingly bearing from shoreward,
   Out to the wild unknown sea,
Left I the loved and the tried ones,
   Still by the parent roof tree.

Clouds were seen floating above us,
   They were so fleecy, the blue,'
Could easy be seen in the distance,
   And softened the light which came through.
Years glided by and a treasure,
   Heaven-sent, came to our hearts;
Adding a new, untold pleasure,
   Naught else in life ever imparts.

Little feet tramped through our dwelling,
   Little hands, still but in sleep,
Left us no time to built castles
   Over which vainly to weep.
How were the hours and the moments,
   Mid-day and evening and morn,
Lovingly, waking or sleeping,
   Lavished on him our first born.

Painted we visions of glory,
   Heard we in praise his dear name;
Sat he within the dim future,
   Throned on the hill-top of fame.
Sadly the vision has vanished,
   Pall now, and bier in its stead,
Bringing to the soul deepest anguish,
   Crush out the life with their tread.

Boy, but in years, when the bugle
  Sounded the call of " to arms !"
Suddenly grown up to manhood,
  Left he his home and its charms.
Blooming with ruddiest feature,
  Vigorous, hopeful and brave;
Strong in high purpose went he,
  Freedom and country to save.

Home! how the life-current gushing,
  Gave to him power anew;
Kindled high hopes that the life-work
  Might not thus early be through.
Shadows crept over his forehead,
  Showing the death angel there;
Slowly but surely erasing,
  Hopes that were bright as the air.

Far from the red field of battle,
  Far from carnage and strife,
Proud to be martyred for freedom,
  Faltered the young hero's life.
Words fail to tell of the anguish
  Felt as they hid him from sight;
This be our solace in sorrow,
  He died in the cause of the right.

Other hearts wounded and bleeding,
  Mingle their tears with my own;
Surely the nation is reaping
  The harvest of sin it has sown.
Father in mercy, oh spare us!
  Slavery surely is dead;
For from her sepulcher, whited,
  Victory, Freedom has led.

                Mrs. G. S. Bradley.
Mt. Pleasant, Wis., Nov. 26, 1863.

THE ATLANTA CAMPAIGN.

The terrible battles of Chickamauga, Lookout Mountain, and Mission Ridge, had been fought, and Rosecrans had safely lodged his victorious legions in Chattanooga.

From Nashville to this city, the country was all our own, but a little further on to the South, Johnston held all the mountain fastnesses, and he defied the further advance of the Union army.

Early in the spring of 1864, one might have noticed in the increased business-like appearance of the "Rock City"—Nashville, that some unusual preparation was going on. Daily, long trains swept across the beautiful iron bridge over the Cumberland, and swarms of soldiers filed out from the depot, and every hill about the city was thickly dotted with tents.

Reviews and drills were no uncommon things, for it was understood that there was earnest work before us. Mighty hosts were gathering, and Sherman was about to march toward the "Gate City." Who could divine the future? Who could tell what the result would be? Who, of all this vast army, would live to witness the triumph of our brave leader?

Alas! that so many must fall to save the country! Why could not the rebels read their doom, ere it should be too late? Why must so many innocent ones suffer? How could the South be so blind?

But we will not anticipate.

LETTER I.

Camp near Fort Negly,
Nashville, Tenn., March 15, 1864.

Arrived in Nashville last Saturday morning, having

been detained in Chicago on account of sickness. Am feeling pretty well at present, though I have rather a bad cold. The weather is quite cool for the time of year, especially the nights, though I am informed that they are rather cold throughout the entire summer. Let me describe my tent, which will perhaps give you some idea of our present surroundings.

Should you approach, and wish to enter, you would be obliged to notice a few strings that hold the door curtains together. You need not stop to knock, but just stick your head in, saying, "How do you do?" I should rise and invite you to a seat constructed as follows: Four stakes are first driven into the ground, cross pieces are put on, and then some thin pieces laid across the other way. Over this is put a small quantity of hay, and then some tent cloth is drawn tightly over the whole and fastened. This is the seat to my writing table, the latter having been made in the same manner, having boards put on the top of the stakes, instead of thin slats. With a newspaper for a tablecloth, and my stuffed seat, it is not a very uncomfortable place for writing.

At my left is a washstand, made after the plan of the table.

For a stove, please imagine a huge sheet iron tunnel placed on the ground, with a small aperture at the bottom for air, and a door in one side, the pipe of the tunnel protruding through a piece of tin in the roof of the tent. This tunnel stove is perhaps one and one-half feet in diameter at the bottom, and tapers down to four or five inches at the top, being, perhaps, two and one-half feet in height. This is a regular military stove, and very good service it does. Of course, you will understand that the stove has no bottom except the ground. On the march, these stoves can be run into each other, like so many basins, thus occupying a small space comparatively.

The tent is about ten feet square, the walls four feet high, and sufficient roof to shed the rain. In one corner is a bunk, made like a common lounge, and filled with hay, on which are laid blankets. For a floor, I have brick, and for a carpet, a few pieces of old tent cloth.

The regiment is now camped about one and one-half miles south of Nashville, and a little to the right of Fort Negley. It is an elevated point of ground and overlooks the city. We can see regiments and batteries encamped in all directions.

Nashville is strongly fortified. There is a vast amount of munitions of war stored here, consequently it is necessary to keep the place well fortified and guarded.

There is considerable sickness in the regiment at present. The weather has been cold and raw, and since coming here the boys have not had as good accommodations as they did at Murfreesboro. It was quite rainy two weeks ago, when they arrived here, and before they could get things arranged in a comfortable manner, many suffered from exposure. The new recruits seem to suffer the most.

Our camping ground is a very pleasant one, and in the summer it must be delightful.

The 22d is likely to fully sustain its well-earned reputation for whittling and carving. The boys are busy at work upon some most beautiful designs. Not only the privates, but the officers have designed some very fine specimens of shell work.

Let the friends at home encourage the whittling propensities, for while the boys are thus engaged, card playing and such things will have the go-by. * * *

G. S. BRADLEY.

LETTER II.

NASHVILLE, Tenn., March 25, 1864.

Just one year ago to-day the fatal disaster at Brentwood occurred, by which so many of the Second Brigade were gobbled up and taken through Dixie. Some of the boys have gone out to-day, to look over the ground again.

It is reported that Morgan, with some eight or ten thousand men, is only some forty miles or so from Nashville. Some of our cavalry force has just been ordered out toward Columbia, to meet him, so it would not be strange if fighting were going on there.

Nashville swarms with soldiers. There are probably 20,000 troops in the city waiting transportation, some going north on furlough, others passing to the front. The 18th Ky. passed through here a few days since, en route for Chattanooga. They are to march the whole distance, as a protection to the railroad. A few days since, the road between here and Chattanooga was cut by guerrillas, and three cars burned.

It is thought that the rebels will make a great effort to intercept our communication with Chattanooga. Could they destroy the railroad, it would inflict great damage on us. The probability is, that troops will be sent by land to keep all raiders out of the way.

Last night and to-day, we have been having a fine rain. It was much needed. Last Tuesday they had over a foot of snow at Stevenson and Chattanooga, a thing never before known so far south.

A refugee just in from southern Alabama, reports that the general impression there is, that the war is going to close the present season, but not particularly favorable to either party. One thing is noticible, which is, that they are giving up the hope of conquering the North. This refugee says that they have a strong hope, that the *peace men* of the North will be able to bring about a compromise of some sort. Says the rebels cannot possibly hold out longer than the present year.

During the last two months, over 4,000 refugees have applied for assistance at the office of Mr. Oviott, agent for that purpose. Of this number, about 1,000 are from this State, especially East Tennessee. They come from Georgia, Alabama, and even from North Carolina. The story they tell of suffering at the hands of the rebels, is a sad one. As a general thing, every man, thus driven out, has his man selected to kill when the war is over. Society in those sections will for years be in a most unsafe condition. Those who have suffered are bound to have revenge. Said one of the refugees from East Tennessee to me a few days since, an intelligent lady: "The government may be satisfied when the rebels return and take the oath of allegiance, but we shall not be, with any such arrangement. We have suffered too much at their hands to overlook it thus."

You ought to hear the soldiers this way talk about Northern copperheads. Said a soldier to me this afternoon: "There is nothing that will make me mad so soon as to think of those copperheads at the North. Here we are fighting the rebels, and some of our people at home are trying all they can to give them aid and comfort. They better crawl into their holes before we return home, or there will be a savage time." Just transport a few from Racine County down this way, and I will guarantee that they will soon have their copperheadism taken out of them or something else. The soldiers declare that they hate them worse than they do the rebels, and they dislike *them* bad enough.

Co. E, is now doing guard duty at the Zollicoffer barracks. Companies I, and E, are guarding the Chattanooga depot. The rest are still near Fort Negley, guarding the various Pikes.

Our sick are getting better—no deaths since my last. It is rather expected that the whole regiment will soon take up quarters in the city, though it is not certain. Our Major surgeon, Henry W. Cansdell, has just resigned, and in his place, we shall probably have Dr. Thomas Hatchard of Milwaukee. He has been with the regiment some six months, as Assistant Surgeon, and is highly esteemed by every one. All the boys have the greatest confidence in him.

G. S. BRADLEY.

LETTER III.

NASHVILLE, TENN., April 2d, 1864.

We are still at Nashville, though we received marching orders two days ago. We were to get two day's rations prepared. No one knows where we are to go, but camp rumor says in the direction of Fort Donelson, as an attack is expected from Gen. Forrest. The boys think they would like to get sight of him again, though not exactly under the same circumstances of just about one year ago. He is represented as being a pretty hard looking man, dressing simply in citizens' clothes. Some of the boys declare they saw him in camp a few days before the battle, selling eggs, which, however, is doubtful.

A large number of troops went down the Cumberland a few nights since on transports, so that the movements of the rebels in that direction will probably be checkmated.

There are a few sick in camp, and some in the hospital, but are getting along well, I believe.

Allow me to say that so far as I am able to judge, the *morale* of the regiment is good. There is no doubt but we have as good fighting material as can be found in the Army of the Cumberland. We have had a good deal of rain lately, so that vegetation begins to look somewhat green. I notice a few peach trees in bloom, but a large portion have been killed by the cold weather this winter.

G. S. Bradley.

LETTER IV.

Extreme front 16 miles south west
of Dalton, Georgia, May 6, 1864.

At last we have reached the "*front*," about which our boys have been talking so long.

Tuesday morning, we broke camp at Lookout Valley, marching some fifteen miles, and camped for the night on the battle field of Chickamauga. As we crossed a spur of grim old Lookout, we saw Chattanooga off on our left, perhaps three miles. The day was quite warm, so that the boys felt somewhat tired when they reached camp, though the roads were not very dusty. Wednesday morning found us once more on the weary march. Camped for the night near Taylor's Ridge, some 12 miles west of Dalton, and about seven miles from Tunnel Hill. Ringgold lay on our left, distant three miles. A heavy picket force was sent out from the several regiments of our brigade. Lieut. Flint, of Co. H, of the 22d, with 400 men was sent to the front of Taylor's Ridge. During the night, our cavalry pickets came dashing down the mountain's side, saying that quite a body of rebels was ascending the hill on the other side. Lieut. Flint reported that he saw a company of rebels on the top about daylight, but they did not show themselves during the day. Yesterday we rested, having been 15 days on the march, with only one day's rest in the meantine. This morning we broke camp at about 7, marching in a south-westerly direction some five miles. Orders were issued to halt and prepare rifle pits. Trees were immediately cut down, rails brought, and an extensive line of pits was made, behind which the 22d will camp to-night. The other regiments have their rifle pits also. The 19th Mich. lies just behind us. This is the first line of rifle pits ever constructed by the 22d, consequently it seems somewhat warlike to us.

It is stated that the rebels are directly in our front, distant some four or five miles. We have been told since coming here that a few rebels were here this morning, but retreated on our approach.

Gen. Thomas is with us, also Kilpatrick. The rumor is, that with a thousand cavalry, he dashed through Dalton this morning, reaching our lines a few hours since.

Officers and men have been cut down to the lowest point in their baggage. Only one valise is allowed to two officers, and one team to each regiment for carrying baggage.

Col. Utley was in command of the Brigade till we reached Lookout Valley, when Col. Ross, of the 20th Conn. took command, that regiment having lately been put into our Brigade. Col. Coburn, of the 33d Ind., will assume command as soon as he returns with his veteran regiment.

The weather is pretty warm at present, though the nights are very cool. I have noticed several quite severe frosts lately. The season is evidently very backward all through the South.

A few of the boys were sent to the hospital in Chattanooga, but I have not been able to obtain their names. It is hard to keep track of such things while marching every day, especially when the sick are in charge of the brigade and not the regiment.

G. S. BRADLEY.

THE BATTLE OF RESACA.

LETTER V.

[From the Madison Journal.]

CAMP NEAR FIELD'S MILLS, ON COOSA RIVER, GEORGIA.
May 17, 1864.

The month of May has been a season of unceasing activity for the 22d Wisconsin volunteers, and Sunday, May

15, will never be forgotten by those soldiers who participated in the terrible struggle. For months we have read of battles, and wandered over battle-fields, looking curiously at the traces of combat, but not until we had marched nearly 250 miles, and nearly 40 south of Chattanooga into the wilds of Northern Georgia, did we see war in its terrible reality. For ten days we have heard the sounds of battle, and slept accoutred for instant action; built four lines of earthworks, only to abandon them at last, and make the assault of the day against the flower of the rebel army, massed behind the finest and strongest works they have yet constructed, upon formidable and natural positions.

May 11th, we made eleven miles, coming up with other divisions of our corps, and with them constructed a double road through Pigeon Gap for our trains, and those of the 15th, 16th and 17th army corps in advance.

May 12th, our corps is held in reserve, and we look on while the seemingly endless lines of troops move forward. Regiments of cavalry gallop past, and batteries of artillery go rumbling by. Our attention is arrested by a distinguished group who gather near us. There is the handsome Butterfield, the one-limbed, spirited Sickles, the fighting Hooker, Palmer and McPherson. Sherman joins them for a moment, then mounts and rides forward with serious, quiet air. Schofield, heavy built, and with all a soldier's look, appears a moment, also the dashing Kilpatrick. Then onward to the front!

At noon we hurry forward for several miles, and form in line of battle, while the war-music of cannon and musketry tells us that the enemy are before us.

May 14th, the 1st brigade of 3d div. 20th A. C., in position to the south of the rebels, are attacked by them, and, after a brief, sharp fight, succeed in repulsing them. Our brigade the 2d of 3d division, was held in reserve. At half past 1 P. M., the battle *really* begins by an attack on Johnston's position by the 4th army corps. We are continually shifted from point to point, and held in readiness. All around the roar of battle goes reverberating through the valley, shells explode sharply high in air, cheers ring up from below, and peals jar the sensitive earth beneath us. Our tremendous army lies massed around the rebel stronghold, and, checking each assault, draw closer the lines of the Union anaconda; every bang of artillery, every crackling volley of musketry cementing in the blood of the bravest the union of the States.

A sharpshooter wounds one of the band, and the wounded are borne by, pale, bloody and ghastly. Goodwin of Co. H, was accidently shot, and his leg amputated. The 1st division under Gen. Williams, pass around to the left, and reach the field just in time to save the 9th Indiana battery, and mowing the rebels by hundreds, drive them in confusion from the field.

Sunday has ever been the day of battle, and having rested from 12 o'clock midnight, after building a strong line of breastworks, we move early in the morning a distance of about six miles to the left around our lines, passing the 23d and 4th corps massed line upon line, and come upon the field of yesterday. There is an ominous silence, and the busy hum of preparation stirs the air.

It is noon; we march through captured rifle-lines, being strengthened by spade and axe, wielded by strong arms, past brigades of troops, till we reach a position in reserve behind Ward's brigade of our division. Half past one—

and while the axe echoes on the ridge above,, and trees topple over, at once the woods resound with rebel yells, and a crash of musketry rings out. The 22d throw off knapsacks, and lie like hounds waiting for the chase.

An officer rides up and asks, "What regiment?"

"Twenty-second Wisconsin," says a man.

"Forward, double-quick up the hill!"

And away we went, over a whole brigade of troops, lying with heads close to the ground to avoid the rain of shot. Shell came crashing and howling, ripping their way like thunder-bolts through the tree-tops; men fall around in the crashing fire; while down across an open valley rushes the regiment, with broken lines but eager steps, while from right, left and front, they pour in grape, canister and bullets.

On up the hill to its crest, where four cannon stand unmanned.

Silas Wright of Co. B, seizes the battle flag of the 102d Illinois, and plants it on the hill. Col. Gilbert, of the 19th Mich., falls, and four men of Co. K, 22d Wisconsin bear him off. The leaves seem alive with balls, and the men fall like grain before the reaper.

Capt. Pugh, of Co. F, charges three different times up that hill to gain the coveted artillery, but from the most formidable breastworks the rebels hurl a sweeping tempest of shot, and men who start up the hill with cheers fall to the earth and hug the sheltering log, while one makes a rampart of dead bodies. Three men lose their brothers. Lt. Dickinson loses his daring boy close by the cannon, and night finds our men holding the position.

A heavy charge and raking fire of artillery succeed on

our left, while our men constitute a reserve. The shots skim close, and men of a regiment rise to run and are ordered back. Not a man of the 22d left his place. For several minutes the firing continues. Then a wild cheer from a thousand throats, and our flag waves from the fort on the left. A third charge by our men nearly in our rear is made with success, and the fight closes to our advantage, and we rest with stacked arms. Suddenly a tremendous fire bursts out in front, and all are ready. It soon dies away and all sleep sweetly, as only the tired soldier, wearied by the excitement of battle, can.

The color guard lose four corporals, wounded; the flag is often hit, and if justice is done, the State of Wisconsin will be proud of her 22d regiment.

During the night, our men secured the cannon, and the rebels evacuated their works, and morning finds us busy burying the dead. Ten men were laid in one trench within the fort where they fell.

We follow the enemy mile after mile, finding hundreds of their dead and wounded lying in the woods, deserted by their inhuman surgeons and officers.

The Army of the West will hold its own in the struggle which is to crush out armed resistance to the Union, and keep pace with the now victorious Eastern Army. This fight has done much to restore harmony in our regiment, and consequently increase its efficiency. With every disadvantage, they occupied the fort, and had there been a proper understanding among us what we were to do, and skill in leadership, we would have accomplished more, but we feel that we did all we could do and have but one name to be inscribed on our flag.

The 26th Wisconsin charged the same position later in the afternoon.

The following is taken from the New York *Herald:*

Sherman attempted to reach Resaca and cut off Johnston's retreat by a flank movement on the left. The wily rebel, however, evacuated Dalton, and fell back. At Resaca he fortified himself in a very strong position. The country in the vicinity is admirable for defence, abounding in hills and thickly wooded. He first formed a line stretching northwest from Resaca. Sherman coming up on the night of the 13th, a general engagement took place the next day. The rebels attempted to turn our left and had their own turned, and were doubled back upon Resaca. Their killed and wounded numbered nearly two thousand, besides 500 prisoners. Our principal losses were in Generals Schofield's and Stanley's commands, who had about a thousand killed and wounded.

THE REBEL POSITION ON SUNDAY MORNING.

The position occupied by the rebel army on Sunday morning was, notwithstanding Sherman's successes on Saturday, altogether more advantageous than that of the previous day. His troops were concentrated on a short line, strongly intrenched throughout its length, with a broad stream with marshy banks covering his centre, which was posted on commanding heights beyond this stream, while his left flank was covered by the strong works that had been constructed with great care and time at Resaca, and his right resting against the river, after crossing a range of hills fully fortified with redoubts, masked batteries and rifle pits. The river in the vicinity of Resaca makes a deep bend to the south, forming a perfect *cul de sac*, across the mouth of which the rebel line extended. The position was such that Johnston's army, with eighty thousand men, at an estimate, was thrown into line of battle but little more than two miles in length. Of course, in a line so compactly formed, a weak spot would be difficult to find.

SHERMAN'S LINE.

The operations of the previous day, in which General Hooker had borne a conspicuous part with portions of his corps, had convinced that officer that the key to this strong position was in the heights on the right of the rebel line, on which they had rested on the previous day. On communicating this impression to General Sherman, Hooker was directed to storm and carry these heights. As one of his divisions, that of General Butterfield, was detached at this time, General Hooker asked to have that division returned to him as preliminary to this assault, a request that was promptly granted, and the gap formed on the right by Butterfield's withdrawal, was filled by an extension of Palmer's line to the right. This position virtually gave Hooker the left of the line, with Howard's corps as a support. The rest of the line remained substantially unchanged.

THE POSITION.

The position that Hooker was to carry, was not a range of hills, but rather a collection of detached eminences of considerable altitude, the intervening hollows being filled with a dense growth of timber and underbrush almost impassable for horsemen, and traversable with great difficulty by infantry. The turnpike road leading from Dalton to Resaca passed through these hills, a portion of them lying on the right and others on the left of that road. On both sides of the road in front of the hills, the country was rolling, and densely wooded. In front of the rebel position was a lofty elevation, covered with heavy timber, filled with their sharpshooters. Our line of battle approaching from the southwest, barely touched the western base of this hill, and then crossed, in a more northerly direction, a narrow valley intervening to another commanding elevation, that had been possessed by us on the previous day, and on which we had planted batteries during the night. The rebel line of battle extended in a circuitous form around the cluster of hills directly back of those particularly noted above, the intervening space between their lines and ours being cleared of its timber. Immediately back of their line, on the right of the road, were two hills—the first wooded, and concealing a battery, the second more remote and cleared at its summit, and having a carefully built redoubt, mounting four guns, which swept the Dalton road with terrible precision. On the opposite side of the road from these heights, was another elevation that had been overlooked at first. It was covered with thick woods in front, but cleared on its rear slope, and was commanded by the rebel masked battery, as well as by their redoubt. On this hill a large body of sharpshooters were concealed by the enemy.

DISPOSITIONS.

While we have been making this hasty and imperfect survey of the field, Hooker has been employed in massing his troops under cover of the hill I have mentioned as in our possession. The divisions of Williams and Geary are ready; but Butterfield has not yet arrived. Everybody is impatient and wondering at the delay. But presently the suspense is ended as the looked-for division emerges from the woods, and moves steadily down the road. It is now noon, and no more time is to be lost; so Butterfield being already in line, is directed to continue his march until within range, and then deploy his division in columns, by brigades, and make a charge at the enemy's position, Geary's and William's divisions to support if needed.

On receiving his instructions, General Butterfield, who was riding at the head of his column with his staff, dashed ahead to survey the ground upon which he was to fight.

THE ADVANCE.

Having now a clear understanding of the work he had to perform, General Butterfield was not slow in entering upon its performance. Entrusting to the brigade commanded by Colonel Wood, the work of taking the hill on the left of the road, Gen. Ward with his brigade, was ordered to charge that upon the right, Colonel Coburn's brigade to act as a reserve to General Ward. These dispositions brought on two seperate battles almost simultaneously, both of them raging throughout nearly the remainder of the day with great fierceness. We shall characterize that in which General Ward led off as the battle on the right, and Colonel Wood's affair as the battle on the left.

THE FIGHT ON HOOKER'S RIGHT.

General Ward soon put his brigade in order of battle, under cover of the advanced hill occupied by the rebel sharp-shooters, and then ordered an advance. Up the hill went the column steadily and bravely, while the rebel sharp-shooters went down the opposite side less steadily, and back to their works. Crossing the summit of the hill, Ward led his brigade on a double quick down the rear slope, across the valley intervening to the base of the opposite hill. This valley was swept by the guns of the redoubt on the remoter height; but so quickly was it crossed by the eager western troops, that the grape of the enemy had but little effect. Yet their guns were played vigorously and earnestly, and continued rolling their iron charges through the valley after the whole column had passed. On gaining the base of the opposite hill, the charging column began to feel the rebel bullets flying about them, as volley after volley was poured down upon them from the rifle pits above. But, nothing daunted, the brave fellows plunged into the woods that covered the face of the hill, and began the toilsome ascent. The reserve brigade, under Colonel Coburn, had, in the mean time, crossed the first hill, and were waiting in line of battle on the inner slope for the moment when they should be needed. Presently the time seemed to have come. Ward's brigade, having approached within easy musket range of the enemy, began returning the compliments they had so moderately received. The roar of this musketry, echoing from hill to hill, and reverberating through the woods, was intensely magnified. It seemed as though Ward had encountered the whole rebel army. To add to the effect, the rebels at this juncture unmasked a battery of four pieces, planted behind an earthwork on the summit of the hill, and began hurling canister at their assailants. But, nothing daunted, the column moved on, firing rapidly as it advanced.

A MISHAP.

Both the brigades of General Ward and Colonel Coburn, though old troops, were in their first action. Their duty had hitherto been to garrison posts or protect lines of railroad, and, although two years in the service, to most of them, this was the first time they had been under fire. It is proper to mention this fact in extenuation of a mishap that occurred at the critical moment to which I have brought the assault, and which came very near proving fatal. The reserve brigade, hearing a few bullets whistling about their ears, and somewhat confused with the deafening roar of the raging battle opposite, fancied their companions cut to pieces, and that the rebel hosts were coming down upon them. Determined not to give way without a struggle, they leveled their pieces, and began firing wildly into the woods on the opposite hill. Ward's brigade, being thus assailed in front and rear, were on the point of retiring, when the staff of General Butterfield, by riding in front of Coburn's men, succeeded in persuading them to desist from firing. Another round would probably have finished the work for the day. As it was, their fire had been nearly as destructive as that of the enemy.

THE FIGHT GOES ON.

General Ward had not been seriously disturbed by this mishap. Apprehending the cause, and confident that it would be quickly stopped, he succeeded with great exertion, in holding his men up to the work, and now moved them directly up to the rebel breastworks. Here, clubbing their muskets, they fought, hand to hand, with the desperate foe, utterly fearless themselves, each striving to mount the works before his comrade. The rebels resisted nobly, but they were overmatched and forced to give way, retiring finally in a rout, leaving their battery of four guns in our possession. In leading the final charge, General Ward was severely wounded in the arm, and was carried from the field, leaving the brigade in command of Colonel Harrison, the senior field officer.

RETURN OF THE REBELS.

The rebels retired but a short distance from their works, when they were rallied by their officers, and receiving reinforcements returned to the fray, determined to re-take their position. Our men were now too feeble to hold the work against the superior numbers the enemy brought against it, and the less so because of the galling artillery fire they opened from the redoubt on the hill in the rear. Colonel Harrison, therefore, wisely beat a retreat, to a small elevation, separated from the main one only by an indentation in the hill like the division of a camel's back. The enemy's work was such that it was impossible for us to bring off the guns we had captured; but by occupying the summit opposite, we were relieved from the rebel artillery fire, while our muskets swept the rebel works so effectually that they could neither occupy them nor get away their guns. And thus our men kept guard over their trophies until night, when an opportunity was afforded of bringing them off the field.

The desperation of this little fight is attested by the fact, that General Ward's brigade lost nearly four hundred men in killed and wounded in the action.

THE FIGHT ON HOOKER'S LEFT.

While the fight above described was in progress on the right of the road, a battle even more desperate was raging on the left of the same road. The brigade of Colonel Wood, it will be remembered, had been detailed to storm the heights on that side of the road. Colonel Wood met with but little resistance in clearing the hill of rebels; but on gaining possession he found the timber on the back of the hill cut away, thus leaving his position open to the gaze of the rebels. The redoubt so often mentioned above also swept this hill with its guns, so that it was not a very safe location, and as the rebels left, their artillery commenced to work. To this we could make no reply, having no guns in position; but Colonel Wood, placing his men under such cover as he could find, directed them to lie down, and the rebels were permitted to fire away until they emptied their magazines, or exhausted their patience.

REBELS MOVING TO THE LEFT.

From his elevated position, during the one-sided fight the rebels kept up with their artillery, Colonel Wood discovered large masses of rebel infantry moving across the cleared fields between the Dalton road and the railroad, as if another attempt was to be made to flank us. The information was quickly conveyed to General Hooker, who promptly ordered Geary and Williams to take positions on Wood's left, extending their line well out to the railroad, in order to meet this apprehended attack. But no attack came from that direction; but very soon Colonel Wood found himself attacked by a whole division of rebel infantry.

ATTACK ON COLONEL WOOD'S BRIGADE.

With the peculiar yell for which the rebel soldiers are so notorious, they came charging on a double quick, up the cleared slope of the hill. The firing from the redoubt had now ceased, evidently to give place to this attack. Colonel Wood promptly had his men on their feet, and ready to receive the attack. Reserving their fire until the assailants were well in range, the command was given to fire, and a more murderous volley was never discharged from an equal number of muskets. A hundred rebels went down at the first discharge; but the column advanced, and nearer and nearer the crest of the hill, they began to return the fire that had been doing such fearful execution in their ranks. For a time, Colonel Wood's men stood their ground with a heroism, that would have done credit to the veterans of a hundred battles; but being without cover and opposed by treble their number, they began to show signs of weakness and a disposition to give way, when help came from an unexpected quarter.

KNIPE SLAUGHTERS THE REBELS.

General Williams, who had been posted on the left of Wood's brigade, in anticipation of the rebel flank movement, on hearing the musketry on his right, had ordered General Knipe, who commanded the brigade on the right of his line, to go to Wood's assistance. Knipe moved off with alacrity, and, crossing the hill from the east, fell upon the rebel flank before they had any warning of his approach. Leading his men in person, he charged directly into the rebel column, the bayonet doing the work of execution when time was insufficient for re-loading, and, without halting his column, fairly pushed the rebel force down the hill with his bayonets, occasionally firing a volley to expedite the rout. This was one of the most gallant deeds of the campaign. The rebels were largely superior in numbers to both Knipe and Wood combined; but the audacity and determination of Knipe's attack defied resistance. The face of the hill was strewn all over with rebel dead and wounded; their brigades were crowded upon one another, and, in inextricable confusion, they were routed and driven from the attack. General Knipe was not content with a single rout, but, following closely on the heels of the fleeing foe, he cut them down at every step. The chase was continued in this manner until the enemy were run into their reserves, concealed in the dense timber, and the attacking party was himself attacked.

GENERAL KNIPE WOUNDED.

Obstinately refusing to give way, the gallant Knipe stood with his little brigade, and contended with a force probably ten times greater than his own. Returning volley for volley, he maintained his advanced position, and would doubtless have continued to do so until reinforcements reached him, had he not fallen severely wounded. His brave men bore him to the rear, and the column steadily fell back to its original position.

CHARACTER OF THE FIGHT.

Though of but short duration, it is seldom that a more desperate fight is witnessed than the one I have attempted to describe so briefly. Its character can be judged from the casualties it entailed. The rebel loss in this charge alone must have been not less than a thousand men. Our own loss was heavy. These men fought with heroism and bravery almost unparalleled. Of General Knipe's staff, every officer was either killed or wounded. Lieutenant Knipe, a nephew of the General, was literally shot to pieces.

But though compelled to fall back, the brigade brought off some trophies of the victory they had achieved. Among these were three battle flags of the 38th and 58th Alabama regiments. They also took a number of prisoners.

CLOSE OF THE DAY'S WORK.

With the exception of another slight advance on the part of Logan's corps, on the extreme right, accomplished without material loss, this was the only portion of the army seriously engaged during the 15th. Our batteries along the entire line had been diligently employed, diverting the enemy's attention to assist General Hooker in his work, but the serious work had been left to Hooker and his corps, and what was assigned them to do was fully accomplished in every particular, as was demonstrated by the subsequent movements of the enemy. General Butterfield, with his division, fought splendidly, and won unbounded praise. The same must be said of Gen. Williams and his veteran division.

RESULTS.

Hooker's loss, during Sunday's battles, was about fifteen hundred men in killed and wounded; and it is supposed that their losses were at least double those of our own. Besides, we took between eight and nine hundred prisoners, four guns and a number of rebel flags. The crowning result of the battle was that it left both flanks of the enemy at our mercy, rendering their position wholly untenable. Under cover of the night, the rebels evacuated Resaca, leaving their wounded and dead behind, with immense stores of ammunition, several thousand stands of small arms, and a large amount of commissary stores.

What the *Herald* correspondent says about Ward's and Coburn's brigades never having been under fire before, is a serious mistake. All of Coburn's brigade had seen desperate fighting at Spring Hill. That there was serious blundering at this battle, no one doubts, but the fault did not rest with Coburn's brigade, and it, besides, should have the credit of capturing the four guns, spoken of above.

We propose now to give Colonel Coburn's reports of the Atlanta campaign, contenting ourself with these, as they convey all that need be said of the weary marches, hard living, and hard fighting, that resulted in the capture of Atlanta.

HEAD-QUARTERS 2D BRIG., 3D DIV., 20TH A. C., }
Camp near Cassville, Ga., May 22, 1864. }

CAPT. JOHN SPEED, A. A. G. 3d Div., 20th A. C.—
Captain:—I have the honor to report the following operations of the 2d Brig., 3d Div., 20th A. C., from the 8th day of May to the 21st day of May, 1864:

On the 9th day of May, the brigade was encamped in Dogwood Valley. Two regiments, the 19th Michigan and the 20th Connecticut, were ordered to march and occupy Boyd's Trail, over John's Mountain, south of Buzzard's Roost. This was done, after a slight skirmish, with the loss of one sergeant of the 19th Michigan, mortally wounded. Three regiments remained there on the 10th, the remainder of the brigade still in their former camp. On the 11th the brigade moved with the division to Snake Creek Gap, some 17 miles, and went into camp near the southern end, and at once began work on the road, making a double track for wagons and a bye-way for troops. On the 12th, the brigade continued the work on the road. At noon, three regiments marched three miles in advance, and encamped in rear of a part of Gen. McPherson's command. The 20th Connecticut and 33d Indiana remained at work on the road during the day, and at night rejoined the brigade. May 13th, the whole brigade marched at daylight, and at about 2 o'clock P. M. went into position in rear of the 15th corps, in the neighborhood of Resaca, having been deployed in two lines. In the evening, the brigade marched to the left and front, about a mile and a half, and encamped for the night in the rear of a part of the 14th corps.

May 14th, the brigade moved forward about 400 yards and relieved a part of the 14th corps—Carlin's brigade in front and to the left. The formation was in two lines deployed. The brigade encamped here for the night on the left of the division. The position of the enemy was in our front and beyond a narrow cleared valley, upon a low wooded ridge covered by fortifications. The 14th corps was severely engaged with the enemy here during the day.

May 15th, the brigade moved in the morning with the

division to the left some two miles, passing the 14th, 4th and 23d corps, and here, having halted, received an order to advance in rear of the right of the 1st brigade, in *echelon*, in two lines, and in their support as an assaulting column on the works of the enemy. On coming to the position where the formation was to be made, it was found to be impracticable on account of the location of a part of the 4th corps on our right. The brigade was then formed in close column of battalion, immediately in rear of the 1st brigade. Soon after, this order was changed, and the brigade was directed to be formed in two lines, in rear of the 1st brigade, which was being done, but before the completion of the deployment, orders were given to advance at once, and as rapidly as possible, to support the 1st brigade, which was making an advance on the enemy's works.

The brigade was moved forward at once in the following order: First line, 85th Indiana, Colonel Baird, on the right, 19th Michigan, Colonel Gilbert on the left. Second line, 20th Connecticut, Col. Ross, on the right 22d Wisconsin, Colonel Utley, on the left. Third line, 33d Indiana, Maj. Miller, in the rear of the 22d Wisconsin. The brigade was thus formed in a narrow ravine very thickly wooded with low and bushy trees, with steep hill sides, and out of view of the enemy and their works. The advance was difficult up this steep hill.

At the time of receiving this order to advance, and throughout the movement up the hill, the 2d division of the 20th corps was moving by the left flank in from six to eight lines from right to left, through my brigade, breaking and intercepting the lines, and preventing every regimental commander from seeing his own troops, or the possibility for the time of managing them. The brigade, notwithstanding moved forward over the hills and onward, carrying some men of the 2d division with them, and losing others of its own men, who were swept with the heavier current to the left.

The summit of the hill is covered with woods, but the slope beyond, and the valley, are cleared in front of a portion of the rebel works, which were situated on the hill beyond, and which here presented, opposite our right, a salient angle receding with a long sweep sharply to our left.

The brigade advanced across a portion of the field to the works, and the left along the woods to its left. This was done under a tremendous fire of artillery and musketry, which killed and wounded many of our men; but they bravely advanced, and planted the colors of the 19th Michigan and 22d Wisconsin in a small fort of the enemy, occupied by four of their field pieces. Such was the fury of the enemy's fire, that the men could not advance further, and here a portion of the 1st and 2d brigades remained during the day, holding this position under the very brow of the rebel earthworks. A portion retired to the left and rear.

Soon after my arrival in the immediate vicinity of the rebel works, Gen. Ward was wounded, and left the field. I took command of the forces then, and made the effort to charge and take the enemy's works, but such was the disorganized condition of the men of both brigades, and the terrific force of their fire, that such charge failed, and nothing more could be done than to hold the place up to the line of their breastworks. In one of these charges, late in the day, the 111th Pennsylvania (Col. Cobham) gallantly participated.

Remaining here until near sunset, I received an order to go to the rear with the men of my command then with me. I returned, leaving the men where I had placed them near the rebel works, and this was approved.

A portion of the brigade having been formed in the rear and to the left after the first charge, I took them by order of General Butterfield, to the left still further, to meet and assist in repelling a charge then made by the enemy upon the left of our position.

The 33d Indiana at once charged forward, and promptly met the attack. After a severe fight, in which the rebels suffered much, they were repulsed, and retired. General Butterfield then directed me to send two hundred men to reinforce the men of my own brigade near the rebel earthworks. This was done under the command of Lt. Colonel Buckingham, of the 20th Connecticut. His force assisted in digging the side of the fort away, and in dragging out four pieces of artillery at night.

The losses of the brigade in the action are as follows: Killed 28, wounded 200. I refer to the reports of the regimental commanders for the names of officers and men killed and wounded, and for acts of distinguished merit.

Early in the action, Colonel Henry C. Gilbert—19th Michigan—was mortally wounded while leading his men up to the rebel works. His life has been gloriously sacrificed to his country in the front rank of his soldiers. Capt. Colmar of the same regiment was killed on the top of their ramparts. Captain Patton and Lieut. Flint, of the 22d Wiscousin, were mortally wounded close beside him.

The conduct of the brigade under the peculiar trying circumstances was excellent. Their determined and gallant charge secured the position so boldly won by the 1st brigade, and together held it under the very muzzles of the enemy's guns five hours in daylight; and their prompt and vigorous action upon the left late in the day, contributed powerfully to repel the fierce assaults of the enemy there.

The brigade encamped on the battle field, a detail making breastworks during the night.

On the morning of the 16th, the brigade marched with the division, passing the railroad near Resaca, and crossing the Conasauga on a temporary bridge left standing by the enemy. At eleven o'clock at night the brigade arrived at Coosawattie river, and crossed soon after on a ferry boat. This was accomplished at half past ten on the morning of the 17th.

At 2 P. M., of the 17th, the brigade marched, leaving a detail of 150 men to complete a bridge [over the Coosawattie, and 250 men as train guard.

Marched till 10 P. M., and encamped with the Division. On the morning of the 18th, the brigade marched towards Cassville, the Division pushing the enemy in front. The 22d was left with the train as a guard. The brigade moved on, having made a march of some 20 miles; encamped on a gravelly plateau, some four miles north of Cassville. Two regiments, the 33d and 85th Indiana, were sent back two miles in the night, and stationed as a guard upon a road intersecting the one to Cassville.

Upon the 19th, a portion of the brigade was ordered to advance with the Division to the right of the road to

Cassville. The 19th Michigan (Major Griffin) and 20th Conn., (Col. Ross) were sent.

The 33d and 85th Indiana, having come up, were ordered to hold the Cassville road and fortify. This they did until 2 P. M. The regiments of the brigade in advance occupied the right of the Division, and supported the artillery, driving the enemy before them, with great promptness and bravery. At 2 P. M. the 33d and 85th Indiana were ordered forward from their position on the road, and at 4 P. M. joined the Division, already formed and advancing upon the enemy.

They were hurried up and placed in position to the right and rear of the Division, which had arrived to a point half a mile west of Cassville. Just at this time, the 19th Michigan and 20th Connecticut were ordered up to support Co. C, 1st Ohio artillery, which took position on an eminence that commanded the enemy's lines on the opposite side of Cassville, and to the east. The 33d and 85th Indiana were moved up and formed the second line in their immediate rear.

At dusk the 19th Michigan and 20th Connecticut were advanced into the town, supported by the 33d and 85th Indiana, which after a skirmish, they held and occupied during the night. The streets were then strongly barricaded, and every preparation made for a strenuous resistance of any attempt to dislodge our forces.

The heights beyond the town were covered by the enemy in long, large numbers, who made extensive fortifications during the night, but evacuated them at daylight.

The brigade occupied the town until 2 A. M. of the 10th, when it moved to the west about a mile and a half and encamped with the Division, the 1st Division of the 20th Corps, relieving us at Cassville.

I here take occasion to return thanks to all my Staff for their activity, and aid, and obeying and executing all orders, and meeting all exigences. To Capt. A. G. Kellam, acting Provost Marshal; Lieut. Crawford, A. A. A. G.; and Lieuts. Booth and Reynolds, my aids, I accord the highest praise for bravery and coolness.

The commanders of regiments did, I believe, their whole duty as soldiers and brave men.

I am very respectfully

Your Obedient Servant,

John Coburn, Col. 33d Indiana,

Com'g Brigade.

HEADQUARTERS 2D BRIGADE, 3D DIVISION, 20TH A. C., CAMP ON CULP'S FARM NEAR MARIETTA, GA., June 28th, 1864.

Capt. John Speed,

A. A. G. 3d Division, 20th A. C.

CAPTAIN:—I have the honor to make the following report of the military operations of the 2d Brigade of the 3d Div., 20th Army Corps, from the 22d day of May to the the 29th of June, 1864, in Northern Georgia.

On the 23d day of May 1864, the brigade being encamped near Marietta, Georgia, with the Division and Corps, marched at 4 A. M. toward the Etowah river, almost due south. The 14th corps marched on a parallel line with ours. The brigade about noon halted at the river to await the completion of the pontoon bridge. This being completed in a short time, we marched across and encamped in line a mile and a half south of the river, the 19th Michigan being on picket duty.

On the 24th of May, the 20th Connecticut volunteers was detailed as train guard. The brigade marched at 7,30 A. M. During the day there was cavalry skirmishing in front. The march was very slow.

At 4 P. M. we passed Burnt Hickory, having come through the gap of that name in the Allatoona hills. The brigade encamped a mile and a half east of Burnt Hickory.

BATTLE OF NEW HOPE CHURCH.

On the 25th of May, the brigade marched towards Dallas at 9 A. M. During the day there was cavalry skirmishing in front. In the afternoon at 2 o'clock the brigade crossed Pumpkinvine Creek.

At 4 P. M. the division arrived in the rear of a position held by the 1st and 2d divisions of the 20th Corps, and in which they had but a short time before been attacked by a heavy force in front, on the Dallas road, near New Hope Church. The brigade was formed in line of battle by battalions in mass, and moved forward on right of the road to support the 3d brigade of this division—a distance of a mile through the woods in the direction of the firing. The 3d brigade bore off to the left of the sound of firing, and I was directed to advance to the front.

This advance, although in woods and hills, was executed as though on the drill ground.

Coming under a rapid fire of artillery, the brigade was deployed in two lines, the 33d Indiana and 19th Michigan in front, the 85th Indiana and 22d Wisconsin in the rear. The brigade was advanced a short distance and halted.

The country just here is an unbroken forest, with undulations from 20 to 30 feet in height. The enemy was posted on one of these ridges and had fortified, having his artillery in position, commanding the ground of our advance. I soon received an order to relieve Robinson's brigade of the 1st division, and began the advance with the brigade, but the 19th Michigan was ordered by Gen. Hooker to halt, and then go to the left and relieve a regiment of the 2d division severely pressed, which it did at once, pouring in a destructive fire.

The 33d Indiana was continued on the advance to the front to relieve Robinson's line; the 22d Wisconsin and 85th Indiana being held in reserve. The line before named had given away and could not be found, but I soon did find the front line, occupied by General Knipe's brigade, and a portion of General Burger's brigade of the 1st division.

General Knipe requested me to relieve his line, their supply of ammunition being almost exhausted. This I did so far as I could with the 33d Indiana and its 550 muskets. This regiment advanced without a falter in line, passing through Knipe's line, and delivering volley after volley, soon silenced the musketry which had been heavy, and was increasing in front.

During this advance, the enemy poured in upon us a tremendous fire of artillery, raking the ground on which we stood. Shells, grape, shot, cannister, railroad spikes, and every deadly missile rained around us.

I aver that no regiment could have borne with more unfaltering daring, this fearful cannonade and musketry fire, than did the 33d Indiana that day. So to, with the 19th Michigan, on the left of the road.

The fight continued until long after dark. A cold and heavy rain closed it, and the men went to work in the darkness to hunt up logs and sticks, with which to make rude breastworks.

The 19th Michigan was relieved at 1 o'clock in the morning. The 33d Indiana continued on the front line and fortified, laboring the entire night.

The losses in the action were as follows: 33d Indiana 3 men killed, 2 officers and 43 men wounded; 19th Michigan, one officer killed and three wounded—Capt Bigelow mortally—3 men killed and 44 wounded; 22d Wisconsin had one officer and eight men wounded and one man killed; 85th Indiana had one officer and six men wounded; making in all one officer and seven men killed, and seven officers and 101 men wounded, a total of 116. Many of the wounded died, among them Capt. Bigelow, of the 19th Michigan, an intelligent, active, energetic and most efficient officer. In this battle, the 2d brigade, while engaged, covered at least a fourth of the entire fighting front of the Corps, and held it until the contest closed in the impenetrable darkness of a midnight storm. Not a gun was fired upon the right, and it boldly held its position there, with the possibility of a flank attack at any moment.

Late at night, the 111th Pennsylvania, Colonel Cobham, came from the left and took position, erecting breastworks on the right, and on his right, the 1st brigade of this division formed and continued the line of works, refusing it almost directly to the rear.

In this battle, Major Miller, commanding the 33d Indiana, and Major Griffin, 19th Michigan, greatly distinguished themselves for coolness and daring.

Early in the morning of the 26th, the 22d Wisconsin and 85th Indiana took their position in the front line, relieving the 33d Indiana and 123d New York. The fortifications were strengthened, and a continued and destructive skirmish fire was kept up, in which the brigade lost two officers and 27 men.

At dark, the brigade was relieved and moved to the right, in rear of the 1st brigade.

May 27th, the brigade moved forward and occupied the works made by the 1st brigade, which advanced some 50 rods and fortified.

May 28th, remained in same camp under a constant skirmish fire, and occasional fire from artillery.

May 29th, remained in camp. At eleven o'clock at night, the enemy made a demonstration on our left, which resulted in a furious discharge of musketry and artillery for nearly an hour. We heard heavy firing at a distance on the right of the army, which proved to be an attack on the Army of the Tennessee.

May 30th, the brigade moved into the front line, relieving the 3d brigade.

May 31st, the brigade remained in the same camp.

June 1st, the brigade was relieved by a part of General Morgan L. Smith's division of the 15th Corps, at 1 P.

M., and with the division marched in rear of the army lines north-east about four miles, passing the 4th, 14th and 23d Corps, encamping on a precipitous and rocky ridge, occupied in front by the 1st division of the 20th Corps.

June 2d, the brigade marched north easterly two and a half miles, and halted in rear of the 23d Corps, forming a single line, and throwing up works with bayonets, cups and plates, in an incredible short time, under a fire from the enemy's artillery.

Here, Major Miller, 33d Indiana, was wounded in the head.

June 3d, the brigade with the division moved still further to the left and north-east toward Akworth, following Hovey's division of the 23d Corps, and in support of it. After moving a mile, we halted near Morris Mill Church, and encamped on the extreme left flank of the army.

The 22d Wisconsin, in support of a battery, erected fortifications. By this movement, the right flank of the enemy was turned and he began to retreat.

June 4th, the brigade moved forward and occupied the line of Hovey's division, which had advanced.

June 5th, remained in camp.

June 6th, the brigade marched at 6 A. M., south easterly about five miles, and struck the Sand Town and Burnt Hickory road. After moving upon it a short distance, the brigade took position at Mt. Olivet Church, near Kemp's Mill, on the left of the road.

The church was burning as we approached, the enemy having just passed to the left and eastward. Pine Knob on the left, and Lost Mountain on the right, were plainly visible from this position.

Here breastworks were erected, beginning at the road and running eastward. The lines were refused on the right of this brigade by the 1st division, 20th Corps, and on the left by the 1st brigade of the 3d division.

The brigade encamped here until the 15th of June, taking upon the skirmish line six prisoners. The rain which began on the first of June continued almost daily. The roads became muddy, and rations scarce, so that the brigade's regular rations were not issued for a short time. While here, the 23d Corps moved to our right and toward Lost Mountain, and the 4th and 14th Corps to our left, toward Pine Knob, on which could be seen the rebel camp.

BATTLE OF LOST MOUNTAIN, OR GILGAL CHURCH.

On the 15th of June, the brigade moved with the division, and, crossing the small stream just below Kemp's Mill, advanced on the road toward Gilgal (wrongly called Golgotha) Church, in a south easterly direction, leaving Lost Mountain to the right and west, about a mile and a half, and halted near a line of the enemy's works, just abandoned, upon the left of the road, and here formed in line of battle in rear of the 1st brigade. The 23d Corps being on the right of our division, and the remainder of the 20th corps on the left. Here the brigade remained about two hours.

At this time the first brigade advanced in line of battle across an open field, broken at right angles to our line, by a ravine a quarter of a mile wide, to a road beyond, where the enemy's skirmishers were posted. They were soon dislodged. The 2d brigade was ordered to advance in support of the 1st brigade in line of battle. The 19th Michigan, Major Griffin, on the right. On its left the 85th Indiana, Col. Baird, the 33d Indiana, Major Miller, on its left, and the 22d Wisconsin, Col. Utley, on the left.

This movement was executed with regularity and promptness. The right somewhat advanced.

On arriving in the wood, a deep ravine was encountered in part of the line, and still further forward, the ground ascended, forming a broken ridge thickly covered with trees.

The 1st brigade met with considerable resistance from the enemy's skirmishers, but advanced, bearing off toward the right, a portion of it crossing the road. Here it was subjected to a tremendous fire of artillery and musketry, coming from what proved to be the enemy's first line of earth works, about 200 yards in front, and tremendous volleys of musketry were returned upon the retreating enemy. The 1st brigade soon exhausted their ammunition, and upon the request of Brigadier-General Ward, I relieved his line, sending the 85th Indiana and 19th Michigan to his relief on the right of the road, and the 33d Indiana and 22d Wisconsin on the left of the road. The troops on the right were subjected for a short time to the same heavy fire the 1st brigade had borne, but having been directed by Col. Baird not to return the fire, it soon ceased. It had by this time become dark. The troops on the left of the road at once began the work of fortification and continued it all night. Those on the right were withdrawn and placed on the left of the brigade and in like manner fortified.

The front of the brigade was composed of the 33d Indiana and eight companies of the 22d Wisconsin. The remainder of the line was refused on the left, along the edge of a ravine, a portion of the 85th Indiana crossing it on the extreme left. An effort was made throughout the night to connect our line with the 1st Division on the left, but such was the darkness and the distance, that it was not effected until after daylight. While with his regiment upon the right of the road, Major Griffin was mortally wounded and died during the night. He was a gallant, faithful and intelligent officer, and nobly did his duty at all times. His death was a public loss. Ten men were wounded in the brigade during the fight. Colonel Baird behaved with remarkable coolness and skill in managing the troops on the right of the road, under a galling and destructive fire, and in withdrawing them almost unhurt, when a want of caution might have sacrificed many of the men.

During the night, one regiment of the 23d corps joined my right, refusing its line square to the rear along the left of the road. The men labored with untiring patience at the earthworks, and by morning built a strong line within 200 yards of the rebel lines, and under fire of musketry and artillery.

On the 16th of June, the brigade remained in the same camp, strengthening the works and skirmishing, the enemy having in many places a near and fatal range upon us from his principal line of works. The loss of the brigade was four killed and twenty-four wounded.

On the morning of the 17th, the enemy evacuated his position, and our skirmishers, at 5 o'clock, occupied his works, which were found to be heavy and strong. The skirmishers were advanced at once, and found the enemy about three miles ahead toward Marietta.

At noon, the brigade with the division, moved forward in advance, forming in line with the 85th Indiana as skirmishers. The enemy was soon found by our skirmishers on a wooded ridge beyond a small stream, and well fortified. The brigade was advanced through a very dense wood about half a mile to a large field, and formed in line between the 2d division on the right, and the 1st division on the left, about 400 yards from the enemy's position.

Earthworks were at once built under a slight artillery fire from the enemy's artillery.

On the 18th of June, the brigade remained in the same camp, skirmishing sharply. Our loss was six in killed and wounded, our artillery in the meanwhile playing with great activity on the enemy.

The rain was excessive.

June 19th, the enemy evacuated his position, and our skirmishers occupied his works at 4 A. M. The works were found to be very strong, with well prepared *abattis*. Six prisoners were captured.

At 10 o'clock, the brigade marched in rear of the division. The rain fell in torrents, notwithstanding which, the brigade advanced a mile and crossed a branch of Nase's Creek, after an hour's delay on account of the sudden rise of the water, which carried away the bridges, and covered the road. Having crossed this stream, we advanced along the road toward Marietta, and formed in line of battle on a wooded ridge half a mile to the right of the road, and in rear of the division already formed in two lines in our front.

The division advanced three-fourths of a mile, finding the enemy in front and on the right flank. A position was here taken, and the brigade again took the front, building fortifications.

During the night, it was moved to the left, building outer works on that line, being under orders to connect with the 2d division, but failed to find it before morning.

On the 20th, the brigade moved again to the front and left, and connected with the 2d division, 20th A. C., building a new line of works.

On the 21st, the brigade was relieved by General Kimball's brigade, of the 4th corps, and advanced soon after with it, connecting on the left with it, building another line of works half a mile in advance.

BATTLE OF CULP'S FARM.

On the 22d of June, the brigade was ordered to march, and did so, at 8 A. M., in support of the 3d brigade. It advanced half a mile, and found the enemy in front posted on a high ridge, with a strong skirmish line in front.

The 3d brigade marched across an open field without resistance. Two regiments of my brigade were ordered to advance through the woods, and form on its left. The 22d Wisconsin and 33d Indiana moved forward in line of battle, at once. The enemy fell back after a short but sharp resistance, and we took a position on a ridge to the left of the 3d brigade. Very soon we received a severe flank fire on the left. The 4th corps not having advanced with us, the left of the 33d Indiana was repulsed at once, and I had the 19th Michigan and 85th Indiana immediately brought up, and formed on the left, and facing in that direction, except on the extreme left, which faced to the front. During this time, the brigade received and gave a fatal fire, which soon repulsed the enemy. I at once requested General Kimball, of the 4th corps, to advance on my left, and connect with my line, which was done with great promptness, and the enemy checked.

About 3 P. M. the enemy charged our line with great vigor, but was repulsed with heavy loss.

In the morning my brigade pioneers had reported under division orders, to Colonel Wood, of the 3d brigade, and were with him the most of the day. The entrenching tools of the division were all given to the 1st and 3d brigades, but notwithstanding this, my men fortified with rails and bayonets, scooping the dirt with their hands and tin cups, until quite a safe work was constructed.

At 5 P. M. the brigade was relieved by Gens. Kimball's and Harker's brigades of the 4th corps.

In this battle the 22d Wisconsin and the 33d Indiana, by their prompt and bold advance, distinguished themselves, and their commanders—Col. Utley and Maj.

Miller. Adjutant Charles H. Porter, of the 33d Indiana, was instantly killed while endeavoring to check the attack on our left. Thus fell in his early manhood a bright, brave, active officer, whose promise was that of a most useful and brilliant career. Captain Burton, Lt. Chandler, and Lt. McKinney of the 33d Indiana, and Lt. Shaffer of the 19th Michigan, were severely wounded during the day.

On being relieved, the brigade in advance of the division marched two miles to the right, to relieve, and reinforce a part of General William's division, of the 20th corps, which had also been severely engaged, the enemy having attacked him soon after his repulse in our front.

On arriving here, the brigade rested four hours, and again advanced to the immediate rear of Knipe's brigade.

The loss in this engagement in this brigade was, one officer killed, four wounded, five privates killed, and fifty-three wounded—in all sixty-three wounded.

The regiments lost as follows:

	OFFICERS.	MEN
33d Indiana,............	4	32
22d Wisconsin,..........	0	12
85th Indiana,...........	0	4
19th Michigan,..........	1	10

On the 23d of June, the brigade, again in advance of the division, moved to the right at 9 A. M., and moving to the east on the Powder Springs and Marietta road, passed Scribner's Female Institute, took position on the left of the road, in front, within musket range of the enemy's works, on the immediate left of Hascall's division of the 23d corps. The brigade was formed in single line, and at once put up earthworks.

This was at a point three miles west of Marietta. Immediately in front was the line of the enemy's works, enclosing that town and Kenesaw Mountain, vast in length, and made formidable by great labor upon strong natural fortifications.

The brigade occupied the camp, taken on the 23d, up to the evening of the 26th of June, in the front. On that day it was relieved by the 1st brigade, and encamped a short distance in the rear.

On the 27th of June, along the whole line of the army, the artillery opened upon the enemy. The brigade was ordered to be ready to move at once. An attack was made on the left by the 14th and 4th corps in great force, but failing of success, we did not move.

On the 28th of June, we remained in the same camp. During this entire time, skirmishing was constantly kept up with the enemy—who was in close proximity—with considerable loss. In the period covered by this report, the brigade did an unparalleled amount of labor, almost daily making lines of works, and this with astonishing alacrity and cheerfulness. In all that constitutes true soldiers, in hard fighting, hard working, long endurance, cheerful bearing, and manly promptness, they filled full the measure of the trying hour. In the battle of New Hope Church, in Dallas Woods, May 25th; of Lost Mountain, of Gilgal Church, June 15th, and of Culp's Farm, June 22d, officers and men vied with each other in heroic daring.

I forward herewith reports of regimental commanders, and with them the list of killed and wounded. In them will be found more especial mention of worthy deeds of the officers and men of my command.

My Staff Officers, during this arduous struggle, rendered me most valuable aid. In the field, Capt. Kellam, Lieuts. Crawford, Booth and Farr, met every required emergency, shrinking from no danger, and cheerfully performing most laborious duties. Lieuts. Buchanan and Harbert, as Quartermaster and Commissary, discharged their duties most acceptably, as also did Lieut. McKnight as Pioneer Officer of the brigade.

The entire losses during this period were as follows: Four (4) officers killed, fifteen officers wounded; thirty (30) men killed, two hundred and seventy-four (274) wounded, and seven (7) missing; making a total of 337

Very respectfully your ob't servant,

JOHN COBURN, Col. Com'd'g Brigade.

HEAD-QUARTERS 2D BRIG., 3D DIV., 20TH A. C., Camp in front of Atlanta, Ga., July 28th, 1864.

CAPT. JOHN SPEED, A. A. G., 3d Div., 20th A. C.—
Captain:—I have the honor to make the following report of the operations of the 2d Brig., 3d Div., 20th A. C., from the 29th day of June to this date:

On the 29th day of June, the brigade was encamped on the Powder Springs road, north side, about 3½ miles west of Marietta, Georgia, behind earthworks recently erected by it. Major-General Butterfield having leave of absence, Brigadier-General Ward assumed command of the division.

On the 30th of June, the brigade remained in the same camp, the enemy remaining as before, close in front, in their works. On the 30th of June, the brigade was relieved by the 1st brigade of the division, and moved a short distance to the rear.

On the 1st day of July, we remained in the same camp, the men washing and cleaning their clothes and arms.

On the 2d of July, remained in same camp.

On the 3d of July, the enemy, at 2 o'clock in the morning, evacuated his position in front, abandoning the lines by which he holds Kenesaw Mountain and Marietta, which our forces at once occupied. The brigade at an early hour moved out with the division on the Marietta road, to the intersection of Sandtown road, three-fourths of a mile from Marietta. Here we came under fire of two batteries of the enemy, stationed south-east of us toward the railroad. The 1st brigade was halted here, and this brigade ordered to advance on the Sandtown road a mile upon a reconnoisance. The enemy was not found upon this road, and a short advance further brought us to the 2d division of the 20th A. C., who were advancing directly east and at right angles to our direction, and skirmishing in front, to our left. The brigade passed the 2d Division, and throwing out skirmishers and flankers, advanced some five miles south to a point quite near the enemy's works, on the left. Here, they appearing in strong force, and opening on us with artillery, we halted. The brigade was formed in two lines and fortified. The shells of the enemy did comparatively little harm, wounding but two men in the brigade. This day we took twenty-five prisoners. (Taken by the 22d Wis.—*Ed.*) At 4 o'clock P. M. the brigade was relieved by Morgan's brigade of Davis' division of the 14th corps, and moved to the right of the road, crossing a branch of the Nick-a-jack Creek, and encamping for the night with the division, at a point near seven miles west of south of Marietta.

On the 4th of July, the brigade moved $2\frac{1}{2}$ miles south, and near to Mill Grove, leaving the rebel works to the left, and encamped here for the night, near portions of the 16th and 23d corps.

On the 4th of July, the brigade moved south-east, passing through the works of the enemy, which had been evacuated the night before, meeting a portion of the 16th corps, which passed to our right. The brigade crossed Nick-a-jack Creek at 2 o'clock P. M. and advanced about two miles, and encamped on a high range of hills overlooking the Chattahoochee River, with the division and corps.

July 6th, we moved about two miles to the left and east, and encamped on the same range of hills, the enemy now being within his last line of works this side of the Chattahoochee River. The brigade remained in this camp until the 17th of July, resting, refitting and preparing for the advance.

On the 10th day of July, the enemy evacuated his position this side of the river, in our front.

On the 17th, the brigade, with the division, marched eastwardly, passed Vining's Station on the Chattanooga & Atlanta R. R., and, going to the river, crossed it at Pace's Ferry, on two parallel pontoon bridges, without resistance, the 14th Corps having preceded ours at this point. The brigade having advanced about three miles, encamped near Nance's Creek, a branch of Peach Tree Creek, and on the Buckhead Road.

July 18th, the brigade advanced toward Buckhead in line of battle some two miles. It having been ascertained that the 14th Army Corps was already in that place, we marched by the flank and encamped near Buckhead for the night, on the right of the road, with the division.

July 19th, the brigade remained in the same camp.

July 20th, the brigade in advance of, and with the division, moved toward Atlanta, due south, and at 11 A. M. crossed Peach Tree Creek with the division, at a point bridged by Newton's division of the 14th corps. Our division had orders to fill the interval between Newton's division and Geary's division of the 20th corps, which crossed to our right and below us. The pickets of the enemy occupied the position we were ordered to assume. Two regiments were ordered to advance as skirmishers. My brigade furnished the 22d Wisconsin, under command of Lieut.-Colonel Bloodgood, who promptly advanced, covering almost the entire front, and leaving but a small space for the 136th New York of the 3d brigade. The skirmishers of the enemy were driven off and pursued for nearly half a mile from out the valley, and over a low range of hills to the south, when the skirmishers halted, joining to those of the 4th corps on the left, and of Gen. Geary on the right, who also advanced.

Peach Tree Creek is a narrow, deep and muddy stream, about forty feet wide and very deep, varying from four to twelve feet, and impassable, except by bridges. The valley is narrow, being about two hundred yards wide at our position, level and cleared. The hills rise gradually from it to the south some seventy feet in four hundred yards. Here these slopes in our front were for the most part cleared, and, except on the left, where there is a small thick grove of pine for a great portion of the space. Passing over the first ridge, a wooded, narrow ravine is reached, and running along its bottom is a small stream flowing toward the west into a branch of Peach Tree Creek, and on this there is a mill. Still beyond the ravine to the south rises the ridge, higher and entirely cleared, and on its top there is a road running by the Buckhead & Atlanta road westwardly by the mill to the river.

Along this road and behind the fences on the crest, were stationed the advance of our skirmishers, overlooking a field about a third of a mile to the south, and covering our division front.

The division was formed in the valley some two hundred yards from the creek, fronting south, the 3d brigade on the left joining the 4th corps, the 2d brigade in the center, and the 1st brigade on the right.

The 2d brigade formed with the 33d and 85th Indiana regiments in front, the former under command of Major Lorin T. Miller, and the latter under command of Lieutenant-Colonel A. B. Crane. The 19th Michigan in the second line commanded by Major Baker, the 22d Wisconsin being on the skirmish line in front.

At about 3 o'clock in the afternoon, I was informed that the enemy were advancing in force in our front. I at once went to General Ward's headquarters and informed him of the fact, and asked leave to advance my brigade to a better position in front. At first General Ward replied that it was against General Hooker's orders, and could not be done, but on second thought directed me to advance if the rebels made a charge.

On returning, I informed Colonel Harrison, commanding the 1st brigade, of the state of facts, and went to the front and ascertained that the enemy were advancing, and at once put the brigade in motion. The 33d Indiana on the right, the 85th Indiana on the left, and the 19th Michigan in rear of the brigade. In advancing we met the skirmishers—22d Wisconsin—being driven in.

Having reached the crest of the first ridge, the line halted as directed before the advance, but seeing the position was eligible, I ordered an advance of the 33d Indiana to the ravine, which was joined by the 85th Indiana, and soon followed by the 19th Michigan.

Upon examining the field to our left, I found that the enemy had driven in the skirmishers in front of the 3d brigade, and were advancing in large numbers on my left flank, and pouring in a deadly fire. I at once refused my left, facing two companies of the 33d Indiana to the left, and rode to Colonel Wood, in command of the 3d brigade, requesting him to hasten his advance on the left, and drive back the enemy. This he did, his brigade gallantly coming up and rescuing my left.

On the right, the 1st brigade, under Colonel Harrison, immediately followed my advance, and moving somewhat beyond it, poured a galling fire into the enemy across my front. The whole line halted for a short time in the ravine. Here the 22d Wisconsin rallied, and from this place the brigade poured into the enemy, who charged in large numbers down the slope. Soon, the enemy being checked, the whole line with the wildest ardor rushed forward to the top of the hill, capturing about two hundred prisoners, and slaughtering the enemy terribly, so short was the range. The enemy fled, but rallied, and three times renewed the attack before night.

The battle was thus continued for four hours.

On reaching the crest of the hill, a portion of the brigade rushed beyond the road, and at once took position, and a portion in the rear, so that at once two lines were formed and almost instantly fortified by rails. The brigade captured one hundred and twenty prisoners and arms.

Here let me testify to the gallant conduct of the two brigades on my right and left—to their promptness and unshaken firmness under the heaviest assaults.

The prisoners gave the information that the enemy in our front was Loring's division of Stewart's corps.

Their dead numbered there alone one hundred and twenty men, and their wounded added would swell their losses to five hundred.

Our men were engaged during the entire night in carrying off the rebel wounded, and the forenoon of the next day was spent by a large detail in burying their dead. My brigade numbered in this battle 1,263 muskets and 52 officers. To all officers and men, are due the honors and gratitude earned by service, valor and enthusiastic devotion to principle, and theirs are the laurels of a victory snatched from the trembling balance of battle, which wavered on either hand of our division.

The commanders of regiments, by their examples, led their men to a result, which could not otherwise have been achieved.

Major Baker, commanding the 19th Michigen, was severely wounded, and the command devolved upon Captain Anderson.

My staff, Captain A. G. Kellam, Inspector, Lieutenant F. C. Crawford, A. A. A. G., Lieutenant Charles A. Booth, Provost Marshal, and Lieutenant Henry C. Johnson, Topographical Engineer, were actively and boldly doing their duty throughout the day.

Lieutenant Crawford, in a signal manner, aided Colonel Crane in managing the 85th Indiana, and Captain Kellam, in every part of the field by his activity and daring, assisted in accomplishing our success. Lieutenant Pliney

McKnight, commanding Pioneers, rendered valuable service in constructing bridges, used by other portions of the army.

The loss in the brigade in this battle is seven officers and 33 men killed, and 169 men wounded and seven missing.

The total losses since the 28th of June up to the 28th of July in killed, wounded and missing, is as follows: 1 officer and 34 men killed, 8 officers and 188 men wounded, and 7 missing; total 238.

On the 21st day of July, the brigade remained in camp on the battle-field, skirmishing with the enemy in front, who at night evacuated his position and withdrew to Atlanta.

On the 22d, the brigade advanced to a position two miles north of Atlanta, and within range of the artillery of the enemy, and went into camp a short distance to the right of the Buckhead road, upon the right of the 4th, and left of the 20th corps. Fortifications were at once made, the skirmishers being advanced half a mile to the front.

On the 23d, the brigade remained in the same camp.

On the 24th, remained in the same place. This day Captain George L. Scott, company I, 33d Indiana, was killed on the picket line while on duty as brigade officer of the day. He was a brave, active, honorable and most faithful officer.

On the 25th, 26th, 27th and 28th of July, the brigade remained in the same camp, skirmishing in front, building a new line of works, and resting under the fire of the enemy's artillery in Atlanta, posted in heavy and formidable works in plain view.

The enemy thus holding to this day with dogged tenacity to this, to him, precious but untenable position.

Very respectfully, your obedient servant,
JOHN COBURN,
Commanding Brigade.

HEADQUARTERS 2D BRIGADE, 3D DIVISION,
20th A. C., ATLANTA, GA. SEPT. 12 '64.

Captain John Speed,
A. A. G. 3d Division 20th A. C.

CAPTAIN :—I have the honor to make the following report of the operations of the 2d brigade, 3d division 20th A. C., for the period from the 27th day of July to the 12th day of September 1864, inclusive.

On the 27th day of July 1864, the brigade being north of Atlanta, was encamped in reserve in rear of the 2d division of the 20th Corps, and remaining there during the day. On the 28th the brigade was ordered to move to the right and reinforce the 15th corps, and marched at 3 P. M., but before arriving at the battle field, was ordered back, the enemy being repulsed.

The 33d Indiana remained in camp under orders as a reserve to the 2d division. On the 27th day of July, the brigade with the division moved to the extreme right of the army, and encamped on the right of the division in a position refused to the right of the Sand Town road, about six miles west of Atlanta, building works.

On the 30th, the brigade with the division moved farther to the right half a mile, taking position on the Sand Town road in the center of the division, in two lines, making earth works.

July 31st, remained in same camp. Davis' division of

the 14th A. C., making a reconnoisance in front to Utoy Creek.

August 1st, remained in same camp.

August 2d, the brigade moved with the division to the left, about five miles, and near the Chattanooga Railroad.

August 3d the brigade moved into the works occupied by a portion of Baird's division of the 14th Corps, on the Turner's Ferry road, and in front of Atlanta.

New works were laid out and commenced at once, two hundred yards in front. The work was continued on the 3d and 4th, and on the 5th the new line was occupied.

August 6th, 7th, 8th and 9th, remained in the same camp.

On the night of the 9th, a new line of works, about three hundred yards in front was laid out and the labor begun. The work was continued on the 10th and 11th of August, as before. On the latter day the brigade moved into the new line of works.

The brigade continued in this position up to the 24th day of August, strengthening the works, and lying in close proximity to the enemy in front, during most of the time keeping up a constant skirmish fire.

During the few days of the latter part of the time, the firing ceased by mutual act of both parties.

On the 26th of August, the 33d Indiana was ordered to march to Turner's Ferry on the Chattahoochee river, to assist in the construction of fortifications for a new camp. The regiment marched in the morning at 6 o'clock, and arrived at the Ferry at noon, and at once commenced the construction of works. The brigade moved quietly with the 3d brigade of this division, at 8 o'clock P. M., of this day toward Turner's Ferry. The pickets were not withdrawn until 2 o'clock in the morning, which was done without observance on part of the enemy.

The brigade arrived at the river about two o'clock in the morning of the 26th, and encamped in single line on the south side of the road near the river, the right resting on the river strengthening the works begun by the 33d Indiana.

These works are in a semi-circular shape, and on a ridge near the river. A pontoon was laid out at the Ferry, in our rear.

At 10 o'clock A. M., on the 27th day of August, the enemy attacked us in front with artillery and musketry, but were soon repulsed. It was supposed to be a reconnoisance by a brigade of infantry, with a section of artillery.

Lieut. Slauter of the 33d Indiana was severely wounded.

In the afternoon the enemy withdrew, leaving their killed and wounded.

On the 28th, 29th, 30th and 31st of August, and 1st of September, the brigade remained in camp, strengthening works and repairing the roads beyond the river running from the railroad bridge to Sand Town.

On the 28th of August, Major Higgins of the 79th Ohio made a reconnoisance in front with 300 men, and found the enemy entrenched at a distance of three miles. After a short skirmish he returned. A portion of my brigade was with him.

On the 2d day of September, at 6 A. M., under orders from Brigadier General Ward, I marched on a reconnoisance from Turner's Ferry to find the position of the enemy. Cavalry was found to be in the city, and we advanced cautiously. I was met in the suburbs by Mr. Calhoun the Mayor, with a committee of citizens, bearing a flag of truce. He surrendered the city to me, saying he only asked protection for citizens and property.

I asked him if the rebel cavalry were yet in town. He replied that Ferguson's brigade was there, but was on the point of leaving.

I replied that my force was moving into the city, and that unless that force retired there would be a fight, in which neither persons nor property would be safe, and that if necessary, I would burn the houses of citizens to dislodge the enemy, that I did not otherwise intend to injure persons or property of citizens, unless used against us.

I ordered my skirmishers to advance, and they moved through the city, the cavalry rapidly evacuating the place. I at once sent dispatches to Brigadier General Ward at Turner's Ferry, and to Major General Slocum at the railroad bridge, of the occupation of the city by my command.

Gen. Slocum came at once to the city. Immediately preceding him came a portion of the 1st and 2d division of the 20th A. C. Gen. Ward directed a portion of my brigade to move up from Turner's Ferry under command of Lieut. Col. Bloodgood of the 22d Wisconsin, which reached Atlanta about sunset, and the remainder, under Major Miller, the next morning.

Soon after Gen. Slocum arrived, he directed me to move my command and occupy the works of the enemy on the south side of the city, to the right of the Augusta railroad. This was done, and Gen. Knipe's brigade was posted on the left of the road, in single line, deployed at intervals of three paces.

Here the brigade has remained in camp until this date.

Some 200 small arms were found in the City Hall, and about 16 pieces of artillery abandoned in the works and burnt with a train of cars. The ammunition abandoned had been fired in the night, and continued to explode with loud reports after we had entered the city, in the forts and among the ruins of the burning shops and buildings where it had been deposited.

The works of the enemy were left almost perfect, and there seemed to have been no attempt at the destruction of anything but the materials of war.

As we passed through the streets, many of the citizens ran gladly out to meet us, welcoming us as deliverers from the despotism of the confederacy.

Others regarded us with apprehension and begged to be spared from robbery. I assured them they would be safe from that.

Many of the buildings we found to have been much injured by our artillery, but such as will be needed for public use can be taken at once with slight repairs.

My command on reconnoisance behaved with remarkable promptness and energy, and deserved to be the first, as they were, of our army to enter the city.

Very respectfully, &c.,
JOHN COBURN,
Commanding Brigade.

LETTER VI.

IN THE FIELD SIX MILES NORTH OF ATLANTA, GA., }
July 21st, 1864. }

Friend T.:—The 22d has again "met the foe." Yesterday P. M., the 4th and 20th A. C., under command of Generals Howard and Hooker, engaged the rebel forces under General Hood, near Peach Tree Creek, four miles north of Atlanta.

Our division advancing in line of battle, the 22d Wisconsin was deployed as skirmishers, and while thus acting drove the rebels nearly a mile across the creek. As they were ascending the hills on the south side, they were met by the rebels in force, who charged down upon them in three different lines of battle at least twenty men deep; but our advanced line of skirmishers, under command of Captain Frank Mead, acting Major of the regiment, held the ground they had taken until they were almost completely surrounded, when Captain Mead gave the order to "rally on the reserve." Our men fell back slowly down the hill, disputing the ground slowly inch by inch, until they met the reserves, when they again rallied and drove the rebels up the hill the second time with tremendous slaughter. The balance of the brigade coming up at this moment, we were enabled to maintain, finally, all the ground we had gained.

The 22d fought well and bravely, and it is a great wonder they were not all taken prisoners, for before Captain Mead gave orders to fall back on the reserve, the rebels were in their front, on both sides of them, and in three minutes longer would have been in the rear of them.

They came down the hill after our men in swarms, but when they went up again their number was considerably lessened, for this morning I counted in front of our brigade 128 rebels, lying stark and stiff, in winrows, ready for the burial party. When I left the regiment, about 10 A. M., our boys were still bringing in bodies.

Our men have by this time fairly "wiped out" all the stain brought upon them by the disaster at Brentwood and Thompson's Station. General Geary, commanding the 2d division of our corps, when he saw from his head-quarters all the rest of the skirmishing line, except the 22d Wisconsin, falling back, and the rebels swarming around us, he is reported to have said: "My God! what do these men mean? 'T is the first time in my life that I ever saw a single skirmish line hold their own against three battle-lines of rebels."

As we were advancing up the hill the second time, one of the privates of company C captured a set of rebel colors, but left them on the ground, and afterwards, when the 26th Wisconsin came up, the flag was picked up by some of their men. Our officers this forenoon tried to obtain the flag, as it is ours by all the rules of war. While the discussion was going on, Captain Speed, A. A. G. of our division, said to Colonel Bloodgood: "Colonel, you need n't care for the flag; the 22d Wisconsin have enough to cover themselves with glory."

The loss of the entire regiment is seven enlisted men killed, and one commissioned officer and thirty-five men wounded. Of those from Racine county killed, were Ingersoll and Mattinore of company H; and wounded, Iverson, Schultz and Holland of company H, and Edwards and Anderson of company F—all slightly wounded. Not a man of company A was scratched, though many very narrow risks were won by members of the company.

Captains Mead and Pugh did their whole duty. Lieutenants Dickinson, Jones and White were ever at their posts, cool and fearless. Colonel Bloodgood, Adjutant Durgin, and, in fact, most every officer in the regiment, have fully proved the falsity of the assertion that they were a set of "*cowardly calves.*" And the men of the ranks have shown to the world, that the 22d Wisconsin has *some* merit left in its columns yet. There is hardly a man to be found in the regiment to-day but what made a telling shot yesterday.

I herewith enclose you an election ticket, which Lew. Dickinson took from the knapsack of a Mississippi rebel.

The heading of the ticket "*Save the Union,*" "*No civil war,*" has some significance. Has'nt it? I understand a great many such tickets have been found on the persons of prisoners captured yesterday. The prisoners say we will have to fight to get Atlanta. We expect to fight to get it, and probably ere this reaches you, Atlanta, the great magnet of this campaign, will be ours.

Yours truly,   RACINE BOY.

LETTER VII.

ON THE SOUTH BANK OF THE CHATTAHOOCHEE, }
NEAR TURNER'S FERRY, Ga., Aug. 31, 1864. }

Do you wish to hear a whisper or two from the old battle-worn 22d? If so, listen awhile and I'll try and tell you where we have been, where we now are, and what we are doing.

After the battle of Peach Tree Creek, July 20th, in which our regiment so nobly did its part in repulsing the rebel charges on our corps, we moved with our division and corps to a position in front of the rebel works around Atlanta, and at a point two and one-half miles northeast of the centre of the rebel den. We remained there building breastworks, abattis, and other defences, and performing our allotment of skirmish duty until the 26th of July, when we were ordered with our division to the extreme right of the Grand Army, and about four miles west of Atlanta, on the Sandtown road. Building two separate lines of breastworks there, within four days, we were returned to our place in the Star Corps, put this time to a position on the Turner's Ferry road, and one and a half miles northwest of the city. Here we remained until the 25th of August, building two very formidable lines of earthworks, and engaging in the meanwhile in some very sharp skirmishing with the rebel pickets, having a man killed occasionally, others wounded quite frequently.

On the 24th and 25th, General Thomas sent all of his supply trains to the north side of the Chattahoochee, and a strong force back to the south side of the river to guard the trains, the railroad bridge at Vining's and all of the ferries for the distance of twelve or fifteen miles along the river. This duty was assigned to the 20th corps, while Sherman abandoned the railroad from the river to Atlanta, and swung his left around so as to let it rest on the south bank of the river near Sandtown, while his right was pushing towards the Macon railroad. This movement completely changes front with Hood's army. Sherman now faces to the northeast, while Hood faces to the southwest. Sherman gets his supplies from Vining's down along the north bank of the river, and around Hood's right flank, and this to the south and rear of his own army, using the steep bank of the rough and muddy Chattahoochee as a guard for his communications. Hood must gather his supplies from the southern part of the State by way of the Macon railroad, now frequently tapped by Kilpatrick, and bring them around Sherman's right, having nothing to protect his line but men. There are few, if any, rebel troops in Atlanta now, and the general feeling amongst the knowing ones is, that Hood will soon be compelled to follow Johnston's example and again draw Sherman on.

Our division, the blue starred one, was detailed to guard this crossing of the Chattahoochee called Turner's Ferry. We came here on the night of the 25th, and immediately commenced fortifying. This precaution which experience has taught us to use invariably, was not unnecessarily taken, for at noon on the 27th, we were attacked by a reconnoitering party of rebels. But after throwing shells at us quite briskly for a few minutes, and sending their skirmishers up so close as to inspect our works, and learn our strength, they retired to the place from whence they came. We cannot now see or hear anything of any rebels near us, except when a "blue coat" straggles outside the lines he is butchered by the chivalry. We have no idea how long we shall remain here, but in all probability until Sherman orders us up to defend Atlanta. We are still hoping and longing for the paymaster to visit us with his agreeable verdancy. There are now eight months' pay due us. But we all feel that a great injustice is being done us by keeping back our pay so long. We are confident it is not because of lack of money, but of sheer negligence of our leaders. The Generals and their staffs throughout the entire army can get their pay whenever they ask for it. Indeed, they have all been paid quite recently, but the private who does all the work for the nominal sum of sixteen dollars per month, must wait and wait through long weary months, must read letter after letter from his dear ones at home, telling of their sufferings for want of what government owes him. *He must wait until the campaign is over to get his pay.*

There may be justice in this, but the men who do the fighting, and who *suffer* through their families at home dependant on their wages for support, fail to see it.

The health of the regiment is, at present, not very good, neither is it very bad. There are very many cases of scurvy in the command, produced by the constant use of salt food and the total lack of any vegetables. Our diet is hard tack, coffee and salt meat, with occasionally an issue of fresh beef. True, we might be a great deal worse off in point of rations, but such an unvarying diet is by no means welcome to the boys, who have worked and fought as Sherman's army has worked during all of this four months' campaign.

Our regiment started from Nashville on the 19th day of April, with over seven hundred men. Now we can only " stack two hundred and ninety muskets. " Where are all the men, do you ask?

They fell by the wayside between here and Chattanooga. Their graves are marked on every battle field between Resaca and Atlanta.

We are anxiously looking for help from the North, to be brought here by the coming draft. We can stand here in our safe shelter, and laugh with vengeful glee to see the shivering victims of the Provost Marshal coming up so reluctantly to our aid in this great struggle. We feel that the repeal of the commutation clause was a blessing sent from Heaven.

* * * * * *

Captain Bones, notwithstanding the hurculean efforts that were made to disgrace him, and the malicious reports that are still being sowed broadcast about him, is still with us, and commanding his old company "K," respected and beloved by all its members, and many others who are indebted to him for manifold acts of kindness.

After having charges preferred against him as long ago as last February, tried by a district court martial, and while awaiting the decision in his case, instead of remaining in the rear secure from all danger, as was his right, he requested permission to take the command of his company. After much cutting of red tape, and against the protest of his enemies, his request was granted, and he fearlessly led his command through all the bloody battles of this roughest of campaigns.

And, when at last, his case did reach the ear of that stern old hero, Major General Thomas, all charges against him were set aside, and by Special Order No. 208, he was honorably restored to duty, and is now with us, and intends to remain until this war is ended, or death or disability takes him from the service.

But I have already written a longer letter than I intended. I hope the next letter you receive from us will be written from Atlanta, and by our worthy Chaplain, now at home.

Mr. Editor, are you tired of listening? Mr. Type-setter, are you tired of following? If so, good-bye.

Yours truly, 23.

LETTER VIII.

Camp of the 22d Wisconsin Vol. Infantry, }
Atlanta, Ga., Sept. 12th, 1864.   }

You are of course aware of the occupation of this proud and haughty "Gate City," by the noble army of the indefatigable and indomitable Sherman. As there are false reports published by some northern papers, concerning the honor, if there be any, of *first* occupying the place, I will simply say that on the 22d ult. the city was formally surrendered to Colonel John Coburn, of the 3d division, commanding the 2d brigade, by the mayor, and protection asked for the defenceless citizens and private property. There was at that time a brigade of rebel cavalry in the city, plundering the stores of all property left. Colonel C. told the Mayor he would give the cavalry one-half hour to leave the place, or he would carry fire, as well as the sword, through the city. At the expiration of that time, a forward movement commenced from the outer works. The skirmishers from our brigade—part of them 22d boys—were the *first* armed Yankees to pass through the streets of the city; but, unfortunately, we left our camp in the morning, upon a reconnoissance, and took no colors with us, and the detachment from the 2d division having a flag with them, when they came up, were "the first to plant the Stars and Stripes upon the Court House," and *their reporters* make capital of it at *our* expense; but *we know*, if the world at large does n't, who were the first to parade the streets of Atlanta. It was a scene of destruction seldom witnessed. In the northern portion of the city, nearly every house is damaged by shell from *Yan-*

kee guns, and some fine dwellings are nearly demolished, shade trees cut down and fences splintered. In nearly every yard is a bomb-proof, or "gopher hole," as the boys call them, in which the families fled for safety when shells came thickest. These "holes" are about six or eight feet deep, and from eight to twelve feet square, planked over and covered with dirt to the depth of three or four feet, with a little doorway upon the south side. I heard of one instance where a family of six or more, with some friends —young ladies of the neighborhood—were gathered, in the afternoon, during the bombardment. A shell of large size came plowing through the covering and exploded in the midst of them, killing five, and wounding nearly all. One old Irish woman remarked in my hearing as we were passing her: "An' sure, I'se belave ye's are bains afther all." At one door I noticed a card in large letters: "United we stand, divided we fall," and white flags without number. Most of the citizens kept well out of sight, and but very little enthusiasm was manifest anywhere, save in the ranks. As the Old Flag caught the breeze from the spire of the court house, such a cheer went up as only a conquering army, flushed with victory, can give. Commencing in the Gate City, it rings out loud and long as it spreads from regiment to regiment, from post to post, and from state to state, and the news carries gladness to every loyal heart in the land. Alas! in this hour of the Nation's rejoicing, thousands of happy hearthstones are made desolate, and places that knew *our brave boys* shall know them no more. The mother, wife, sisters, and "friends so dear," shall look and wait in vain for the return of their country's brave and noble defenders. Unhappy thought! cruel, stern reality! And yet, the sacrifice is worthy. To die in defence of Justice, Freedom and Right, is *glory* and *honor* enough. Sooner die a thousand deaths upon gory fields, than submit to the reign of *southern despots*, or *yield an inch to their infernal desires*. The *Right* must prevail; Liberty's Banner, purified in the nation's blood, shall yet wave triumphantly over *all* this fair land. The rights of *all* shall be emblazoned upon her folds in letters of fire, and the United States of America will sustain a name not second to any nation on the earth—" The *pride* of the *free*, the home of the brave." This war *cannot stop* till our flag floats *triumphantly* from every spire, from every mountain top; till every chain is broken that binds human limbs and reduces *man*, created in the image of his Maker, to the level of the brute. Slavery, the curse of our nation, must be plucked out, *root and branch*, and and the tree of Liberty firmly planted, before we can have *lasting peace*. It matters not if "Little Mac" is nominated and elected to the executive chair, which I cannot believe will be the case. Peace cannot be had with "chains and slavery;" and a conquering, noble and brave army, *submitting to the dictations of a weaker power*—to these miserable butternuts, whom we've driven from one stronghold to another, against almost insurmountable obstacles. Do you think the army in the field will submit to their dictation? Never! If such were to be the case, the *war is just begun*. But I will not dwell longer upon this subject. I have no fears but "Honest Old Abe" will fill the chair at the White House another four years, and will *see* this thing through, despite southern foes and *northern traitors*.

We are now in camp near the formidable works that surround the city, and bade defiance to us so long. The 20th army corps garrison the city, while the army is in camp, in a line from Decatur to the Chattahoochee River, at Turner's Ferry, via this city.

The recent order, expelling *all citizens* from the place, is now being carried into effect. All those who are connected in any way with the rebel army, to go *South*, others go North. A long train of government wagons, filled with these *happy families* (?), started for Rough and Ready this morning, where they are taken by Hood's wagons under a flag of truce. The city is to be "*purely* a military depot." For the present, we are enjoying hugely the season of *rest* we were so much in need of—preparing for the "fine winter's campaign."

ATLANTA CAPTURED.

THE GREAT MOVEMENT OF SHERMAN'S ARMY PRECEDING THE EVENT.

The news of the capture of Atlanta marks the progress our armies are making in the work of crushing the rebellion. It sends a thrill of joy to every loyal heart, dispels all gloomy forebodings, and brings up the masses to the support of our glorious cause, which is now so grandly in the ascendant.

The movement of General Sherman, which commenced on the 26th ultimo, is thus explained by a correspondent:

"The 20th corps received orders on Friday last to

march from its position on the extreme left of the army, and on the Chattanooga railroad, to the rear along the railroad, and take up position in the *tete du pont*, covering the railroad bridge across the Chattahoochee river. This was done with some display on Friday afternoon, the purpose being, I suppose, to give the enemy an idea that we were about to evacuate.

"The 23d corps held the right, near East Point, and on the advance of the army, Schofield moved at dark by the right flank to the west of East Point. The rest of the army followed, the 4th corps in the rear, silently taking an affectionate leave of the railroad which had almost miraculously fed it, and which had bountifully provided the whole army with 20 days' rations for the hazardous movement."—*Daily Paper.*

SHERMAN'S OFFICIAL REPORT—OUR LOSS 1,200—REBEL LOSS 300 KILLED, 250 WOUNDED, 1,000 CAPTURED—24 CANNON AND MANY SMALL ARMS FALL INTO OUR HANDS.

WAR DEPARTMENT, Sept. 4.

To Major-General Dix:

General Sherman's official report of the capture of Atlanta has just been received, dated Aug. 25th, five miles south of Atlanta, 6 o'clock yesterday morning. It had been detained by the breaking of the telegraph lines, as already reported.

"Our army withdrew from about Atlanta, and on the 30th made a break on the East Point road, and reached a good position from which to strike the Macon road. Howard was on the right, near Jonesboro; Schofield on the left, near Rough and Ready. Howard found the enemy in force near Jonesboro, and intrenched his troops within half a mile of the railroad. The enemy attacked him at 3 o'clock in the afternoon and was easily repulsed, leaving his dead and wounded.

"Finding strong opposition on the road, I advanced the left and centre rapidly to the railroad, and made a good lodgment and broke it all the way from Rough and Ready down to Howard's left, near Jonesboro, and by the same movement interposed my whole army between Atlanta and that part of the enemy intrenched in and around Jonesboro.

"At the first we made a general attack on the enemy at Jonesboro, the 14th corps, General Jefferson C. Davis, carrying the works, with 10 guns and about 1,000 prisoners. The enemy retreated south, and we have followed him to his hastily constructed lines near Lovejoy's Station.

"Hood, finding me on the only road that could supply him, and between him and a considerable part of his army, blew up the magazine in Atlanta, and left in the night. The 20th corps, General Slocum, took possession of the city. So Atlanta is ours, and fairly won.

"Since the 5th of May, we have been in one constant battle or skirmish, and we need rest.

"Our losses will not exceed 1,200, and we have over 300 rebel dead, 250 wounded, and over 1,000 prisoners.

W. T. SHERMAN."

A later dispatch from General Sherman, dated on the night of the 3d, at Atlanta, says:

"The enemy destroyed seven locomotives and eighty-one cars, loaded with ammunition and small arms and stores, and left fourteen pieces of artillery, mostly uninjured, and a large number of small arms. Deserters are coming into our lines. E. M. STANTON,
Secretary of War."

ATLANTA

Is comparatively a new place, formerly called Marthasville; but in 1847 it was incorporated, and its name changed to "The City of Atlanta." In 1850, its population only amounted to 2,500 souls. It is situated on a high ridge, six miles west of Decatur, 101 miles northeast of Macon, and is the point at which the Western and Atlantic, the Macon and Western, and the Georgia Railways connect. And this, taken in connection with the fact that it was settled by men of northern extraction, and intelligent emigrants from Germany, is what has made Atlanta a place of bustle and of business. In importance, it is second to none in the South. Manufactures of all kinds of arms and munitions of war until recently, flourished in Atlanta, as they now do in Macon. Its entire population at present may be set down at 100,000, for that number will include the rebel army, the militia, the citizens, the refugees, the negroes, the prisoners and the spies. Martial law has been proclaimed and every living thing has been *Hood*-winked *General-ly* by the authority supposed to be vested in *Bragg*. It is not doubted that affairs in Atlanta will be speedily improved by the Government of the United States, and Major-General W. T. Sherman is taking *active measures* in that direction every day!

The Atlanta editor of the Mobile News, says: "I can

give you no idea of the excitement in Atlanta. Everybody seems to be hurrying off, and especially the women. Wagons loaded with household furniture and everything else that can be packed upon them crowd every street, and women, old and young children innumerable, are hurrying to and fro, leading pet lambs, deer, and other little household objects of affection, as though they intended to save all they could. Every train of cars is loaded to its utmost capacity, and there is no grumbling about seats, for even the fair ones are glad to get even a standing place in a box car. The excitement beats anything I ever saw, and I hope I may never witness such again. But in the midst of all this the soldiers are cool, and cheerful, and sanguine."

FACE OF COUNTRY.

The face of the country in Georgia is undulating. Hills overgrown with clumps of woods, and valleys traversed with noisy creeks; and hills and valleys relieving each other at short intervals, mark its face just like so many wrinkles. Much of the soil will hardly repay the labor of cultivation. The rich lands are on the Chattahoochee and South rivers, and Peach Tree, Nancy's, and Utoy creeks, and will produce, so the farmers say, from 1,000 to 1,500 pounds of cotton to the acre, and from eight to ten barrels of corn, where that article is cultivated. Wheat is always an uncertain crop in this country. What is known as the gray lands will not produce over 700 pounds of cotton, or eight barrels of corn, or twenty-five bushels of wheat to the acre.

SOUTHERN TRASH.—The "poor whites" of the South

are in most cases as ignorant as the emancipated slaves, and as incompetent for the franchise. The Springfield Republican says:

"The general ignorance in the South is absolutely appalling. We never half comprehended it till the war brought us into contact with the masses of the poor whites. Of eighteen thousand rebel prisoners at Point Lookout, Md., not long since, only about two thousand could read and write. And this is the average condition of the white men of the South, untaught in the first rudiments of learning, debased, brutal, and with no ambition for anything better. The planters and tradesmen of the South have educated their children, but they have taken no interest in the general education of the people; indeed have discouraged it, from the prevailing sentiment that ignorance and slavery is the proper condition of the laboring classes."

A Nashville correspondent of the *Watchman and Reflector*, writing from that city, after glancing at the retribution which has everywhere followed the footsteps of wrong in the several insurrectionary states, thus speaks of the manner in which the various classes at the South are punished. They are certainly having at least a portion of their punishment in the present life:

"I have seen the children of once wealthy slaveholders clad in the coarse "negro cloth" which formerly was only used by slaves.

I know that once wealthy slaveholding families have often been forced to live for months on corn bread and a little bacon—formerly the diet of none but the slave.

I know that once wealthy slaveholding ladies are now obliged to work hard for a living; that they are forcibly separated from their husbands; that their children are wrested from them by conscript officers; that they are sometimes obliged to fly and sometimes driven from their homes; that they are occasionally pressed by hunger to save their lives by begging, and (God pity them) by worse; that their little daughters can at some places be seen without shoes and stockings, while the negro children at their sides are comfortably clad; that their word is doubted and their petitions refused when their former slaves are believed and protected; that they are compelled to endure without a word, the insolence of blacks which a few years ago they would have punished by stripes till the blood ran down the culprit's back in streams.

I know that wealthy slaveholding ladies have been halted by soldiers once their own slaves, and obliged to show their passes!

In truth, there is hardly any humiliation that the negro formerly endured, that the slave holder and his parasites, "the poor white trash," do not now undergo. A negro soldier telling how he had forced his old mistress to stop and show her pass, said, "Halt, is de sweetest word I ever spoke."

The poor whites were the slave-hunters of the hard old times. They hunted the runaways with bloodhounds. They have been hunted with the same dogs by conscript officers.

The fugitive slaves were compelled to hide in caves, and holes, and in the depths of forests and swamps. So have the poor whites. The slaves were arrested wherever found and flung into prison. So have the poor whites. The slaves were whipped and shot for trying to escape. So have the poor whites. The slaves were forced to fly from their homes and families. So have the poor whites.

The slaves were driven like sheep to the slaughter, into the deadly cane brakes of Louisiana and other States. So have the poor whites been driven into the still deadlier trenches of Virginia and Georgia.

Truly, the Lord liveth and heareth the cry of the poor, and avengeth those who call on him in their distress!

ANECDOTES OF SHERMAN.

While a regiment was moving by Sherman's headquarters—a tent, fly and a fence corner, near Kenesaw Mountain—one of the soldiers observed a Major General lying asleep by the roadside. He spoke very loudly to his comrades, saying: "There's the way we are commanded—officered by Major Generals who get drunk and lie in fence corners." Sherman heard him and sprang to his feet. "Not drunk boys," he said quietly, "but I've been up all night, and I'm very tired and sleepy." He got on his horse, and, followed by his staff, rode away.

An order was promulgated directing all civilians to leave Atlanta (North or South) within twelve days. On the day of its issue a gentleman entered Sherman's office and enquired for the General. The latter answered, very promptly, "I am General Sherman." The colloquy was very nearly as follows:

Citizen—General, I am a Northern man from the State of Connecticut; I have been living at Atlanta for nearly seven years; have accumulated property here, and as I see that you have ordered all citizens to leave within twelve days, I came to see if you would make an exception in my case. I fear, if I leave, my property will be destroyed.

General Sherman—What kind of property do you own, sir? Perhaps I will make an exception in your case, sir.

Citizen—I own a block of stores, three buildings, a plantation two miles out of town, and a foundry.

General Sherman—Foundry, eh! what have you been doing with your foundry?

Citizen—Have been making castings.

General Sherman—What kind of castings? Shot and shell, and all that kind of thing?

Citizen—Yes, I have made some shot and shell.

General Sherman—You have been making shot and shell to destroy your country, have you? and you still claim favor on account of being a Northern man! Yes, sir, I will make an exception in your case; you shall go South to-morrow morning at sunrise. Adjutant, see that this order is carried out. Orderly show this man the door.

Citizen—But, General, can't I go North?

General Sherman—No sir. Too many of your class there already, sir.

SHERMAN TO A SOUTHERN MINISTER.

The following letter is characteristic of its author, and is an interesting sketch of one of the many pleasing episodes of the war. How very agreeable it must have been to a rebel minister, one clothed with the authority of the church and defending the most unholy cause! We can almost see him as he reads the missive:

ATLANTA, GA., SEPT. 16th, 1864.

Rev ——————— Confederate Army:

DEAR SIR;—Your letter of September 14 is received. I approach a question involving a title to a "horse" with deference for the laws of war. That mysterious code, of which we talk so much but know so little, is remarkably silent on the "horse." He is a beast so tempting to the soldier, to him of the wild cavalry, the fancy artillery, or the patient infantry, that I find more difficulty in recovering a worthless, spavined beast, than in paying a million of "Greenbacks;" so that I fear I must reduce your claim to one of finance, and refer you to the great board of claims in Washington, that may reach your case by the time your grandchild becomes a great grandfather.

Privately, I think it was a shabby thing in that scamp of the Thirty-first Missouri who took your horse, and the colonel or his brigadier should have restored him. But I cannot undertake to make good the sins of omission of my own colonels and brigadiers, much less of those of a former generation. "When this cruel war is over," and peace once more gives you a parish, I will promise, if near you, to procure out of Uncle Sam's corrals a beast that will replace the one taken from you, so wrongfully; but now it is impossible. We have a big journey before us and need all we have, and, I fear, more too; so look out when the Yanks are about and hide your beasts, for my experience is that all soldiers are very careless in a search for title. I know that Gen. Hardee will confirm this, my advice.

With great respect, yours truly,

W. T. SHERMAN, Maj. Gen.

A PRUSSIAN OFFICER IN SHERMAN'S ARMY.

I wish to say a few words about Captain Dilger, or "Leatherbreeches," as he is familiarly called. When the war broke out Captain Dilger was an artillery officer in the Prussian service. A short time after the battle of Bull Run, an uncle of Dilger (a merchant in New York) wrote that the present was an opportune time to visit America, &c.

Dilger was desirous of studying war as carried on here, and procured a leave of absence for a year. As soon as he arrived he joined the Army of the Potomac as an artillerist and commanded a battery. As his year drew to a close he managed to get his leave indefinitely extended, and has just been ordered to Cincinnati to be mustered out of the service, the term of his battery, the first Ohio Artillery, having expired.

He came out here with his battery with General Hooker, and by the name of "Leatherbreeches," became known to every officer and soldier in the army of the Cumberland. In all the battles which had occurred from Lookout Mountain to Peachtree Creek, Dilger has been on hand. He is first to open fire on the eve of battle, and takes his guns nearly up to the skirmish line. So often has he done this that some officer sometime ago, presented him with bayonets for his pieces.

"I saw him throughout the entire afternoon of the 20th ult., during which time he hurled the most frightful destruction into the rebel ranks. At one time he took "smooth bores" up to Gen. Johnston's line of battle, and for half an hour poured a raking fire of grape and cannister into the enemy in front of Hooker. He at one time became the target for three rebel batteries, and lost seven men during the day. He fires by volley when he "gets a good thing" and the acclamations of the infantry drown the reverberations of the cannon's roar upon all such occasions.

"He is a fine looking young man, speaks French, Italian and German fluently, and English with ease. He wears close buckskin breeches, with top boots, and stands by his guns in shirt sleeves during the battle. He has elicited the admiration of the whole army by his coolness and intrepidity when in action, and for his skill as an artillerist he has been made the recipient of numerous letters of acknowledgement from Generals Thomas, Johnson, King, Baird, Brannan, and others.

DEPARTURE OF COL. COBURN.

Shortly after the taking of Atlanta, Colonel Coburn, who had endeared himself to the brigade in a very strong manner, took leave of us to the regret of every one.

The following is his

FAREWELL.

Head-Quarters 2d Brig., 3d Div., 20th A. C., }
Atlanta, Ga., Sept. 20th, 1864. }

Soldiers of the Second Brigade:—My term of service has expired, and I am about to be separated from you. We have been associated as a brigade almost two years. We have borne in that time all the burdens, and endured all the trials and hardships of war, together. This especially has made us friends—such friends as only suffering and trial together can make. In that time, you have shared an eventful part in the great struggle of the age. In Kentucky, Tennessee and Georgia, you have nobly illustrated the history of your own states of Indiana, Michigan and Wisconsin. That history cannot be written without a record of your calm patience, disciplined endurance and heroic daring.

The bloody and desperate battle of Thompson's Station, and the successful fights at Franklin, Tennessee, gave early proof of your valor; while in the past campaign at Resaca, Cassville, New Hope Church, Golgotha, Culp's Farm, Peach Tree Creek and Atlanta, you have in the front of the fight borne straight onward your victorious banner.

At Resaca, your flag was the first to wave on the enemy's ramparts.

At New Hope Church, the fury of your onset redeemed the day's disaster.

At Peach Tree Creek, your charge rivalled the most famous feats of arms in the annals of war; and at Atlanta, your ranks were the first to climb the works of the enemy and take possession of that renowned city.

The 33d Indiana, at Wild Cat, fought the first battle and won the first victory gained by the Army of the Cumberland, and the united brigade fired the last shot at the flying foe, as he fled from his stronghold in Atlanta.

But not alone in the stormy and fiery fight have you been tried. You have, by long marches, by herculean labor upon field works, by cheerful obedience, by watching that knew no surprise, and by toil that knew no rest or weariness, eclipsed the fame of your daring in battle, and placed high above the glitter of victorious arms, the steady light of your solid virtues. We have lived together as brethren in a great common cause. We part, our hearts glowing with the same patriotic ardor.

And hereafter, when the war is over, and the light of home is smiling around you, we will have no prouder memories than those associated with this brigade.

Your comrades in arms are sleeping beneath the clods of the valley, from the Ohio to Atlanta, and from Atlanta to Richmond.

Faithful, patient and brave, they have given to their country and to God whatever martyrs and heroes can give.

And as, one by one, they fell out from your glorious ranks, they have added new testimony to the sacredness of your cause.

My friends, and soldiers, farewell.

JOHN COBURN,
Colonel 33d Indiana Vol., commanding Brigade.

CORRESPONDENCE WITH HOOD.

Upon arriving in Atlanta, General Sherman issued an order that the city was to be held for military purposes, consequently the citizens must leave.

The following conveys the intentions of General Sherman:

> HEADQUARTERS POST OF ATLANTA,
> ATLANTA, Ga., Sept. 5, 1864.
>
> GENERAL ORDER
> No. 3.
>
> All families living in Atlanta, the male representatives of which are in the service of the Confederate States, or who have gone south, will leave the city within five days. They will be passed through the lines and go south.
>
> All citizens from the North, not connected with the army, and who have not authority from Major-General Sherman, or Major-General Thomas to remain in the city, will leave within the time above mentioned. If found within the city after that date, they will be imprisoned.
>
> All male residents of this city, who do not register their names with the city Provost Marshal within five days and receive authority to remain here, will be imprisoned.
>
> WM. COGSWELL,
> Colonel Commanding Post.

In order to allow the inhabitants a chance to leave the city, General Sherman proposed an armistice of ten days, which was accepted by General Hood—then encamped near Lovejoy's—in the following letter:

Headquarters Army of the Tennessee,
Office Chief of Staff, Sept. 9, 1864.

Major-General Sherman, Commanding U. S. Forces in Georgia:

General:—Your letter of yesterday's date, borne by James W. Ball and James R. Crew, citizens of Atlanta, is received. You say therein, "I deem it to be to the best interest of the United States that the citizens residing in Atlanta should remove," etc. I do not consider that I have any alternative in the matter. I therefore accept your proposition to declare a truce of ten days, or such time as may be necessary to accomplish the purposes mentioned, and shall render all the assistance in my power to expedite the transportation of citizens in this direction.

I suggest that a staff officer be appointed to surperintend the removal from the city to Rough and Ready, while I appoint a similar officer to control their removal farther south; that a guard of 100 men be sent by either party, as you propose, to maintain order at that place, and that the removal begin next Monday.

And now, sir, permit me to say, that the unprecedented measure you propose, transcends in studied and ingenious cruelty all acts ever before brought to my attention in the dark history of war.

In the name of God and humanity I protest, believing that you will find you are expelling from their homes and firesides the wives and children of a brave people.

I am, General, very respectfully,
Your obed't servant,
J. B. Hood, General.

Official—Mc A. Hammett, Lieutenant, etc.

The following is General Sherman's reply:

      Hd. Qrs. Mil. Div. of the Miss.,
    In the Field, Atlanta, Ga., Sept. 10, '64.

General J. B. Hood, Commanding Army of the Tennessee, Confederate Army:

GENERAL:—I have the honor to acknowledge the receipt of your letter of this date at the hands of Messrs. Ball and Crew, consenting to the arrangements I had proposed to facilitate the removal south of the people of Atlanta, who prefer to go in that direction. I inclose you a copy of my orders, which will, I am satisfied, accomplish my purpose perfectly.

You style the measure proposed "unprecedented," and appeal to the dark history of war for a parallel, as an act of "studied, ungenerous cruelty." It is not unprecedented; for General Johnston himself very wisely and properly removed the families all the way from Dalton down, and I see no reason why Atlanta should be excepted.

Nor is it necessary to appeal to the dark history of war, when recent and modern examples are so handy. You, yourself burned dwelling-houses along your parapet, and I have seen to-day fifty houses that you have rendered uninhabitable, because they stood in the way of your forts and men.

You defended Atlanta on a line so close to the town, that every cannon shot, and many musket shots from our line of intrenchments, that over shot their mark, went into the habitations of women and children.

General Hardee did the same thing at Jonesboro, and General Johnston did the same, last summer, at Jackson, Miss. I have not accused you of heartless cruelty, but merely instance those cases of very recent occurrence, and could go on and enumerate hundreds of others, and challenge any fair man to judge which of us has the heart of pity for the families of "brave people."

I say it is a kindness to those families of Atlanta, to remove them now at once from scenes that women and children should not be exposed to; and the brave people should scorn to commit their wives and children to the rude barbarians, who thus, as you say, violate the laws of war, as illustrated in the pages of its dark history.

In the name of common sense, I ask you not to appeal to a just God in such a sacriligious manner—you who, in the midst of peace and prosperity, have plunged a nation into civil war—"dark and cruel war"—who dared and badgered us to battle, insulted our flag, seized our arsenals and forts, that were left in the honorable custody of a peaceful Ordnance Sergeant, seized and made prisoners of war the very garrisons sent to protect your people against negroes and Indians long before any overt act was committed by the "to you," hateful Lincoln Government, tried to force Kentucky and Missouri into the rebellion in spite of themselves, falsified the vote of Louisiana, turned loose your privateers to plunder unarmed ships, expelled Union families by the thousand, burned their houses, and declared by act of Congress the confiscation of all debts due Northern men for goods had and received.

Talk thus to the marines, but not to me who have seen these things, and will this day make as much sacrifice for the peace and honor of the South, as the best-born Southerners among you.

If we must be enemies, let us be men, and fight it out

as we propose to-day, and not deal in such hypocritical appeals to God and humanity.

God will judge me in good time, and he will pronounce whether it will be more humane to fight with a town full of women, and the families of a "brave people" at our backs, or to remove them in time to places of safety among their own friends and people.

I am, very respectfully, your obedient servant,
W. T. SHERMAN,
Major General commanding.

The mayor of the city also uttered his protest, which called forth another strong letter from General Sherman, but the people had to leave, and Atlanta became strictly a military post.

THE PREPARATION.

The army fairly cut loose from Atlanta, was to start across the state of Georgia on a long and tedious march. This plan was fully elaborated by General Sherman, and when laid before the War Department at Washington, it received their full approval.

During the first ten days of November, everything in the shape of a locomotive or car on the Atlanta & Chattanooga R. R. was used to its utmost capacity in transporting north those who were unfit for the long tramp; also, supplies that would not be needed. A great deal of machinery, forage and stores, that had accumulated at Atlanta, Rome, and other places—all surplus artillery, baggage, wagons, and in fact everything that would impede a rapid march across the country, was sent back to Chattanooga. In the place of such things, the cars brought back recruits, convalescents and furloughed men; also ordnance supplies.

On the night of November 11th, the last train of cars left for the north, and the Grand Army, with thirty days rations on the wagons, was prepared to "march to the sea."

Besides the four corps of infantry, there were four brigades of artillery, two horse batteries and two divisions of cavalry. All were equipped with great care, and thus with some 60,000 men, Sherman was prepared to commence one of the most important movements of the war, a movement that would be likely to occupy a large place in the public attention, and also cover many interesting pages in history.

A few extracts from Sherman's Special Order No. 120 will show what he proposed to do, and how he expected to do it:

HEAD-QUARTERS MILITARY DIV. OF THE MISSISSIPPI, }
IN THE FIELD, KINGSTON, GA., Wednesday, Nov. 9. }

1. For the purpose of military operations, this army is divided into two wings, viz: The right wing, Major-General O. O. Howard commanding, the 15th and 17th corps. The left wing, Major-General H. W. Slocum commanding, the 14th and 20th corps.

* * * * * * *

4. The army will forage liberally on the country during the march. To this end, each brigade commander will organize a good and sufficient foraging party, under the command of one or more discreet officers, who will gather, near the route travelled, corn, or forage of any kind, meat of any kind, vegetables, corn meal, or whatever is

needed by the command; aiming at all times to keep in the wagon trains at least ten days' provisions for the command, and three days' forage. Soldiers must not enter the dwellings of the inhabitants, or commit any trespass. During the halt, or a camp, they may be permitted to gather potatoes, turnips and other vegetables, and drive in stock in front of their camp. To regular foraging parties, must be entrusted the gathering of provisions and forage at any distance from the road travelled.

5. To army corps commanders, is entrusted the power to dettroy mills, houses, cotton gins, etc.. and for them this general principle is laid down: In districts and neighborhoods where the army is unmolested, no destruction of such property should be permitted; but should guerrillas or bushwhackers molest our march, or should the inhabitants burn bridges, obstruct roads, or otherwise manifest local hostility, then army corps commanders should order and enforce a devastation more or less relentless, according to the measure of such hostility.

6. As for horses, mules, wagons, etc., belonging to the inhabitants, the cavalry and artillery may appropriate freely, and without limit; discriminating, however, between the rich, who are usually hostile, and the poor or industrious, usually neutral or friendly. Foraging parties may also take mules or horses, to replace the jaded animals of their trains, or to serve as pack mules for the regiments or brigades.

In all foraging, of whatever kind, the parties engaged will refrain from abusive or threatening language, and may, when the officer in command thinks proper, give written certificates of the facts, but no receipts; and they will endeavor to leave with each family a reasonable portion for their maintenance.

* * * * * * *

By order of Major-General W. T. SHERMAN.
L. M. DAYTON,
Aid-de-Camp.

The following order, issued by General Slocum, will furnish additional facts relative to the march:

HEAD-QUARTERS 20TH CORPS,
ATLANTA, GA., November 7th, 1864.

(*Circular.*) When the troops leave camp on the march about to commence, they will carry in haversack two days' rations salt meat, two days' hard bread, ten days' coffee and salt, and five days' sugar. Each infantry soldier will carry sixty rounds of ammunition on his person. Every effort should be made by officers and men to save rations and ammunition; not a round of ammunition should be lost or unnecessarily expended. It is expected that the command will be supplied with subsistence and forage mainly from the country. All foraging will be done by parties detailed for the purpose by brigade commanders, under such rules as may be prescribed by brigade commanders. Pillaging, marauding, and every act of cruelty or abuse of citizens, will be severely punished. Each brigade commander will have a strong rear guard on every march, and will order the arrest of all stragglers. The danger of straggling on this march should be impressed upon the mind of every officer and man of the command. Not only the reputation of the corps, but the personal safety of every man, will be dependent, in a great measure, upon the rigid enforcement of discipline, and the care taken of the rations and ammunition.

By command of Major-General SLOCUM.

H. W. PERKINS,
Assistant Adjutant-General.

The route decided upon by General Sherman was evidently through the richest section of the State, and should he make toward Savannah, he would be able to destroy the railroad running from Macon to Savannah, the main artery of the State, also many other branches of vital importance to the confederacy.

On the morning of the 12th, the 14th corps moved out of Kingston, leaving simply a brigade to look after the last shipment of things North.

In the afternoon, the following was sent as a parting message, "All is well," and the wires were then cut, and Sherman's army was really cut off from the outer world. The railroad track was all torn up from Kingston to the Chattahoochee, also every building that could be of any service to the rebels.

The several corps were then concentrated near Atlanta, and the work of destruction went on rapidly.

On the evening of the 14th, the torch was applied to everything valuable, store-houses, machine shops, and depot buildings. For many hours, huge, dense columns of black could be seen going up from different parts of the city, and the heavens were lighted up in a most magnificent manner by the grand conflagration. Several of the railroad buildings, which could not be burned, being built of stone or brick, were demolished by battering rams.

Next to Richmond, perhaps no city had furnished more

war materials than Atlanta, and now every one felt that it should no longer remain a stronghold for traitors. The destruction was complete.

Shortly before leaving the city, the following was issued:

HEADQUARTERS MILITARY DIVISION OF THE MISSISSIPPI, IN THE FIELD, KINGSTON, GEORGIA, NOV. 8TH, 1864.

SPECIAL ORDERS,
No. 119.

The General Commanding deems it proper at this time to inform the officers and men of the 14th, 15th, 17th and 20th corps, that he has organized them into an army for a special purpose, well known to the War Department and to General Grant. It is sufficient for you to know that it involves a departure from our present base, and a long and difficult march to a new one.

All the chances of war have been considered and provided for, as far as human sagacity can. All he asks of you is, to maintain that discipline, patience, and courage which have characterized you in the past, and hopes through you to strike a blow at our enemy that will have a material effect in producing what we all so much desire —his complete overthrow.

Of all things, the most important is that the men, during marches and in camp, keep their places, and not scatter abroad as stragglers and foragers, to be picked up by a hostile people in detail.

It is also of the utmost importance, that our wagons should not be loaded with anything but provisions and ammunition. All surplus servants, non-combatants, and refugees, should now go to the rear, and none should be encouraged to cucumber us on the march.

At some future time, we will be enabled to provide for the poor whites and blacks, who seek to escape the bondage they are now suffering under.

With these few simple cautions in your minds, he hopes to lead you to achievements equal in importance to those of the past.

By order of Gen. W. T. SHERMAN.
L. M. Dayton, Aid-de-Camp.

On the 15th, the whole army, in four separate columns, marched eastward.

A few days subsequent to this, the following characteristic proclamations appeared:

To the People of Georgia:

Arise for the defence of your native soil! Rally around your patriotic Governor and gallant soldiers. Obstruct and destroy all the roads in Sherman's front, flank, and rear, and his army will soon starve in your midst. Be confident. Be resolute. Trust in an over-ruling Providence, and success will soon crown your efforts.

I hasten to join you in the defense of your homes and firesides. G. T. BEAUREGARD.

Richmond, Nov. 18.
To the People of Georgia:

You have now the best opportunity ever yet presented to destroy the enemy. Put everything at the disposal of our Generals, remove all provisions from the path of the invader, and put all obstructions in his path.

Every citizen with his gun, and every negro with his

spade and axe can do the work of a soldier. You can destroy the enemy by retarding his march.

Georgians, be firm, act pomptly, and fear not.

B. H. Hill.

I most cordially approve the above.

James A. Seddon, Sec'y of War.

The above is from a Senator in the rebel congress.

And here follows one from the lower house:

Richmond, Nov. 19, 1864.

To the People of Georgia:

We have had a special conference with President Davis and the Secretary of War, and are able to assure you that they have done, and are still doing, all that can be done to meet the emergency that presses upon you. Let every man fly to arms. Remove your negroes, horses, cattle, and provisions from Sherman's army, and burn what you cannot carry.

Burn all bridges, and block up the roads in his route. Assail the invader in front, flank, and rear, by night and by day. Let him have no rest.

Julian Hartridge,	Mark Blanford,
J. H. Reynolds,	Gen. N. Lester,
Jno. T. Shewmaker,	Jos. M. Smith.

It is said there was great rejoicing at Richmond, when they heard of the intention of Sherman to march off into the interior of an enemy's country. The rebel papers declared that he could never get through—that they would soon get him just where they wanted him. They declared that Hood had out generaled him at Atlanta, and that he was now simply trying to make his escape.

We shall see.

THE SAVANNAH CAMPAIGN.

In order to present as vivid and correct a picture as possible of our "long tramp" across the State of Georgia, we shall make copious extracts from our journal. Perhaps it may not be as readable as the narrative style, still a journal form is calculated to present our daily life during "Sherman's march to the Sea," so we invite you to live over with us a march, that will ever occupy a conspicuous place in history.

Just before leaving Atlanta, the following was announced:

HEADQUARTERS 2D BRIGADE 3D DIV. 20TH
A. C., ATLANTA, GA., NOV. 9TH, 1864.

CIRCULAR:

I hereby assume command of the 2d Brigade, 3d Division, 20th A. C.

Highly appreciating the compliment of being placed in command of officers and men of such sterling quality as compose this brigade, my highest ambition will be to exercise all the ability and energy within my power, in sustaining its present proud record, and securing for it, the reputation in camp and field, of being excelled by none in the service.

To do this, I rely with confidence upon the harmonious and hearty co-operation of all concerned.

DANIEL DUSTIN.
Col. 105th Ill. Inft'y.

LETTER VIII.

HEADQUARTERS 22D WISCONSIN,
ATLANTA, Ga., Nov. 11, 1864.

DEAR HOME FRIENDS:—Perhaps ere this, you have been

informed that a movement for an extended campaign is in progress. When I reached Atlanta last Sabbath, I was at once informed that the 20th corps had already taken up its line of march, and had encamped for the night some three miles out of the city, on the Macon railroad. The 22d regiment was soon found, but they were just breaking camp to march back to their camping ground southeast of the city.

Whether this movement was simply a *blind* or not, no one knows. The probability is, that we were called back for the protection of the city, the 17th corps not coming up as soon as expected. That morning just about daybreak, the pickets of our brigade were fired upon, and there was a brisk little fight. The bullets came whistling over the camp in quite a lively manner. One man of the 33d Indiana was killed, and one taken prisoner, and some two or three wounded.

Our present camp is a very pleasant place, just inside the breastworks built by the rebels.

There are two forts near us, one on either hand. The rebels had a line of works entirely around the city, and on every hill along the line was a fort, some of them very strong.

The voting in our regiment passed off very quietly. It stands as follows: Lincoln, 372; McClellan, 10.

The next morning, a little after daylight, we were suddenly aroused from our slumbers by the report of artillery on the extreme left of our brigade. The rebs had opened fire on the 85th Indiana, from a hill perhaps three-fourths of a mile distant. Our men were under arms in a few moments, valises and boxes were packed, horses were saddled and stood pawing at the doors of our tents, where they remained till about noon. In a short time, the firing on our left ceased, but it was only to be opened with greater energy on our right. It was reported that the rebs had three brigades of cavalry, but our skirmish line held them back, and soon our artillery sent them flying out of sight.

Since the taking of Atlanta, our boys have seen very quiet times till a few days since.

All is excitement now about the coming campaign, and we are expecting every day to be on the wing. It is very evident that some great movement is at hand. Some think we are going to one place, some to another, but we are evidently going to do something, and you may rest assured that Sherman will make his mark again. He is abundantly able to hold Atlanta, and still protect his communications, but in my opinion, it would be far better to evacuate this city, burn it, at least all the public buildings, effectually destroy the railroad as far back at Resaca, then send out two strong columns, one toward Augusta, and the other toward Macon, destroying both of these railroads, and Atlanta would cease to be a place of any importance. The rebels would not be able in a long time to repair the several roads, and thus the city would not be of any particular use to them. If Atlanta is held, it will require a large force here, and a large one all along the line toward Chattanooga. It will not pay to do this, but destroy Atlanta and its railroads, and at least 50,000 men could be spared, either to aid Grant, or go on an extion to the gulf.

The health of our regiment is good at present, and evething goes off pleasantly.

Colonel Bloodgood has shown himself to be an able

man, and his officers have great confidence in him. Great efforts were made at one time to crush him, but he has triumphed nobly, and some of those who were opposed to him have apologized, saying they were sorry they acted the part they did. Some who tried hard to ruin him, have themselves been compelled to leave the service in disgrace.

The 22d lost some very able officers during the difficulty, but it has good ones left, and to-day the regiment stands high in the 2d division. It has borne itself nobly on several hard fought battle-fields, and its ranks have been sadly thinned, though it has lost but few officers killed.

Captain Wm. Bones is brigade inspector, and Captain Kellam is A. A. G. on Colonel Dustin's staff—Colonel D. now commands our brigade—and Captan May is acting major of the regiment. Colonel Bloodgood was in command of the brigade a short time, and gave very excellent satisfaction. G. S. BRADLEY, Chaplain.

THE MARCH.

Nov. 15th.—Orders came last night for us to move to-day. The 20th, 17th, 15th, and 14th corps have been organized into an army, called the Army of Georgia, the 20th and 14th forming the left wing, the 17th and 15th the right wing. We march in four columns. The organization is as follows: 20th corps commanded by General Williams; 17th, General Blair; 15th, General Osterhaus; 14th, General Jeff. C. Davis; left wing, General Slocum; right wing, General O. O. Howard; 1st division, 20th corps, General Jackson; 2d, General Geary; 3d, General Ward.

Broke camp about 9 A. M., and marched out beyond the fortifications south of the city a short distance, where we rested till about 4 P. M., taking dinner in the mean time, when we commenced the grand march through the enemy's country. Our course lay in the direction of Decatur.

Nov. 16th.—Marched all night, stopping about every half hour for awhile; we being in the rear and subject to all of the stoppages, none of us had much sleep. I fell asleep on my horse several times in spite of myself. Have travelled some 15 miles. If last night's march is a fair specimen of the campaign, it will be a hard one for both man and beast.

From Atlanta and for full five miles, I saw but just one house left standing, and that was soon in flames. We saw the light for many miles after passing it.

Went into camp just before dark, a short distance from the main road. Just as we came into camp, one of the boys found a large box of corn concealed down by the spring; so our horses were well cared for. Also found plenty of sweet potatoes. For supper our bill of fare was as follows, viz: bacon, sweet potatoes fried, hard bread and coffee with sugar. Was very hungry after such a march. We are now 22 miles from Atlanta. One of the citizens along the way informed me, that this movement of our army was entirely unknown to the people where he lived. The country through here was formerly owned and worked by rich planters, but exhausting the soil, they divided their large plantations, selling to poor men, and moved to Mississippi or Alabama, to put the land there through the same exhausting process.

By the road side, resided a family of Smith's. The following conversation occurred between one of the married daughters and one of our soldiers;

"Is your husband in the rebel army?"

"Of course."

"Was he conscripted?"

"No, sir, he volunteered; *I would not have a man if he had to be conscripted!*"

As a general thing, the buildings are very poor; now and then a pleasant, substantial mansion is seen. This is a great country for sweet potatoes and yams, the only difference between them being in the quality of the two, the sweet potatoes being finer.

Thursday, Nov. 17th.—Reveille at 3:30 this morning. Had a good night's rest—the best since I left the North. Last evening the camp fires of the 14th corps could be seen nearly opposite us some eight or ten miles to the right. Between the different corps and on the flanks, are some six to eight thousand cavalry scouring the country, eating up not only every green thing, but almost every dry thing. This will undoubtedly be looked upon as the biggest raid of the war.

We are now striking through the very heart of Georgia. All intend to live well during the campaign.

The country this side of Yellow river is more level, and the soil less red than on the other side of the stream. We are getting into a fine country.

It is reported that some 1,400 Georgia militia were

through here a few days since, and that they stopped about 20 miles from where we camped last night. There had lately been 15,000 troops, but they had then left, going towards Jonesboro.

Friday, Nov. 18th.—Stopped for dinner at a place called Social Circle, taking its name from the formation, a number of years since, of social parties for drinking. It is on the Atlanta and Augusta railroad, and about 40 miles from the former place and 136 from Augusta. Some of the troops were engaged in destroying the track, while the rest of us were enjoying our dinner; some were feeding their horses and mules from a corn crib near by; some were making a raid on a barrel of sorghum; while others went after pigs, chickens, &c. The troops had a hard march yesterday and last evening, as there was a continual stopping of the trains. Travelled all night till 2:30 this morning, when we went into camp some five miles the other side of the Circle.

1:10 P. M. Dinner over, we have come along. Some are now tearing up the track, while others are guarding the trains. Files of troops go on each side. The people at the Circle had heard of the raid night before last, so all the cars are taken south, and the people along the road have undoubtedly run off a good deal of their stuff, still there is plenty of forage left for us. Foraging parties are sent out each day on the flanks, while everything is taken along our track as we come to it. The question, I think, is never asked how much the farmer needs for his subsistence, but all is taken—literally everything. These foraging parties bring in cattle, horses, sheep, pigs, sweet potatoes, corn, bacon, sorghum, wheat flour, corn meal, honey, &c.

3:30 P. M.—Are now at Rutlege, a little station on the railroad, seven miles from Social Circle and nine from Madison. This morning there were a few rebel cavalry here, but they left in a hurry.

By order of General Slocum, the freight depot was burned, also another railroad building near, and a line of smoke was seen for a long distance along the track.

Reached camp about four and a half miles from Madison; camped on the plantation of Hon. Mr. Jones, formerly member of Congress from Georgia. His plantation comprises 2,000 acres. When he heard of the approach of the Yankee army, he immediately mounted his horse and left. Said to his overseer that it would not do for him to remain at home, as he had made too many speeches against the North when in Congress.

He had just completed the digging of about 1,000 bushels of sweet potatoes, but in a short time after our arrival none were left. He had also large quantities of corn, wheat and oats, on hand, which our army freely used.

Several of his negroes joined us, concluding they had worked long enough for Mr. Jones.

NOVEMBER, 19.

Broke camp about daylight, and after marching a short distance, were ordered to halt and tear up and burn the railroad track. The entire forenoon was spent in this manner, the track being torn up as far as Madison. It was quite interesting to see them tear it up. A whole regiment would get hold of a long strip and turn it completely over. Fence rails were piled on and fire applied. At times the track had the appearance of a huge furrow going over. All the railroad buildings in Madison were burned, also the Market House, said to have been used lately for a slave whipping post. Our soldiers were quite loud in their denunciation of the vile system, and the torch was applied with a hearty good will.

Madison is one of the prettiest places I have seen in the South. It is in the midst of one of the richest sections of Georgia, and most of its inhabitants belong to the upper class. Many who reside here own extensive plantations in Mississippi or Alabama. As I passed a house, a lady, sitting on a piazza, inquired:

"When do you think this thing will be over?"

"I do not know, but I hope soon."

"Well," said she, "I think our people are very foolish to continue the war any longer. We are not subdued in spirit, but we are *whipped*, and we might as well own up. We *hate* you, but you now have the power in your own hands, and sooner or later we must come under."

"Supposing you could gain your independence," I inquired, "what advantage would it be to you? Would you not be just as well off under the old government?"

"No, I don't think so."

"Why not?"

"Well I don't suppose it would make much difference with us as individuals, but then you know our government has just as much pride as you have."

"Don't you think Southern people have had wrong ideas about Northern people and Northern sentiment?"

"Yes, I suppose they have to quite an extent. So far as I have seen your army, I am quite well pleased with the soldiers. They seem to be under excellent discipline—much better than our soldiers."

Something was then said on the slavery question, when she remarked that she had no doubt that slavery was a curse to the country—that the South would be much better off without slaves.

"What do the people about here think of so many of them joining our army?"

"O, we are all glad of it, for your army has taken about all we have to live upon, and the less niggers we have to take care of the better for us."

"What kind of an idea did the people generally have of the Yankee soldiers?"

"We were all told that they were *awful bad men*, but they have treated me very kindly indeed."

She seemed to be quite an intelligent woman, and very ready to communicate her ideas of matters generally. She thought the war would have ended before this time, had it been left to the peope; but the big men of the South had everything to lose if they failed in getting their independence, so the war must go on.

"I don't know" said she, "what in the world the people through here are going to live upon, for your army is taking everything."

Sunday, Nov. 20th.—Camped last night about five miles south of Madison, on the road leading to Milledgville. Had a good night's rest. Broke camp at 5 P. M., and marched about 15 miles, camping for the night within a few miles of Eatonton. Rained considerable last night, thus rendering the roads quite muddy.

Nov. 21st.—Rained again nearly all night. This part of Georgia appears to be more productive than any other we have seen. The well filled corn, wheat, and oat cribs prove it. It is also a good cotton region, though but little has been raised since the war commenced. The few people seen, all say that nearly every one is in the army who is fit to go.

It is quite interesting to see the troops of negroes that press into our lines. They frequently come, bringing with them a lot of mules or horses. Night before last, some twenty negroes got together, took 40 of their masters mules and horses, and come over to us. They had been sent off into the swamps with them, but concluded it would suit the Yankees pretty well to get hold of such things, so they came in. The feeling is almost universal among them to fall into our army. They all seem to have the idea that we are down here to set them at liberty, or that the war is in behalf of the blacks. They very readily tell us where anything is concealed, and seem well pleased when we find various articles. Several have told me that they would be glad to go along with us, but could not on account of their families.

So far we have all enjoyed the campaign very much indeed. There is a certain sort of excitement about it that keeps one's interest alive all of the time. We are constantly seeing new places and things, and the monotony of camp life is no longer felt.

One of the 22d, Jack McLain, in company with another young man was out foraging a few days since, armed simply with revolvers. As they neared a house, they noticed a man dart behind a barn, but thinking it was one of our own men after a chicken, they boldly pushed on, but had gone only a short distance, when "whiz" went a bullet by their heads. Wheeling their horses, they made for our lines as fast as possible.

No house escapes the general pillage. The soldiers rush into every one not under guard, and pick up whatever suits their fancy. It is sad to see the work of ruin.

Every house containing cotton is burned by general orders, the boys remarking simply, "Here goes for King Cotton."

Our corps separated at Madison, the 1st and 3d divisions going toward Milledgville, while the 2d under Geary struck off toward Athens to destroy the railroad that way, the men taking five days rations with them—their wagons being left for the other division to guard.

The most of the inhabitants whom we find along our march, seem very gloomy over the present aspect of affairs. The fall of Atlanta was a stunning blow to them, however much their leaders and papers may try to smooth over the matter. They had evidently built strong hopes on the success of their army in Georgia, but when they saw Johnston continually driven back, and then Hood so badly used up at Atlanta, they began to open their eyes and perceive, that the "*Yankee army was bound to go where it pleased.*"

Marched about fourteen miles to-day, and camped at night, within about eight miles of the capital of the state. Have had a very hard day's march, owing to the rain. Rained all night last night and most of to-day. We broke camp about daylight, the rain pouring down in torrents all of the time. It has been the most disagreeable day's march I have had since entering the service. We camped last night within some two miles of Eatonton, a village that contained before the war perhaps 1600 whites—some 4000 whites and blacks. The railroad buildings were all burned, being in flames as we passed.

Went into camp about 2 30 P. M.; to-day, the boys being pretty well tired out working their way along in the rain and mud.

Tuesday, November 22d.—had a very windy, chilly night. I slept very well till toward morning, when I felt too cold to sleep. Yesterday some of the boys of the 3d brigade, while out foraging, were fired upon and some of their horses wounded. Some of the 22d, out several miles on the flank, represent a terrible consternation existing in every direction. The people are running off their horses and mules as fast as possible, but if they leave it for their slaves to do, we shall get the most of them. We have already quite an army of blacks along with us, both men, women and children.

Our camp was on quite a hill—a very windy, bad place. We expected to move at 8 A. M., but falling in the rear, we had to wait for the other divisions to move, which kept us there till nearly night. Being without tents, we suffered all day from the cold. They have burnt up all the fencing everywhere around here. The soldiers seem cheerful and happy, and all, or nearly all, are pleased to have a part in this, the *grandest affair* of the whole war. I heard one say, a day or two since, that he would not have missed it for fifty dollars. At present, all live sumptuously, it being a rich country through here.

MILLEDGEVILLE, Ga., Nov. 23.

Arrived in this place this morning about 5 o'clock, after marching all night. We crossed Little River, a branch of the Oconee, just before dark yesterday, our former camp being about a mile on the other side. Had a most unpleasant march last night, the weather being very chilly. There were many bad places in the road, so our men had to stop continually. We crossed the river on a pontoon. It was entirely impossible for me to keep awake, and I fell asleep many a time on my horse, and continued so till, losing my balance, it would wake me up. When within about two miles of the city, I was so thoroughly chilled and sleepy, that I got off my horse, tied him to a fence, and lay down by a fire, where I fell asleep in a few minutes. After staying there awhile, I went on toward the city. The various regiments were very much scattered when we got into camp; very many soldiers had straggled, and did not come into camp till long after daylight, they having lain down by the road-side and gone to sleep. Several mules were killed during the night's march, and some of the wagons tipped over, and some had to be abandoned, being broken. We passed directly through the city, near the State House, and camped a little south of the city. We occupied the house of a widow lady for our head-quarters. She seemed quite pleased to have us take up our abode there, as that would afford her ample protection while we stayed. She gave me prices, as follows:

Coffee $18 per lb., sugar $7 per lb., ham $4 per lb., bacon $3.75 per lb., butter $7 per lb., lard $4 per lb., wheat flour $1 per lb., beef steak $1 per lb., cotton cloth $5 per yard, jean $15 per yard, corn meal $8 per bush., tea not to be obtained.

The location of the Capitol is a very pleasant one, and it seemed a pity to burn such a building. Perhaps it will not be done.

We found quite a large quantity of muskets packed in boxes in the main entrance hall. While looking around the building, I heard a loud explosion, and on going to the window, I saw the arsenal on fire, and soon it was completely wrapped in flame. It was a large brick structure, standing a short distance from the capitol. In it were found various articles—gun slings, huge pikes, a short, heavy knife or saber, &c. The burning was a magnificent sight. In the magazine, another brick building, standing still further off in another direction, was found quite a quantity of ammunition. I saw six wagons engaged in drawing it to the river, into which it was thrown. The building itself is fire-proof, and will probably be blown up after the troops get away.

I was much disappointed in the size of the place, supposing that being the capital of such a state, it would be a large place, but it contained before the war only some 2,500 inhabitants. There has long been a strife about removing the seat of government, Atlanta and Macon each striving for it, so that people in Milledgeville dare not invest property there, hence it could not grow. Business has been very dull for a year or so, merchants not being able to procure goods. So much for the *paper blockade.* As we entered the place, the penitentiary was burning. One of the prisoners who came into our army, a man sentenced there for life, having been implicated in a murder case with five others, in Adairsville—informed me that about a week before our arrival, Gov. Brown came in and made a speech to the prisoners, there being 150 confined at the time, telling them if they would volunteer they might be released from prison. All but 25 of them enlisted, though most of them were Union men, this prisoner said, but they thought they would stand a better chance to run away if in the army. A day or two before we came, the keepers all fled, leaving the balance of the prisoners to look out for themselves. There were some women left—

very hard cases. One of them dressed herself in federal uniform and entered our army.

There were but few houses left in the place unsacked, everything being taken that the soldiers could get hold of.

November 24.—Left Milledgeville about 8 o'clock A. M. Crossed the Oconee on a good bridge, and then waited for other troops to go ahead of us, till near 11 o'clock. Our course now is in a north easterly direction, apparently toward Augusta. It is a rough, uneven country, the timber mostly pine. Fence rails, for the most part, are made of pine. As a general thing the plantations are well fenced—much of it twelve rails high. *It makes excellent fire wood* as we pass along. The soil must be rather poor through here, judging from the amount of sand it contains.

Marched some twelve miles—coming rather slow on account of bad places in the road.

To-day is Thanksgiving day all over the North, and our friends are probably enjoying themselves. Many prayers will go up from numerous public congregations, as well as private individuals, in our behalf. While our friends at home are enjoying their pleasant dinners of good things, we are far away on the weary march. What a difference in our conditions.

Nov. 25th.—Last night, the rebels burnt a bridge, or rather several acres of wide swamp where we must pass. Some of the planters near, protested strongly against this, telling the troops that it would only make it worse for them, for while our army might be delayed, our soldiers would have all the more time to sack their plantations. They were right in this. It will do the rebels no good to burn bridges, for we have a pontoon train with us, and a bridge can soon be put across any stream. Some of our boys out foraging this morning were fired upon, probably by the squad of rebs who set fire to the bridges. It is getting quite dangerous for small squads to go out far from the main column. Regular parties are sent out every day after horses and mules. Lieutenant Knowles, of the 22d, has charge of one party, and has thus far been very successful. As we were riding along to-day, Captain Bones said to a colored man riding leisurely along on a horse, "Whose horse is that?" The negro, not understanding him, began to tell to whom he himself belonged.

"I don't care anything about whom you belong to, but I want to know whose horse that is?"

"O, he belongs to the crowd."

Colonel Dustin and the rest of us all burst out laughing, thinking that the Captain did not get much the start of the negro that time.

Saturday, Nov. 26th.—Marched some twelve miles yesterday. We shall probably now all along have more or less skirmishing with the enemy, for we are in the very heart of their country. There was a rumor in camp yesterday that Grant had taken Richmond with very heavy loss to himself. The rumor comes, of course, through rebel sources. The report is very much doubted, but all hope it is true. When some of the people along the road heard of the election of Lincoln, they exclaimed, "O dear, we shall still continue to have war!" So far as I have been able to find out, the idea of the inhabitants is, that slavery lies at the basis of the whole trouble. People have told me that they went to war for the purpose of making their institutions more secure.

Whole families are frequently seen coming in on the cross roads, with some old mule team and wagon, having on board what few household matters they could get together. I have frequently seen them patiently waiting for our trains to come along, so that they could fall in. While the whites are in perfect consternation, the blacks hail our approach as a day of jubilee. It is almost the universal belief among the blacks, that we are marching through here to liberate them, hence they will give us any information desired.

Our progress to-day has been rather slow on account of bad places in the road. As a general thing, the roads are dry and nice, there being so much sand in the soil that the mud soon disappears.

I should dislike living in this part of Georgia very much indeed. It is a timbered country, but the land is poor. It looks extremely lonesome all through here. Have seen but very few young men in the country, and am told that nearly all are in the army. In many places, the women have the most of the work to do. Some of the best negroes have been put into the rebel army, still there are many left. Some plantations seem to swarm with little woolly heads.

Reached camp at Sandersville a little before dark, having marched about eighteen miles. We are now about twenty-seven miles from Milledgeville. Quite sharp skirmishing has been going on all day from where we camped last night. In some places along the road, I noticed rebel breastworks of rails thrown up, and trees were felled across the road. Some of Wheeler's troops kept ahead of us. There was skirmishing all through the village here. The 14th corps entered the place about the same time the 20th did, and both had part in the skirmishing. Saw one big rebel lying dead in the church, shot through the breast. Our boys were just putting him into a rough coffin, and his grave was being dug near the church. Our loss was slight.

Sabbath, Nov. 27th.—Broke camp at 8:30 A. M. Had a very pleasant camping ground last night. Slept warm for the first time in several nights. 'Tis a most lovely day—wish we could stop and have services.

In the night, the 1st and 2d divisions were sent off in the direction of Augusta, to destroy the railroad. It comes within some three miles of Sandersville. This place contained about 1,000 inhabitants, and is the county seat of Washington county. As we marched along, I noticed the jail and court house on fire. Struck the railroad in a short time, and found it in flames as far as we could see either way. Many blacks have joined us to-day. Women came with large bundles on their heads, children also carried quite large packages on their heads, and some of the larger ones carried the little ones. All seemed bent on having their freedom, poor, ignorant, miserable people! They little know the hardships before them. Many of them come into our ranks with expectations that will fall far below realization. Our soldiers urge them to go along with us, without stopping to think how they will manage to make their way to a land of freedom.

We now have some sixty rebel prisoners along with our division, including six officers, one of whom is a Colonel, the result of yesterday's skirmishing.

Lieutenant Knowles, of the 22d, captured a rebel while on picket yesterday, coming upon the fellow before he was aware of it.

Monday, Nov. 28th.—Yesterday we marched from Sandersville to Davisboro, about fifteen miles; had quite a pleasant day's march—camped for the night a little distance back from the railroad in an open field, but near a piece of woods. We usually camp in line of battle, so as to be prepared at a moment's warning for any emergency. Davisboro is a small village, surrounded by rather a pleasant country. Broke camp this morning about daylight, marching in the direction of Louisville.

11:30 A. M.—Are now resting in the woods a short distance from the river near Louisville. Quite heavy skirmighing is going on just in our front. Our brigade has the advance to-day. I was riding along in company with General Ward, when the skirmishing became so warm that we had to halt. I could see the smoke of the guns in the woods. It is supposed that the enemy have some 2,500 cavalry ahead of us. They burnt all the bridges across the big swamp in our front last night, and are now probably disputing our further passage.

Some of the boys are saying that they are glad we are in the advance of the corps to-day, for if they have to fight at all, they rather go in at first than be brought up as reserves.

After skirmishing for awhile, it was discovered that the firing on the other side of the swamp came from our own men of the 14th corps, they supposing us to be rebs on this side, and we supposing the same thing of them.

It seems that they crossed further up the river, and entered Louisville early in the day. Seeing the bridges on fire, they sent a guard of men down to put it out, and they fired in upon our advance cavalry. General Ward coming up just at this juncture, ordered the cavalry back, and two companies of the 33d Indiana to advance. Thus the 33d was pitted against another Indiana regiment of the 14th corps. They fired a few volleys, when some daring fellow of the 33d ventured across on the burning stringers of the bridge, and the whole thing was soon explained. Had this occurred in the night, most serious results might have followed, but as it was no one was hurt.

Some of the southern people express great surprise at the election of Lincoln. Said they had been led to suppose that he could not possibly be elected, and that we already had in the field about every man. The largeness of our army is a perfect wonder to them.

Nov. 29th.—Staid on the other side of the river last night so as to cover the trains till the bridges could be fixed. The swamp proved to be a very bad place to cross, the teams not all getting over till about dark to-day. Just before dark last evening, word came into camp that the rebs were pressing in our rear, and that Capt. Bones had been fired upon. It seems that he had gone out that way all alone, to see if any pickets had been left by the other brigades, and was riding along in rather a leisurely manner, when he noticed a head looking out carefully from behind a tree. Reining his horse to the side of the road to get a better view of the fellow, the rebel at once rode out and ordered him to halt, being at a distance of about six rods. The Captain wheeled his horse towards camp at once, discovering about the same time two other rebs on horses, who also commanded him to halt. Two of them fired upon him, the third one's gun failing to discharge, and then commenced a race for life, but the rebs did not dare to follow far, as it would bring them too near our main force. Captain Bones is a brave, dashing officer, but it was a foolish thing for him to venture towards the rear all alone, as there are plenty of the enemy hovering about, to pick off any one who may happen to be so unlucky as to fall within their reach.

Col Dustin thought him unwise thus to expose himself, still he commended him for his bravery.

Several companies of the 22d were at once ordered into line of battle and sent to the rear, and soon the entire brigade was thrown around the trains. The night passed off quietly, however.

Our present camp is but a short distance this side of the swamp, on a very low, wet piece of ground, the water actually standing on some portions of it. It was expected last night when we broke camp on the other side, that we should travel all night again, but some of the divisions sent to destroy the railroad failing to come up, it was deemed best that we camp within reach of the pontoon, so as to protect it.

Nov. 30th—The artillery went forward last night, but was ordered back, it being feared that we might be attacked during the night. Four guns are now in position just opposite us on the other side of the road.

Thus far we have been very fortunate as to sickness. There are a few complaining, though there is nothing serious I believe.

Wish we could get some letters from home while camping in this swamp. How anxiously the loved ones far away will wait for letters from us! Shall we ever meet again?

Dec. 1st—Broke camp last night about 8 o'clock, marching only about five miles, but it took us till one o'clock this morning. It was an awful road to travel in the night, many places being so muddy as to be almost impassable, and then to add to our trouble, the night was exceedingly foggy and dark, so that one could not tell where to go only as he followed closely the one ahead of him. Not having felt very well during the day, it was a very hard night's work for me, producing a sickness at the stomach. Col. Bloodgood and others were affected in a similar manner. Getting into camp so late, we simply spread our tents on the ground and lay down in the chilly, cold open air, still I slept quite warm and well, considering the circumstances.

Passed through Louisville during our march, but did not stop. Saw many chimneys standing as evidence that fire had faithfully been doing its fearful work. It once contained 2,000 inhabitants, but it is almost entirely deserted at present, the people taking the most of their effects with them. Our stay in the swamp is already having its effect upon the men by way of cough. Were this a rainy time, I hardly see how we could possibly get through these swamps.

Shortly after daylight this morning, Corp. Witham of Co. G, brought in a rebel prisoner under the following circumstances: He went out after wood, and seeing a persimmon tree, he shook it, the noise of which started up a sleeping reb near by. There was a loaded musket by his side, and he had all his accouterments on. Witham was not armed at all, but putting his hand to his pocket as if about to draw his revolver, he marched boldly up to the fellow, when the reb said in a hurry, "I surrender," and he brought him in. The fellow seemed very much surprised at his capture.

A colored man and his wife with two children have just

passed me. The children were astride a poor old horse, the mother leading it, and the father pushing on ahead. And here comes another woman on horseback, with a little boy behind her and a small child in her arms. She tells me that she has been with the army since it was in Marietta—that her husband was a teamster.

A squad of rebel prisoners has just gone along, and among the number, I noticed some very young looking boys. Some of the men are very confident that we shall never be able to get through to the coast. Kilpatrick a few days since cut the railroad between Augusta and Millen. The bugle is sounding, the troops have mostly passed, and we are the rear guard, so we are elected for another night's work. These night marches are very severe on the men, but they cannot be avoided.

For breakfast had chicken, goose, fresh pork, sweet potatoes, hard bread and coffee with sugar.

Broke camp at 7 o'clock A. M. The country through here is very thinly settled. After leaving camp, we travelled for two hours before coming to a house. When we do come to one, it is generally that of a wealthy planter with plenty of negro cabins near. The soil is very sandy, and the principal production is corn. This is emphatically a pitch pine country. Most of the houses we see through this section are deserted. Along at first, as we started out of Atlanta, the people mostly staid at home, but this way they have left.

Dec. 3d.—Marched about 15 miles yesterday on the Millen road, passing through some very pleasant country. Saw one splendid plantation. The Mansion House was a very fine one, the best we have seen on the march, and the grounds around bore evidence of much taste in the proprietor, Dr. Jones, formerly professor in Oglethorpe University, but for awhile past a Major in the rebel service. He was taken prisoner a few days since.

Reached camp about dark and spent a very pleasant night.

The boys do not very often put up their tents, but lie down by good fires, with their blankets over them. We generally put up our headquarter tents every night. Camped last night 11 miles from Millen.

Now and then, we pass a school house, and some very good ones too, but as a general thing, the population is too scattered for schools. During the day, I stopped to feed my horse from a big corn crib, the overseer telling me that he had about 3,500 bushels on hand when our army first commenced passing, worth about $8,00 per bushel, but there would be nothing left in a few hours. On the north side of a large open square, was a row of corn cribs, on the east the mansion house, on the south, a row of negro cabins, and on the west the road along which our troops passed. The plantation employed 16 hands. The overseer remarked, that the women and children of the country must suffer very much after we go away.

The Confederate government calls for a tenth of all they raise. What would our northern farmers think to be thus taxed?

About five miles from Millen, we stopped for dinner, and while it was preparing, in company with Adjutant Durgin, I visited the rebel prison just in our rear about half a mile, where our prisoners have recently been confined. A space of about twenty acres was enclosed by setting pine posts upright in the ground, about fourteen feet in height. Around this log enclosure, were forty sentry boxes, entered from the outside by means of ladders, the only entrance to the prison being on the south side. The ground is dry and sandy, and through the center runs a fine stream of water—its only redeeming feature. On the north side of this stream are numerous huts where our poor boys have lately been kenneled. About 8,000 were confined here. They were moved from Andersonville four or five weeks since, and had but just got fairly located, before they had to remove again to get out of our way. The huts were built in all manner of shapes. Some had walls of logs, with a covering of timber, and over these a good layer of sand. Some had walls of turf, again others were cut into the ground perhaps two feet and then covered, some times with pine slabs, sometimes with sand, and some were simply thatched with pine boughs, while others were bare sheds. It made my heart ache to look upon such miserable hovels, hardly fit for our swine to live in, and here our brave soldiers had to stay. No wonder that 635 graves were counted near by, and all this in five weeks. If ever I felt indignant, it was when I stood in one of those sentry boxes and looked over the acres thus covered with these huts. Many of our soldiers visited the spot, but it was only to go back muttering louder curses on Jeff. Davis and all his murderous crew. Through the middle of this mass of huts, was a row of bake ovens, each having two good sized arch kettles set for heating water. Near the entrance way was a small building, or rather the roof to one, set on posts, under which our soldiers were punished, I conclude, as stocks for the feet were lying near. I counted holes enough for seven persons, and they appeared to be well worn. Also noticed a lot for the neck. I never knew before that our soldiers had to undergo this barbarous method of torture, but there was no mistaking the fact now.

Around the inside of the stockade, was the "dead line" perhaps a rod and a half distant, beyond which it was death for any man to pass.

Sunday, Dec. 4th.—More cannonading this morning, but as yet we get no information relative to it. Broke camp about 8.30 A. M. There is a rumor that Savannah is ours—did not learn by what forces, but I do not credit it. Marched about 12 miles yesterday. Some of our forces, yesterday morning, struck off toward Waynesboro, in order to destroy the railroad, although it was first cut by Kilpatrick, several days ago. The destruction of the railroads through Georgia will prove a serious loss to the rebels, for many of their supplies are drawn from this state. It will prove a tedious work for them to wagon their corn over such an extent of territory.

I think it is not the design of Sherman to get into any fight back here from the coast, any more than actually necessary to clear the way. We have not the transportation to spare to carry wounded men, and to leave them in the hands of the rebels would be worse than death itself. The mere raid, living upon the country as we do, will quite as effectually bring the southern people to terms. It is much better to conquer by destroying property than life.

Reached camp in the evening, having travelled perhaps five miles. The road has been very bad indeed—swamp again. In some places our horses went in so deep we had to hold up our legs pretty well to keep from getting wet. In some instances horses stumbled and threw their riders into mud and water.

News has just come in that Kilpatrick had quite a lively little fight last night, which explains the cannonading heard, resulting in the capture of two guns and fifty prisoners. A soldier of the 5th Ohio, foraging to-day, saw three of our men with their throats cut from ear to ear. Said they had no other wounds. They had evidently been captured while out foraging, and thus inhumanly butchered.

A few days ago, four men of the 55th Ohio were found hanging by their necks in the woods, with a piece of paper attached to one of them, stating that the hanging was done by members of company F, 21st Georgia.

Monday, Dec. 25.—Had a very good night's rest, though I was somewhat cold before morning. There was a little distant cannonading during the evening. Broke camp at 7 A. M., it being a beautiful morning.

Several of the buildings on the plantation where we camped, were set on fire just as we left. Our men have many exciting things to talk about. I have just been listening to the story of a negro who says he concealed three of Stoneman's men in the swamp at the time of his famous raid through here, they getting separated from their command, and he fed them there for several weeks. At length he secured some good horses for them, took them twelve miles and told them to go on.

"How does it happen," I asked him, "that all you colored people seem so willing to help the Yankees?"

"O," said he, "I knew that they were trying to set us free, and I was not afraid of them."

Yesterday an orderly, connected with the 3d brigade of the 2d division, went out foraging in company with three others. After gathering what they wanted, they took the stuff out to the main road near a church. Here they found four of our men lying dead, having been shot in the breast. Some negroes were burying them. The rest of the orderly's company went back after something, leaving him to watch their forage. Being gone longer than he thought they ought to be, he started out to see what was the matter. Having gone some three miles, riding leisurely along, he heard somebody say "halt," but supposing it at first to proceed from some of his own men, who were trying to frighten him, he did not feel alarmed, but in a few minutes he discovered quite a party of rebel cavalrymen a little distance off. They said "come this way," but he wheeled his horse in a hurry, saying as he did so, "can't do it boys," and started for our lines. Five of the rebels started at full tilt after him, and having better horses than he, continually gained on him, firing their carbines as rapidly as they had a chance. They followed him till they could distinctly hear the rumbling of our wagon trains, when they turned back. His companions have not yet come in, and are probably in the hands of the rebels.

Reached camp a little after dark, having marched about 15 miles. The road has been very good. Our path lay through the pine openings or plains—nothing but pine. Yesterday we passed through a beautiful forest of live oaks. It really looks cheerful to see green trees this time of year. We are now about ten miles from the Savannah River, and nearly 60 from Savannah.

December 6th.—Reached camp to-day about 4 P. M., our brigade being in the advance again. Saw but few houses to-day and those belonging mostly to the poorer class. In several places the rebels had felled trees across the road, thinking thus to impede our progress, but such things do not hinder us, for the infantry can march around them, and our pioneers will have everything out of the way by the time the trains wish to pass.

Our course lay in a southerly direction along the river, at a distance of about five miles, so the rebels had all their labor in vain—we did not wish to cross. We seem now to be making toward Savannah, still we may turn off at any moment.

This morning our breakfast consisted of turkeys, chickens, fresh pork and other usual things.

Some days the soldiers have all they can possibly eat, then again they suffer for rations. Our camp to-night is in the forest, with the tall, murmuring pines above us.

About the worst thing one meets with in a soldier's life, are the lice, or "gray backs." It is almost impossible to keep clear of them. Generally, as soon as the soldiers get into camp, lots of them may be seen here and there with their shirts off, looking after gray backs, or, "skirmishing," as they have it.

Was informed a day or two since that this expedition comprises some 73,000 men, and 100 cannon, Kilpatrick having about 7,000 men under him. We go in four columns, and each forages at least five miles on either side, thus we lay waste a strip of country 40 miles wide. No one, without being here, can form a proper idea of the devastation that will be found in our track. Thousands of families will have their homes laid in ashes, and they themselves will be turned beggars into the street. We have literally carried fire and sword into this once proud and defiant State.

Broke camp about 1 P. M. Just after we left we had

quite a piece of swamp to cross, and here the rebels had cut down trees again across the road. It seems very foolish for them to do such things, for they are very small obstructions indeed.

The 14th corps must have cut the Charleston and Savannah railroad by this time, which will make quite a difference in the supplies of that ill-fated city to which we are hastening.

Marched about six miles to-day. Bad places in the road again. Did not see a house after leaving Springfield till near our camp ground. The country is very level through here.

A rumor prevailed to-day, that the Colonel of an Illinois regiment, mounted infantry, was lately found hanging by the neck in the woods, and that Kilpatrick had declared he would serve the rebel Colonel now in his hands in the same way.

Have heard more or less cannonading all the afternoon. It must be at or near Savannah. To-night we are twenty-one miles from the city.

Dec. 2d.—Broke camp at two A. M.—marched twelve miles—got on the wrong road, and consequently had to march further than we otherwise should—went too far to the right, striking the road traveled by the 17th corps. Had a good road most of the way—pine plains still. Have seen no wealthy plantations lately. Came to one place where the proprietor was a well-to-do sort of planter and a strong *Union* man. For the last two months, he had secreted himself from the rebels who had been hunting for him, but hearing of our approach, he came out of his hiding place, with the intention of going along with our army and getting North if possible. Transportation was given him and his family, and the boys made him up a purse of $130,00. He seemed a great deal affected when the money was handed him, saying with tears in his eyes, "Gentlemen, I most heartily thank you for this, for I never expected to meet with such kindness."

Saturday, Dec. 10th.—Broke camp at 7 A. M., striking the railroad 10 miles from the city. A portion of the 1st division were destroying it as we passed. This morning just as the head of our column hove in sight, a train of cars was seen coming around the curve on the long bridge from Savannah, but it at once turned back. Our cavalry started forward, hoping to capture the train, but the steam horse was a little too fast for them. There has been cannonading all the forenoon in our front.

Come to a halt about noon, being distant from the rebel works just about one mile. We lay in the woods till nearly night, when our brigade was ordered into camp a short distance to the right near the railroad. And here we are at last before Savannah.

LETTER IX.

Hd. Qrs. 22d Wis., five miles up the River,
Above Savannah, Dec. 15, 1864.

Without doubt, friends will be glad to hear of our safe arrival before the city of Savannah. It is now a little over four weeks since we broke loose at Atlanta from all communication with the North, and during that time we have made our way through the very heart of Georgia, for the distance of some 350 miles. Our march has been a most triumphant one, and to-day we are knocking for admittance into the great stronghold of the southeast. Arrived here the 12th. Our brigade has not lost a man by sickness since we left Atlanta, and there have been but very few unable to march.

Dr. Bennett has just informed me that they have only about 50 cases at the division hospital.

Last Sabbath orders came for the 22d to take up its position on the river, to support battery I, 1st N. Y., all under command of Colonel Bloodgood. Our force lay back under cover of the trees till about dark, when they took their positions on the bank, and proceeded to throw up proper works. The boys marched with a hearty good will, being well pleased at being sent here for this purpose. The night passed off very quietly, but about 8 A. M. on Monday, word was passed along the lines that three boats were coming down the river, one of which was thought to be a gunboat. On they came with their rebel rag proudly fluttering in the morning breeze. They proved to be two steamers, the Sampson ahead, then the Resolute, followed by the gunboat Macon. When within range, our batteries opened upon them. Perhaps a dozen shots were fired, before the gunboat made any reply, when she sent some 32 pounders bounding over at us, most of them falling short, but some struck in the bank just under the battery, and some went high above us. One went directly over the house where Colonel Bloodgood had his headquarters, and others crashed through the trees near the house, making the limbs fly in a lively manner. None of us were hurt in the least, for when we saw the white smoke from their guns, we either jumped down behind our breastworks, or got behind the big trees near the shore. This artillery duel was kept up for about half an hour, when some of our shot passed through the wheel house of the Resolute, also striking both the other boats, causing so much confusion amongst them that the Samson backed into the Resolute on one side, smashing her wheel house, and the gunboat behind smashed in the stern. Being thus disabled, she blew off steam at once, and we felt certain that her show of resistance was over. The other boats, however, made no effort to take off the crew, but steamed up the river as fast as possible. The steamer was at once taken possession of by Colonel Hawley, of the 3d Wisconsin, who was at this time occupying the Island between us and the boat, word being sent him by Colonel Bloodgood that the boat was disabled. We captured 7 officers and 33 men, who were loud in their curses at the other boats for thus deserting them in the hour of their danger. During the night, a party of sailors from the 22d Wisconsin, under command of Lieutenant Dickinson, of company A, towed the Macon to this side of the river, and workmen were at once put at work upon her to get her once more in running order. She has an excellent engine, but the rest of the boat is not worth much. She will, however, answer a very good purpose in transporting troops from point to point. She is now in charge of Colonel Bloodgood, Lieutenant Dickinson still remaining on board with his sailors to manage her.

Of course, we feel a little proud of the capture. Yesterday the rebel gunboat down the river attempted to shell her, but was unsuccessful. Last night, however, we moved her further up the river for safety.

Our present location is a beautiful one. I should be content to live in such a paradise as this all the rest of my life. The bank is sufficiently high above the water to afford a beautiful prospect up and down the river. We can see the church spires of the city from near our headquarters. At every hour in the day, small boats can be seen running over to the Island, so the boys are having a fine time. A fishing party has gone out for a pleasant time. While I write now, the gunboat down the river is thundering away at something. Every discharge jars the house, and we can distinctly hear the bursting of the shells. We are all in the best of spirits.

Friday, Dec. 16th.—The gunboat is inclined not to allow us much peace, as shells have been flying quite lively most of the day. One man of the 3d Wisconsin was to-day killed on the Island. A shell passing through the breastword, took the top of his head off.

The rebels have also been shelling our forces on the Island; so that it was deemed necessary to send over a section of our artillery to silence them. They seem to have something of a force on the Carolina side, and there has been more or less skirmishing with them all day. It is the intention to-morrow to send some troops to drive them off and get possession there. The 3d Wisconsin went over yesterday to reconnoiter, but finding the enemy rather too strong, Colonel Hawley hastily returned to the Island.

You need not expect that Savannah will fall immediately, for it is strongly fortified and defended by a good force, probably 15,000 men. We could probably take their whole works by direct assault, for we far outnumber them as to men, but it would result in a heavy loss to us.

You may rest assured, however, that Savannah will fall sooner or later. Their outer line of works is about four miles from the city, and we have works within 400 yards of theirs. Our sharpshooters prevent the working of some of their guns in the day time, so in the night they pitch a few shells into us here and there.

While we have been staying at the river, the rest of the brigade have been doing skirmish duty near the rebel works.

The cheering news came to us to-day that 20 tons of mail matter await the 20th corps on board the gunboat below Fort McAlister. So we shall soon hear from home.

Truly yours,   G. S. BRADLEY.

LETTER X.

Tuesday evening, Dec. 20th.—This afternoon the gunboats ascended the river to a point nearly opposite us, and sent their shells over this way, some of the pieces striking very near our house, and some exploded near the regiment, but many of the boys went right on with their preparation for supper, not even getting behind a tree. Some of us, a little more timorous, either got behind the big oaks, or under the breastworks. They quit about dark and went down the river, but seem to be banging away at something again this evening. There was pretty constant cannonading all of last night. The gunboats shelled the 2d division, who were preparing works for some of the large guns we have just received from the fleet; some 40 being wounded and nine killed. There has been some skirmishing on the Carolina shore to-day, one man having his leg shot off by a cannon ball; another being wounded in his arm, and a third one killed.

There has been a rumor to-day that they are evacuating the city, but the report is not credited. It is stated by a deserter that the inhabitants are very anxious that the city should be surrendered, probably fearing that if they hold on, it will share the fate of Atlanta.

Before this reaches you, the telegraph will probably have informed you of a glorious victory or a terrible defeat, for we are just on the eve of most important events. The storm is about to burst, and the throats of more than 100 cannon along our lines will not be opened, we trust, in vain, although many of our brave boys must fall.

Yours just before the battle,
G. S. BRADLEY.

AT SAVANNAH.

I need not tell you that Savannah is ours, for the papers have already told you this in big letters, and you have had your rejoicing over the glorious news.

On Monday, Dec. 19th, the rebels opened with heavy cannonading all along their works, and it was kept up nearly all day, our guns but seldom replying. Tuesday it was the same, the gunboat down the river, in an especial manner paying us its compliments in the shape of huge 64 pounder shells. About 2 o'clock on Wednesday morning, a small reconnoitering party of the 2d division, 20th A. C., General Geary's command, crawled stealthily up to the rebel works near one of their large guns, getting up to the very muzzle, it being too dark to clearly distinguish objects. For a moment they dropped down under the works, fearful that the rebels might take the alarm and pour in upon them. After waiting a short time, they ventured to peep over the works and listen, but could neither see nor hear any one. Then they crawled clear over and found that the line of works was entirely evacuated. Some of the number were sent back to report, and soon our troops along the 3d division line were notified, but could hardly believe what was told them, suspecting it to be some trick of the Johnnies. They even went so far as to want to trade coffee for tobacco, with the supposed rebs, but the 2d divisions stoutly affirmed they were no Johnnies but veritable Yankees. Gen. Ward soon mustered his forces and pushed on toward the city, but Gen. Geary was a little ahead of him, and received the surrender of the city, Gen. Sherman being absent at Hilton Head at the time.

On looking over their fortifications, a single line of works about $3\frac{1}{2}$ miles from the city, it is evident that they could not have maintained much of a fight. Still nature had helped them very materially, there being swamp all along their line of works. In some places there were rice swamps, over which they had let the water at high tide and then shut down the gates. In charging their works, we should have been obliged to go right through these swamps in the face of a galling fire from both musketry and heavy guns. The works were quite well supplied with heavy ordnance, mostly 32 pounders. There were two guns directly in the road on which we advanced into the city. The woods along the road near us frequently showed the marks of their shots.

When we retired to rest Tuesday evening, we expected that the morrow would witness a most bloody day, but instead, our army triumphantly entered the city without any opposition.

Savannah is one of the oldest cities in the country, and is really a beautiful place, being finely shaded by the live oak. On some of the streets, there are two rows of trees through the center, with a wide path between them, and a row near each side walk, thus giving to the city a very cheerful appearance.

Were it not for the chilly air, one might almost be led, on walking through the city, to think it mid summer, so green are the trees. As a general thing the streets are wide, and frequently intercepted by small public squares well set out with trees, and often ornamented with some monument. On one of them, I noticed a most beautiful white marble one to the memory of Pulaski; on the east side is the simple word PULASKI; on the south it reads as follows:

PULASKI.

THE HEROIC POLE, WHO FELL MORTALLY WOUNDED FIGHTING FOR AMERICAN LIBERTY AT THE SIEGE OF SAVANNAH, 9TH OF OCTOBER, 1776.

On the west, also the simple word PULASKI; on the north, Savannah, 9th Oct., 1779, and directly under this is the figure of Pulaski falling from his noble steed, all of which is very finely executed. The shaft is perhaps near

40 feet in height, surmounted at the top by the statute of the hero, the whole of white marble. Around the monument, is a substantial fence, the posts being in the shape of cannon, each surmounted by the representative of a large solid shot.

The prospect up or down the river is a fine one, the bank on which the city is built being high above the water.

I shall perhaps be able to give you a more complete picture of the city after I have seen more of it. The number of inhabitants has been about 30,000, about half of them remaining, among whom are many very strong Union men, and you need not be surprised if before long you hear of a decided Union movement this way.

The 22d regiment was at the rice mills till Saturday morning, when we had orders to abandon them and join our brigade near the city. On Friday evening, Colonel Dustin informed Colonel Bloodgood that the 22d was now all alone at the river—that Wheeler's cavalry, numbering several hundreds were within a few miles of us, and that our pickets better be strengthened. You may imagine that we did not like the idea of being gobbled very well. The men thought of Brentwood.

The night, however, passed away without alarm, and Saturday morning found us on the move to the city, with colors flying and music playing. During our stay at the river, about 7,000 bushels of rice were threshed.

December 27th.—It being the general impression that we should remain in Savannah for the present, our boys went to work immediately to put up good quarters, but yesterday just at night orders came for us to be ready to move to the north side of the river. This movement is probably for the purpose of stopping rebel raids along the river, so annoying to our boats.

The impression now is that we are soon to enter upon another campaign, perhaps toward Charleston.

All are in the best of spirits over our own success, also over the good news from Nashville and other quarters. Truly, this winter's work is telling hard against the rebellion. Yours truly,

G. S. BRADLEY,

Chaplain 22d Wis.

GEN. SHERMAN'S DISPATCH.

SAVANNAH, Ga., Dec. 22, 1864.

To His Excellency President Lincoln:—I BEG TO PRESENT YOU, AS A CHRISTMAS GIFT, THE CITY OF SAVANNAH, WITH A HUNDRED AND FIFTY HEAVY GUNS AND PLENTY OF AMMUNITION, AND ALSO ABOUT TWENTY-FIVE THOUSAND BALES OF COTTON.

W. T. SHERMAN,

Major-General.

GEN. FOSTER'S DISPATCH.

STEAMER GOLDEN GATE, }
SAVANNAH RIVER, Dec. 22d, 7 P. M. }

To Lieut.-Gen. Grant and Maj.-Gen. Halleck:—I have the honor to report that I have just returned from General Sherman's head-quarters, in Savannah. I send Maj. Gray of my staff, as bearer of dispatches from General Sherman to you, and also a message to the President.

The city of Savannah was occupied on the morning of the 21st. Gen. Hardee, anticipating the contemplated assault, escaped with the main body of his infantry and light artillery, on the evening of the 20th, by crossing the river at Union Causeway, opposite the city.

The rebel iron clads were blown up and the navy yard burned. All the best of the city is intact, and contains 20,000 citizens who are quiet and well disposed.

The captures include 800 prisoners, 150 guns, 12 locomotives in good order, 190 cars, a large supply of ammunition and materials of war, 3 steamers, 33,000 bales of cotton safely stored in warehouses.

All these valuables—fruits of an almost bloodless victory—have been, like Atlanta, fairly won.

I opened communication with the city with my steamers to-day, taking up all the torpedoes we could see, and passing safely over others. Arrangements are made to clear the channel of obstructions. Yours, etc.,

J. G. FOSTER,
Major-General.

SHERMAN'S MARCH TO THE SEA.

BY REV. G. S. BRADLEY, CHAPLAIN 22D WIS.

And still the war along the border
  Had forces in deadly array,
And we knew by the distant camp-fires,
  That many had gathered that way;
And we heard the wild notes of the bugle,
  That sounded o'er river and lea,
And a rider then told us in haste,
  That Sherman would march to the sea.

And when we saw our banner of Stars
    Flung out to the breezes so gay,
Our patriot blood within was stirred,
    And we could not remain away.
Hastily taking the last adieu,
    With weeping by cottage and tree,
We followed fast our leader so brave,
    For Sherman must march to the sea.

And up the wild heights of Resaca,
    Our columns were hurried that day,
But many a *brave* slept by that fort,
    And sad was the work of the fray.
Then Kenesaw frowning with cannon,
    And thick as the rebels could be,
Soon fell by the hands of our legions,
    For Sherman must march to the sea.

Golgotha, Dallas Woods, and the like,
    Where bullets were showered like hail—
Our men stood like tried heroes that day,
    And we made the enemy quail;
Then southward we hurried to battle,—
    Peach Tree fell by river and lea,
And the country all caught the glad sound,
    As Sherman marched down to the sea.

Then out from Atlanta we hurried,
    Its grim walls all battered and black—
Nothing was left to rebeldom there,
    Naught but ruin along our track;
And our banners were flung to the breeze,—
    We knew we should march by river and lea—
That our journey would take us afar,
    As Sherman marched down to the sea.

Then we heard the loud champing of steeds,—
    The clatter of hoofs by the way—
And we knew our columns were marching,
    Striking tents at break of the day;

And rumbling of trains fell on our ear,
   And we thought of what was to be,
Away in the dim, distant future,
   As Sherman marched down to the sea.

As in the swamp and tangled morass,
   Our troops were hurrying through,
Often the booming of cannon was heard,
   The sharp rattle of musketry too ;
And we knew our comrades were falling
   By many a river and tree,—
And the life-tide fast away ebbing—
   As Sherman marched down to the sea.

But bright did our bivouac fires blaze
   In the deep old forests of pine,
And we lay ourselves down on the ground,—
   Our pickets well guarding the line.
O 'twas wearisome marching so long,—
   Such tramping by river and lea—
But our hearts were brave as brave could be,
   For Sherman would march to the sea.

How often we thought of the future,
   And prayed for the ending of strife,—
That brother might visit with brother,
   And troubles no longer be rife ;
Yet, while traitor flags flaunted the breeze,
   Insulting the stars of the Free,
We buckled anew our saber's keen blade,
   For Sherman must march to the sea.

Let rebels have stockade or fortress,
   Well mounted, and guarded and manned,
We knew nothing could hinder the way,
   Which our old Tecumseh had planned ;
And loudly echoed the bugle and drum,
   That marshaled our troops on the lea,
And cheer upon cheer went up from the men,
   For Sherman would march to the sea.

Hark ! what meaneth that booming away—
   That crossing the pontoon below ;
Can it be the traitors have fallen,
   And this their salute as they go ?
But the morning scarcely had broken,
   With fog upon river and lea,
When we knew by "Forward boys ! Forward !"
   That Sherman *had* marched to the sea.

And the black throated cannon were still,
   Yet pointing to the northward, they lay,
While the city from flames had been spared,
   And rebels were now far away ;
And then there was shouting and joy,
   To think fair Savannah was free !
To our God will we utter our thanks—
   As Sherman marched down to the sea.

LETTER XI.

SAVANNAH, Ga., Dec. 28, 1864.

It may be well, perhaps, to review briefly some of the more striking points of the campaign just now brought to a close.

After the fall of Atlanta, it began to be talked about in northern papers that Sherman was preparing for some great move, how, when, or where, no one knew.

Finding himself so nicely out-generaled in the loss of the " Gate City," Hood determined he would punish Sherman by stopping his supplies. His communications must be cut in the rear and his mighty army would soon be starved out of their stronghold, and there is but little doubt but Sherman's gigantic stride across the broad State of Georgia, if not produced, was, at all events, precipitated by Hood's severance of railroad communications between Atlanta and Chattanooga, forcing the evacuation of the former stronghold. From Chattanooga, Hood threw himself on Florence, and there began to feed and shoe his troops, and to reinforce and mobilize his columns, so as to play a still grander game in Tennessee. His plan was carefully elaborated. First, he seized Corinth, and Beauregard held it in force. This move opened a line of supplies by the way of the Corinth and Mobile railroad, through the length and breadth of Mississippi and Alabama. Right and left on the railroad line, he received contributions, and rapidly got forward troops, food and forage, ammunition and clothing. The mending of the railroad between Corinth and Tuscumbia perfected his communications.

These preparations were made with the apparent intent to force Sherman out of Atlanta. Sherman did go out of Atlanta; but unfortunately for Hood, went out on the wrong side. About the middle of November, the latter's preparations neared completion; but Sherman's were already completed. While Hood was chuckling over both retrospect and prospect in Northern Alabama, Sherman with the instinct of genius, and the skill of a thoroughbred soldier, reversed the tide of fortune, took the offensive, and, out of the nettle danger, plucked the flower safely.

Everybody recollects how summarily General Sherman and his handful of invading Yankees were to be disposed of, after leaving Atlanta. Trees were to be cut down, bridges were to be burned, all forage for man and beast was to be destroyed, the country was to be desolated and the difficulties that beset Bonaparte on his famous and disastrous visit to Moscow, were to have been repeated in the State of Georgia in the year of grace 1864. That was the programme written out and printed at length in all the southern papers. Hospitable graves were the only hospitable and welcome openings that awaited him of the blue coat on the road from Atlanta to Savannah! So said the fulminating proclamations of Governors, Generals, editors and all. But the gallant Sherman says it was an "agreeable journey."

Probably but very few people in the south dreamed that Sherman could make his way through the entire length of Georgia, without greater interruptions than he experienced.

We were often suprised at the abundance of everything eatable, and it was evident to every one that the south could not be starved into submission.

But if we could destroy their railroads—the great arteries of the south—we should most effectually operate against Richmond, Charleston, and other strongholds, though hundreds of miles away.

While Grant has been holding the *hydra headed monster—rebellion* at bay, near Richmond, Sherman has been SKINNING and *carving* and taking out the vitals in Georgia, and soon you will hear of his plowing up South Carolina.

And he will not do it with a one-horse affair either, but setting his coulter deep, he will cut their secession roots and turn up a better soil. Do you say it is terrible thus to destroy property? So it is, but better thus than to desr oy life.

Do you say that the women and children of the south must suffer? Undoubtedly, but how can the rebels be punished at all without a great deal of suffering somewhere. So far as the *women* are concerned, we might as well spare our pity, for they are the worst secessionists, and why should *they* not suffer?

They have urged on the brutal treatment of Yankee prisoners. They have personally insulted these poor men, and would you now spare them a proper amount of suffering? We say no. Let them understand that secession means something more than a holiday parade.

Our heart has often been pained as we have witnessed the cruelties and devastation of war. As we have looked over plantations laid waste, houses burned, and the people turned out as beggars into the streets, our hearts have relented, but right over on the other hand we have thought of the thousands in the prison pens of Charleston, Andersonville, Salsbury, Libby and other places, and then we have said, let *ruin* bring them to their senses, if nothing else will.

You will notice in the rebel papers that they now declare the fall of Savannah no particular loss to them—that they will now have an additional force to concentrate at some other point.

Well, they have certainly rather a happy way of looking at all their mishaps, as "blessings in disguise." But it will not go down with the masses at home. Such raids as the one through Georgia will make the war a *reality* to the people of the south as perhaps nothing else can. The people at home will be completely discouraged, and the soldiers in the field will feel the same when they hear of the destitution of their families. Let the south build as many air castles as people please, but one fact stands out apparent to every one who has been where we have, that the rebellion is fast tumbling to ruins. Sherman is knocking the bottom out.

But my letter is already sufficiently long, yet I want to quote an extract from the correspondence of the New York Herald, which is as follows:

"On the evening of the 12th, Howard relieved Hazen's second division of the fifteenth corps, by a part of the seventeenth corps, and threw it across the Little Ogeechee, towards the Great Ogeechee, with the view of crossing it to Ossabaw Island, and reducing Fort McAlister, which held the river. The enemy had destroyed King's bridge across the Great Ogeechee, and this had to be repaired. Capt. Rees, topographical engineer of Howard's staff, with the Missouri engineers, prepared the timber and bridged the one thousand feet of river during the night, and on the morning of the 13th, Hazen crossed and moved towards the point where Fort McAllister obstructed the river. Kilpatrick, in the meantime, had moved down to St. Catherine's Sound, opened communication with the fleet, and asked permission to storm Fort McAllister; but Sherman did not give his consent, considering it questionable whether the cavalry with the poor facilities, and small supply of artillery, could succeed.

THE FORT CARRIED BY HAZEN.

Learning that Hazen was to storm the fort on the afternoon of the 13th, I visited the right of the line, and at 1 o'clock joined Generals Sherman and Howard, at Dr. Cherne's rice mill, on the Ogeechee, opposite Fort McAlister. I found Sherman on the roof of the mill, surrounded by his staff and signal officers Bekley and Cole, waiting to communicate with Hazen on the island. While patiently waiting for Hazen's signals, Sherman's keen eye detected smoke in the horizon seaward. Up to this time he had received no intelligence from the fleet. In a moment the countenance of the chieftain lightened up, and he exclaimed:

"Look! Howard; there is the gunboat!"

Time passed on, and the vessel now became visible, yet no signal from the fleet or Hazen. Half an hour passed and the guns of the fort opened simultaneously with puffs of smoke that rose a few hundred yards from the fort, showing that Hazen's skirmishers had opened. A moment after Hazen signalled.

"I have invested the fort and will assault immediately." At this moment Sickley announced. "A signal from the gunboat." All eyes are turned from the fort to the gunboat that is coming to our assistance with news from home. A few messages pass that inform us that Foster and Dahlgreen are within speaking distance. The gunboat now halts and asks:

"Can we run up? Is Fort McAllister ours?"

"No," is the reply. "Hazen is just ready to storm it. Can you assist?"

"Yes," is the reply. "What will you have us to do?"

But before Sherman can reply to Dahlgreen, the thunders of the fort are heard, and the low sound of small arms is borne across the three miles of marsh and river. Field glasses are opened, and, sitting flat upon the roof, the hero of Atlanta gazed away off to the fort. "There they go grandly; not a waver," he remarks.

Twenty seconds pass, and again he exclaims:

"See that flag in the advance, Howard; how steadily it moves; not a man falters. * * There they go still; see the roll of musketry. Grand, grand."

Still he strains his eyes, and a moment after speaks without raising his eyes—

"That flag still goes forward; there is no flinching there."

A pause for a minute.

"Look!" he exclaims, "it has halted. They waver, no! it's the parapet! There they go again; now they scale it; some are over. Look, there is a flag on the works! Another, another. It's ours. The fort's ours!"

The glass dropped by his side, and in an instant the joy of the great leader at the possession of the river and the opening of the road to his new base, burst forth in words:

As the old darkie remarked, "dis chile don't sleep tonight." And turning to one at his side, Captain Andereid, he remarked: "Have a boat for me at once, I must go there," pointing to the fort, from which half a dozen battle flags floated grandly in the sunset.

And well might William Tecumseh Sherman rejoice; for here, as the setting sun went down upon Fort McAllister reduced, and kissed a fond good night to the Starry Banner, Sherman witnessed the culmination of his plans and marches, that had involved such desperate resistance and risk—the opening of a new and shorter route to his base. Here at sunset, on the memorable 13th of December, the dark waters of the great Ogeechee bore witness to the fulfilment of the covenant Sherman made with his iron heroes at Atlanta, twenty-nine days before, to lead them victorious to a new base.

Yours truly, G. S. BRADLEY.

VICTORY.

BY JULIA ADELAIDE BURDICK.

I.

Victory!
Thunder it, cannon and resonant bell!
Echo it, mountain-side, hill-top and dell!
Trumpet and bugle the loud pean swell!
  Victory! Victory!
Booming of cannon and bursting of shell,
Haste, to our foeman the great tidings tell!
  Victory!

II.

Victory!
Wave, happy flag, over fortress and fleet!
Army and navy exultingly greet!
City to country the glad news repeat!
  Victory! Victory!
Fly with it, freemen, the poor bondman meet,
Strike the last fetter in twain at his feet!
  Victory!

III.

Soldier, the weary day's suffering through!
Patriot, everywhere dauntless and true!
Nation, unflinching to dare and to do!
  Victory! Victory!
Lift up your voice and welcome anew
Ruler as wise as the land ever knew!
  Victory!

IV.

Victory!
Flash it with lightning, o'er highways of wire!
Speed it, ye steeds with the red heart of fire!

On with it, white ships, and never more tire!
Victory! Victory!
Beacons on rampart and redan and spire,
Signal triumphant the Nation's desire!
Victory!

v.

Victory!
Thunder it ocean and river and lake!
Echo it strands that the mad waters rake!
Fly with it winds till the universe shake!
Victory! Victory!
Heaven and Earth into melodies break,
Morning hath broken, awake, O awake!
Victory!

IN MEMORIAM.

TUNE—*Just before the Battle.*

Inscribed to Mrs. THOMAS PLACE, whose son, EUGENE, fell a martyr to his country in the autumn of 1864.

BY MRS. G. S. BRADLEY.

Farewell home, and farewell mother!
Hear you not the country's call?
Well I know your heart will falter,
Fearing your loved boy will fall.
Surely, mother, you'll withhold not
Service for a hundred days.
Duty to the country, mother,
In my mind all else outweighs.

THE STAR CORPS.

> *Farewell home and all its treasures:—*
> *Glad I leave you for the fight;*
> *God will love your boy, dear mother,*
> *More if he sustain the right.*

In the tear-gemmed eye, dear mother,
Well I read your anxious fears,—
Know that fancy leads the spirit
Where the battle-field appears ;—
Shows among the slain and dying,
Him who gladly leaves you now ;—
And well I know the struggle, mother,
Ere you can submissive bow.

> *Yet, dear mother, I must leave you,*
> *For the country's honor bright,—*
> *God will love your boy, dear mother,*
> *More if he sustain the right.*

Fancy, too, will often picture
Him the subject of disease,—
Till the pain and anguish, mother,
Doth the weary soul release.
Many more must fall, dear mother,
Ere shall cease this conflict wild ;
Though you've nobly given Luther,
Hold not back your second child.

> *Let me go, tho' I may, mother,*
> *Pass forever from your sight;*
> *God will love your boy, dear mother,*
> *More if he sustain the right.*

* * * * * * * *

Farewell home, and farewell, mother !
Far removed from loved ones all,
I am sick and I am dying,
Dying, lest the country fall;
One by one the brave boys going,
Tells the value of the prize ;

'T is well, if from our ashes,
Liberty and Union rise.

> *Farewell, loved ones! Quell the anguish*
> *That makes the heart so wildly swell;*
> *Keep in mind the cause of Freedom,*
> *That for which your loved boy fell.*

Well I know that you will miss me,—
Sad indeed will be each heart,
When the flash along the wire
Shall to you the news impart.
O, how you will weep, my mother,
Thinking of my lonely lot,—
How no kindred ones around me,
Stood beside my dying cot.

> *Farewell, father, farewell mother!*
> *All my kindred fade from sight!*
> *God will love your boy, dear mother,*
> *For he died to save the right.*

You will come and bear my body
Back to rest with loved ones gone,
While the stream of life, tho' sluggish,
Will the tide of years roll on.
You will often think of GENIE—
Sometimes wish me back again,—
But oh! you would not wake me, mother,
Life hath so much grief and pain.

> *Farewell Father! farewell Mother!*
> *All my kindred fade from sight,*
> *God will love your boy, dear mother,*
> *For he died to save the right.*

Mt. Pleasant, Wis.

Extract from Colonel Dustin's Report of the Savannah campaign:

HEADQUARTERS 2D BRIG. 3D DIV. 20TH A. C.
Savannah, Georgia, Dec. 27th, 1864.

To *Captain John Speed*,
A. A. G. 3d Division 20th A. C.

SIR:—I have the honor to transmit my report of the operations of the 2d brigade, 3d division 20th A. C., from the time I assumed command on the 9th day of November to the 21st day of December. I also transmit herewith the reports of my regimental commanders, embracing the time from the occupation of Atlanta, on the 2d day of September, to the capture of Savannah on the 21st inst.

By special orders from Corps Headquarters, I assumed command of this brigade on the 9th day of November, my own regiment, the 105th Illinois, still remaining in the 1st brigade. I thus relieved Lieut. Colonel Crane, of the 85th Indiana, the ranking officer of this brigade. Col. Crane was in command but for a few days, and to relieve him from the necessity of making a separate report as brigade commander, it may be here stated that nothing of particular interest occurred while he was in command, excepting that on the 5th day of November the brigade moved out on the McDonaugh road for the distance of two miles, and then encamped. On the 6th, it was ordered back to its original position near Atlanta. Before returning, and just at daylight on the morning of the 6th, a dash upon our picket line was made by a squad of rebel cavalry, and one man from the 33d Indiana veteran volunteers was killed. Early on the morning of the 9th of November, our lines were disturbed by artillery firing from the enemy, who had placed two guns in position at a point, a short distance to the right of the Decatur road. From this point, some fifteen or twenty shells were thrown into our lines, some of them bursting within and close upon the encampment of the 85th Indiana. The brigade was promptly under arms, but the firing soon ceased, and no farther demonstration was made in our front.

On assuming command of the brigade, I found it organized as follows:

Regt.	Comdg. Officer.	Aggre'ate strength.
33d Indian Vet. Vols.	Lt. Col. Burton.	636
22d Wisconsin Vols.	Lt. Col. Bloodgood.	711
19th Michigan Vols.	Lt. Col. Baker	703
85th Indiana Vols.	Lt. Col. Crane.	640
	Grand Aggregate,	2,690 men

Of this number, the total present was 1,531.

Number of muskets present 1,222.

I found the 19th Michigan detached, and on duty in the city of Atlanta, reporting to Col. Crane, 107th N. Y. Volunteers, commanding a provisional brigade.

On the 14th, I announced the brigade staff, as follows:

Major Wilson Hobbs	85 Indiana,	Surgeon in Chief.
Capt A. G. Kellam.	22d Wisconsin,	A. A. A. G.
Capt. Wm. Bones	22d Wisconsin,	A. A. I. G.
Capt. D. J. Easton	19th Michigan,	A. A. D. C.
Lieut. H. C. Johnson	33d Indiana, Top. Eng.	A. A. D. C.
Lieut. L. M. Wing	19th Michigan,	A. A. Q. M.
Lieut. W. S. Harbert	85th Indiana,	A. C. S.
Lieut. C. A. Booth	22d Wisconsin,	Prov. Mar.
Lieut. H. C. Brown	85th Indiana,	Brig. Amb. Offi-
Lieut. John Hart	33d Indiana,	Brig. Pioneer Offi-

From the 10th to the 15th, the command was busy in preparing for the new campaign.

Nov. 15th, pursuant to orders of the day before, the brigade moved out from Atlanta at 9 A. M., taking the Decatur road.

The 3d division in the rear, and the 2d brigade in the center of the division.

* * * * * * * *

Dec. 10th, broke camp at 7 A. M., and marched to within five miles of Savannah, on the Savannah and Augusta dirt road, crossing the Charleston and Savannah railroad, ten miles from the latter place. Here our advance coming upon the enemy, our troops went into position. The 2d brigade being in reserve, went into camp in good season, in rear of the line of the 1st and 3d brigades of our division.

Dec. 11th, remained in position until dark. In obedience to orders from Corps Headquarters, the 22d Wisconsin was detached and sent to Gibbon's plantation on Savannah river to support a battery and blockade the river. At dark the brigade moved forward into the first line, connecting the right of the 1st brigade with the left of the 3d brigade of our division, and midway between the dirt and railroad, the general direction of the line of battle being nearly north and south.

Dec. 12th, remained in position. The battery supported by the 22d Wisconsin, attacked three boats attempting to pass the blockade. One, being a gunboat, the other side-wheel steamers—one armed. The unarmed boat was disabled by the battery, and the other two abandoned her, our forces immediately taking possession of her and her crew.

The 22d Wisconsin at the river took possession of the rice mills on the river, and details from the regiment commenced operating them, contributing very materially toward relieving the embarassment of the Subsistence Depot, on account of the scarcity of supplies. This work was energetically prosecuted under direction of Lieut. Harbert, A. C. S., of the 2d brigade, by details from the brigade.

Dec. 13th. line of battle connected and advanced—2d brigade again in reserve.

Dec. 14th, by direction from corps headquarters, two regiments, the 85th Indiana and 19th Michigan, Lt. Col. Crane commanding, made an expedition eight and a half miles into the country with twenty-four wagons, returning in eight hours with the wagons loaded with stores.

Dec. 15th, remained in position.

Dec. 16th, at 7 A. M., brigade moved to the left of the Augusta dirt road, occupying partially completed works just then evacuated by the 2d brigade 1st division 20th A. C. (Col. Carman), connecting on the right with the 1st brigade of our division, and on the left with the 1st brigade 1st division 20th A. C., picket line 500 yards in advance of line of battle, and within 500 yards of the enemy's line of battle.

Dec. 17th, remained in position. Details from the regiments were set to work, and the unfinished breastworks in front of the brigade, put into good condition for defense.

Dec. 18th, in position—nothing of importance occuring.

Received the following order from division headquarters:

HEADQUARTERS 3D DIVISION, 20TH A. C.
Near Savannah, Ga. Dec. 18th, 1864.

Circular:

To-night each brigade commander will send out to his front a reconnoitering party to ascertain every avenue to the enemy's position. A written report of the investigation will be sent to these headquarters by 9 A. M. to-morrow.

By command of
Brig. Gen. W. T. WARD.

John Speed, Capt. & A. A. G.

In pursuance of which, after a careful personal examination of the ground by the Colonel commanding, the following report was made:

HEADQUARTERS 2D BRIG. 3D DIVISION 20th A. C.
Near Savannah, Ga. Dec. 20th, 1864.

CAPTAIN:

I have the honor to submit the following report for the information of the General commanding.

This brigade (2d) has three (3) regiments in line, the 22d Wisconsin being detached, and upon duty at Gibbon's plantation on the Savannah river.

The right of our line rests upon the Savannah and Augusta dirt road, connecting with the left of the 1st brigade of this division (Col. Smith), the left connecting with the right of the 1st brigade, 1st division of this corps (Col. Selfridge), with a front of seven hundred and forty (740) yards—the general direction of our line of battle is a little east of north, and is very well fortified.

Our front is covered by a picket line of two (2) commissioned officers and one hundred and seventy (170) men, connecting on right and left as indicated above, and is four hundred (400) yards in advance of the line of battle—the intermediate ground being covered with pine. The ground is dry, with no serious obstacles to an advance in line of battle.

In front of the entire length of our picket line, is an open space—probably eight hundred (800) yards in width on our right, and gradually widening towards the left. The enemy's line of battle—fortified—is just on the edge of the woods upon the opposite side of the open space just referred to, and continues towards the left, along the edge of the woods—about half our brigade front. From this point toward the left, their line is plainly visible in this open space.

In front of the right of our picket line, there is an almost impenetrable slashing of timber, one hundred (100) yards in width, and extends towards the left, nearly half the front of our brigade. Between this slashing and the rebel skirmish line, there is a basin of water from 75 to 100 yards in width, the depth of which has not been ascertained. This basin of water widens and evidently deepens toward the left, where are three floodgates, plainly visible, indicating that this basin of water has been used for purposes of irrigation.

On the 19th inst, I made a careful personal examination of the ground. The same has been done by other officers of my staff and command.

The ground to within a short distance of the enemy's picket line has, I think, been very thoroughly explored.

I have reason to believe that between the rebel skirmish line and their line of battle, there is a ditch or canal extending from the bridge on the main road toward the river.

In my judgment an advance in our front for the purpose of assaulting the enemy's works would be extremely difficult and its success doubtful.

This report was very fully confirmed by facts transpiring with the evacuation, except perhaps the distance between the picket line of this brigade and the enemy's line of battle.

Dec. 19th, upon the application of the Colonel commanding, permission was granted to build a new line of works 500 yards in advance of the old, and the line laid out.

From this new line, our musketry, together with the artillery assigned to that part of the line would have greatly controlled, if not rendered quite untenable, the enemy's lines in our front.

Dec. 20th, work on new lines commenced by details from the regiments, and energetically prosecuted through the day and night.

Dec. 21st, early in the morning, it having been discovered on the left during the night, the enemy's works in their front had been evacuated, our skirmish line was advanced under direction of Lt. Col. Crane, 85th Indiana, division officer of the day.

Finding the works in our front empty, the brigade was immediately moved forward, being the first to occupy the enemy's works in front of our division.

After halting in the works two hours, the brigade was marched forward, and went into its present position, one mile north-west from the city, the brigade being in the center of the division, two regiments on the line, and one in reserve.

The picket line of the brigade occupies the line of rebel .

works spoken of above, and consists of one commissioned officer and eighty-five (85) men.

Dec. 25th, the 22d Wisconsin was relieved from duty on the river and rejoined the brigade.

During the march, the brigade destroyed about ten (10) miles of railroad track. Being without the usual facilities for doing this, it was done under considerable disadvantage and much hard labor. It was, however, accomplished most effectually, and reflected credit upon officers and men for their energy and zeal.

I have the honor herewith to forward the Reports of Major Hobbs, Surgeon in Chief of the brigade; Lieut. Wing, A. A. Q. M., and Lieut. Harbert A. C. S.

From Lieutenant Wing's report, it will be seen that the whole number of horses and mules, and the amount of forage procured on the march, is as follows:

Horses, (36), thirty-six.

Mules, (32), thirty-two.

Number pounds of corn (99,312) ninety-nine thousand, three hundred and twelve.

Number pounds of fodder (66,720) sixty-six thousand, seven hundred and twenty.

Lieut. Harbert's report shows the following subsistence stores taken from the country:

150 head of beef cattle.

475 sheep.

8,000 pounds fresh pork.

2,000 " " bacon.

10,000 " " poultry.

5,000 " " honey.

3,000 " " corn meal.

2,300 " " flour.

6,600 bushels of sweet potatoes.

33 barrels of sorghum.

To the constant energy and systematic industry of Lieutenants Wing and Harbert, the brigade is under especial obligations, which I take pleasure in here acknowledging.

Lieut. Harbert so managed his department, that when the supplies of the other brigades of the division were exhausted, he still had on hand two days' rations of hard bread, having, in the meantime, satisfactorily supplied the troops with daily issues of sweet potatoes.

I have to express my gratification with the faithful, efficient, and gentlemanly manner in which I have been assisted by my staff officers.

For more particular remarks in regard to the execution of the duties of the different staff departments, I desire to refer to the Letter of Advice of the brigade Inspector, a copy of which is herewith transmitted.

In closing this report, I desire to say, that while my position has been somewhat embarassing by being separated from my regiment, and placed in command where I was comparatively a stranger, I am exceedingly well pleased with the brigade, and do not hesitate to pronounce it one, of which any brigade commander may well be proud.

* * * * * * *

Very respectfully, your obed't servant,

DANIEL DUSTIN,
Col. Commanding Brigade.

LETTER XII.

SOUTH CAROLINA SHORE, OPPOSITE SAVANNAH, GA.,
January 6th, 1865.

Perhaps it may be interesting to friends to know that we are now on the sacred soil of South Carolina, and it may further be interesting to know how we got here.

On Saturday morning, Dec. 31st, orders came for the 3d division to move across the island to the north side of the Savannah river. We were soon on the march, crossing the first channel on a rebel pontoon, and soon we reached the further side of the island, it perhaps being about a mile across. As we came in sight of the rebels on the main land, they opened fire on us, wounding several men of the 105th Illinois. They had taken possession of a house, and were sharpshooting from the windows. Leaving the teams in a safe place, a ten pound rifle Parrot was drawn to the shore by hand, and a few shells pitched into the Johnnies, some of which went through the house, others killing several of their horses under a barn close by. It was certainly amusing to see the rebels get out of that house. Soon our pontooniers were at work, but the wind blew so hard it was impossible to lay the bridge, the channel being very wide here.

Shortly after we reached the island, a cold, drizzling rain come on, and there we had to stand and take it till after dinner, when orders came for us to move back to our old camp west of the city. On reaching it, lo and behold, the first division had moved in immediately on our leaving in the morning, and so we were left out in the cold. The 31st Wisconsin, under command of Colonel West, however, very kindly invited us (22d Wis.) to quarter with them for the night, which we did, though pretty well crowded.

The next day in the afternoon, we were once more ordered to the Carolina shore, every one supposing that the pontoon had been completed, but on reaching the place, we found that there was a fair prospect of staying on the island all night, so tents were put up. The night was very chilly, the ground freezing some.

At four o'clock the next morning, the regiment was ordered back to the dock in the city, to take a steamer across the river. There they stood in the cold till about daylight, when they embarked—all except the teams, which still remain on the island—and soon the Carolina shore was reached.

You probably remember that during the first year of the war, a negro pilot took possession of a small steamer in Charleston harbor, while the officers were on shore, got up steam, passed out directly under the guns of Sumpter and Moultrie, giving the proper signal, and then with a white flag flying, approached our fleet and turned over the steamer to Uncle Sam. The name of this pilot was Robert Small, and that of his boat, the Planter. The boat was appraised at $30,000, half of which, by an act of Congress, was given to this pilot, and he was also made captain of the boat. Captain Small is a mulatto, short, thick set, full face, bright, keen eyes, and withal a smart looking man.

The Planter is a boat of 375 tons, and has lately been undergoing $40,000 repairs at Philadelphia, so Captain Small informed me. The boat is one of the trimmest little steamers I have ever seen, and is kept in very fine order. Most of the crew are colored, the mate being white, also a few others.

The 22d had the honor of being transported in the Planter, and all saw the man who at the time made such a stir in the papers.

While on board the boat, I fell in with a man recently from Charleston, who informed me that the lower part of the city was most terribly cut up by our cannon. Said the business part of the city was destroyed, and that the upper part was completely crowded with inhabitants, several families living in one house. Thought we could easily take the city by throwing a good force into the rear— that we need not fire a gun, if we could only manage to cut off their communication. Was confident, also, that Wilmington would soon be in our possession. He further said that the people that way had now no expectation of ever gaining their independence, and that could the question be left to them, the war would cease, and all be back in the old Union.

Whether this be true or not that way, it is undoubtedly the case in Georgia. A great many have expressed themselves as thoroughly convinced of the hopelessness of their cause, and are now anxious to have the war close, and they return to their allegiance once more.

There is more Unionism in Savannah, than in any place we have been in yet. The people seem to be glad that we have come.

As I was standing on the wharf a few days since, looking at the steamers puffing up and down the river, a citizen remarked to me : " It seems like a new life to us here in Savannah to have your army come. For a long time, the river has been still, only now and then a small blockade runner coming in. We feel that we now breathe a new and purer atmosphere. I shall have to tell you a little incident about myself. I have been in the confederate service—was in Atlanta in the militia, at the time you opened such a tremendous cannonading from all your guns. It made terrible work with us. In one case, one of your shells struck in our ditch, passing directly through four men. Shortly after the taking of Atlanta, the militia were sent home by order of Governor Brown, and I returned to Savannah. When the troops were again called for, I concealed myself, being determined that I would never fight any more, for I have always been a Union man. Was a merchant here. For some time before the Yankees came to Savannah, *I was sick*, (?) no one except particular friends being allowed to enter my house. Well, the morning you entered the city, a cousin of mine came to the house, knocked, and on telling his name was admitted. He hurried at once into my room saying, you need not be afraid to go out into the streets now, for the Yankees have come. I jumped out of bed, *tore off my blister plaster*, and rushed out into the streets. *I felt well right off*, and I have not seen a sick day since."

Without doubt some of this Unionism is assumed, as the confederate cause is completely given up; still I think from all I can see and hear, that there is a good deal of genuine Union sentiment in the city of Savannah, and our advent was undoubtedly a day of great rejoicing. Of course, many have an eye to business, and they well knew that so long as the rebels held the city, trade would remain dead. Their large warehouses would remain empty, and soon poverty would stare them in the face. *Thus the people of the South are being compelled to accept of Uncle Sam's protection—coerced.*

There is a rumor that the 20th corps is to be divided up between the other corps, but for what reason I cannot say. We are now camped about six miles north of the city, with a sufficient force to repel any attack that the rebels may be disposed to make. Between us and the river, is a very extensive rice swamp, much of the rice still remaining on the land in shocks.

We are probably the advance troops in the great campaign just about to commence. It is thought that we may remain here four or five weeks, but I should not be surprised if we start in two weeks.

One thing is certain, if we march through South Carolina, *the people will fare no better than those of Georgia.* Every soldier in the army feels a sort of hatred against this State, and consequently it will be pretty hard to restrain them in their foraging expeditions.

Every one says, "let South Carolina know what war is. Let her be forced to experience some of the horrors, she was so willing to have visited upon the border States."

By the time Sherman's army gets to Charleston, probably there will be a *good deal of Unionism* in this thoroughly rebel State.

There are but few sick in our regiment—none I think dangerous. Colonel Bloodgood is in the hospital, having been quite unwell most of the time since our arrival at Savannah, and in fact most of the time since leaving Atlanta.

Captain May is now in command of the regiment, he having been acting Major during the campaign. He is a fine officer, and highly esteemed by the entire command.

Our hospital steward, C. Tockterman, has lately been commissioned Assistant Surgeon in the 38th Wisconsin, and Proctor Scofield is now our hospital steward. It is a most excellent appointment.

Yesterday a reconnoitering party of 150 men of our brigade, was sent out under Captain Crawford, a division staff officer, for the purpose of examining roads, getting barges, &c., 38 men being detailed from the 22d under command of Lieutenant Bones. They went out some seven miles, encountering no rebels anywhere.

The day our brigade crossed the river, some of our men hunting hogs came upon a few rebel scouts and fired upon them, mortally wounding and capturing one of them.

Without doubt, there is now a perfect consternation all through South Carolina, as news of our present movement has gone far and wide.

The weather for the most part has been rather warm, still we have had our chilly nights and snapping frosts.

To-day it rains, still the boys are busy fixing their little cabins.

We are all in the best of spirits, and hope that before next "New Years," this terrible war will be over, our country saved, and we all at home.

    Yours truly,   G. S. BRADLEY.

LETTER XIII.

HD. QRS. 22D WIS., 2D BRIG., 3D DIV., 20TH A. C., }
  PURYSBURG, S. C., Jan. 18, 1865. }

At 8 A. M., yesterday, we broke camp and marched to this place, arriving about 3 P. M. By water, we are about 25 miles from Savannah, and about 20 by land.

The place contained perhaps half a dozen dwelling houses previous to our arrival, but only three now remain, viz: one occupied by Colonel Dustin and staff, one by our headquarters, and the other by a colored family.

Purysburg is on the Savannah river, and is somewhat famous in the history of the Revolutionary struggle, as being the headquarters of General Lincoln for a while.

On our arrival, we found an earthwork thrown up on the river bank, behind which was an old cannon mounted on a huge pair of wheels. This cannon was thickly crusted on the inside with rust, it probably having descended from Revolutionary times, and was simply placed there in position as a sort of Quaker gun.

We took our position yesterday afternoon, unsuspecting any rise of water, though we found the road just ahead of this place impassable by reason of floodwater. During the night, the water continued to rise so that some of the 85th Indiana had to move three times before morning.

Colonel Crane, sleeping in a bunk in his tent, remained till daylight, when he found himself out quite a distance in the water, and they had to go in after him with a horse.

We found that the water had completely covered the road for quite a distance over which we came, thus hemming us in entirely. Several teams started out early this morning down the river bank after rice straw, but after going a short distance, were compelled to return. So here we are to-night on an island, the only boat within reach being a little skiff, able, perhaps, to carry four men.

A steamer was expected up the river to-day with supplies, but did not come.

The prospect now is, that we shall have to remain here for the present—at least, till the freshet goes down somewhat. This freshet is supposed to be caused by rains in the up country, or possibly the extensive melting of snow in the mountains. They are probably having their " January thaw " up that way.

By the time this reaches you, its contents will not be contraband news, and perhaps I am entirely wrong in the programme, but my impression is as follows: The 20th corps will move up this side of the Savannah river, the 14th the other, while the 17th and 15th corps, having gone to Beaufort by water, will strike off and form a junction with us this way, and we shall then move on Augusta, after which Charleston and Wilmington can be attended to at our leisure. Perhaps we may make simply a feint towards Augusta, and really strike a more vulnerable point of rebeldom.

At any rate, the next few weeks will tell one way or the other. Sherman will soon add another chapter to history.

Thus far in South Carolina, we have seen nothing but the everlasting pitch pine. Now and then a farm house is seen, but the settlements are very few indeed. The soil is, of course, sandy and poor.

Crows are very numerous, especially in the vicinity of the rice swamps, and immense flocks of blackbirds complete the picture. A short time since I had the privilege of seeing my first alligator. He was about seven feet in length, and really looked a little ugly.

A few of the 22d have been left in the hospital at Savannah, but there are, I believe, no serious cases. Probably all of them will be able to communicate with their friends, so I need not stop to enumerate them.

I may not have a chance to write you again for the present, but I trust you will ever hear a good report of the old 22d.

Yours truly,   G. S. BRADLEY, Chaplain.

LETTER XIV.

PURYSBURG, S. C., Jan. 25, 1865.

For a few days past the weather has been chilly, and the nights freezing cold. Our long and hard rain storm cleared off with a cold snap; it feels and looks like snow to-day, and if we were North it would certainly come. Yesterday orders came for us to make ourselves as comfortable as possible where we now are, as there is no immediate prospect of an advance, on account of the awful roads. The water has in a good degree gone down, still it runs over the road in several places, both in front and rear. It will probably require two weeks of good dry weather before we shall think of moving. If, in the mean time, our Northern friends are impatient at our present slow progress, all I have to say is, that I wish them no worse punishment than to be obliged to march just one day through South Carolina swamp and mud at the time of high water.

Several scouting parties have been out in different directions. One day last week we opened communication with Foster's forces at Pocotaligo, some thirty miles from Purysburg. Most of the parties sent out have usually returned in company with a good supply of beeves, sheep &c.

It is a sad mistake that the people make in leaving

their houses, for their property would not suffer near as much if they remained.

It is understood that the 14th corps have taken up their position at Sister's Ferry, a place some thirty-five miles above here. The 19th corps will garrison Savannah.

Our mails lately have been very small, at least, some of us have received but few letters. Perhaps our friends North became discouraged about us, thinking we were lost somewhere in Georgia, and thus neglected to write. Don't serve us so again, for Sherman will bring us all out safe. You need not believe more than a hundredth part of what the rebels say about us.

By the way, the picture in Harpers of January 7th, of the capture of the *Resolute*, in which the 22d played so conspicuous a part, is a very poor affair. Davis did not do himself justice.

Of late, our hearts have been greatly cheered by the good news from other quarters.

Knowing how interested everybody at home is in hearing from the army, I shall try to keep you posted while our communications remain open. In a few days we shall probably cut loose from all connections with the outside world, and be lost again for a short time somewhere within the shell of rebeldom. We may not be able to catch Hardee, but we shall probably drive him into his "tactics," to say the least.

We are now about 40 miles from Branchville. Whether we shall go there or not, no one at present knows. Old Tecumseh—I suggest that this be the *sobriquet* of our brave Commander Sherman—keeps his counsels to himself. Some may be pretty good at guessing, and hit the nail on the head, but the General himself is *very close.*

We may make a feint towards Augusta, causing the enemy to send a large force there, while we slip in behind, cut the railroad and then taking Branchville at our leisure, march toward Charleston.

Possibly we may strike further north to Columbia, and then swing around to the east again. I have no doubt but Sherman has his plans matured on a big scale, and this will be another campaign worthy of a conspicuous place in history.

Yours in an enemy's country.

G. S. BRADLEY.

EXTRACTS FROM JOURNAL.

Sunday, January 29, 1865.

Broke camp at Purysburg, at 7 A. M., and marched 17 miles, camping for the night on Roberts' plantation, in a big cornfield.

Heard some cannonading and musketry just before reaching camp. It was either the gunboats shelling the woods along the river, or more likely, the 1st division, skirmishing with the enemy near Robertsville.

The troops that preceded us left but very few houses standing. We saw many in smoking ruins as we came along.

I have noticed one thing during this winter's campaign which is a disgrace to the army and its leaders. The houses of the poor are almost universally sacked and burned, but many of the richest have a guard at once placed over them and are thus spared from the general ruin. This is entirely wrong.

Monday, January 30.

Another, bright, clear, cold morning. Froze quite hard

during the night, but as the sun comes peeping through the quiet pines, it seems cheerful once more.

I am sitting by our bivouac fire, and all around I can see the pleasant cheerful fires of hundreds, and can hear the hum of many voices.

Slept well last night—better than for several nights past.

Dreamed that I was captured by the rebels, but they treated me very kindly. Don't care though about its coming to pass.

Broke camp quite early, reaching Robertsville about noon—distance two miles, making us now about 45 miles from Savannah. This is a pleasant little village, about five miles from the river, containing a very neat church, with a steeple and town clock, a store or two, and about 15 dwelling houses. The inhabitants had all left except a few negroes.

As the 1st division came near this place on Sunday, the 3d Wisconsin was sent ahead as skirmishers. They encountered the rebels near the village and were fired upon, but they steadily advanced, and as the rebels turned to run, they poured in upon them, causing a general stampede. General Sherman, waiting at the landing five miles from here, had ordered the 1st division to signal their safe arrival here by cannon shots, so they gave the signal by turning their guns upon the retreating foe, thus accomplishing a double purpose.

From all that we can learn, there are perhaps about two brigades of Wheeler's cavalry hovering near us, their camp to-night being about two miles from ours.

After reaching camp, Lieutenant Knowles, of the 22d, with some 40 men from the brigade was sent out on a foraging expedition, and while a few of his men rushed ahead to get the first pickings from the plantation, the rebels suddenly dashed in between them and the main party, and they were probably taken prisoners, none, however, from the 22d. Lieutenant Knowles informed me that his party had some pretty hard fighting for awhile.

Tuesday, 31st.—The last day of January, and here we are, camped in a pine forest away up the Savannah river in South Carolina.

God grant that this cruel war may soon be closed, and all be permitted once more to enjoy the sunny smiles of home, and no longer disturbed by the clangor of strife and the sight of blood. God grant that soon the day may come when our nation, purified and strengthened by this baptism of fire and blood, shall arise to a higher and better life—when the foul blot of human chattelism shall be swept away, and no traitor dare again to lift his finger against the government.

Feb. 2d.—Broke camp at 7 A. M., marching toward Lawtonville. When within some two miles of the village, we found the rebels disposed to fight us. The wagon train was ordered to stop, and the several brigades were sent ahead to feel the enemy.

There was a large swamp across which we must pass, and here the rebels took their stand. The skirmishing, however, commenced some three fourths of a mile before we reached it.

Gradually they fell back, and our men advanced. Getting within some 50 rods of the swamp, a line of battle was formed in the following order:

In the centre was our brigade, on the right, the 1st, on the left the 3d.

Our line was as follows: 85th Indiana on the right, then the 22d Wisconsin, then the 19th Michigan—the 33d Indiana being absent at the time, arriving, however, about dark.

This line of battle was formed about 3 P. M., and was about half a mile in length. All advanced in gallant style. I should not, however, forget to mention that this line was formed in an open field in plain sight of the rebels in the woods. We had a skirmish line ahead, and at a given signal, off our brave men dashed on the double quick, the rebels firing their pieces and retreating in a hurry. By the time the woods were reached, not a rebel could be found, and we pursued once more the quiet tenor of our ways.

A few men were killed and several wounded. Marched about 15 miles to-day. Some of our skirmishers found the following posted in a conspicuous place:

"Yanks, you better leave this country, for France and England have recognized the Southern Confederacy, and Lincoln is ordered to withdraw his troops from our soil."

Poor deluded Southern Confederacy!

An officer lately informed me he had heard there was a regular organized party in the army, for the destruction of property in South Carolina. There is a most terrible feeling on the part of our soldiers in this respect, and nothing will prevent the ruin of the country.

We camp to-night within a few miles of the 15th corps, and General Sherman's headquarters are close at hand.

The 17th is also a little further to the right—the 14th has been moving up through Georgia on the other side of the river, but will probably cross over soon—if they are not already over. Thus we are laying waste a wide extent of territory. To-day passed a splendid mansion. In front was a most beautiful flower garden. In the several rooms, was furniture of the costliest kind. I noticed a very fine piano, chairs, mirror, &c.

But in a short time, all was demolished, and the mansion was fired, but just about this time, General Ward came up, and ordered the fire put out. While this was being done, the torch was applied in another part of the house, and while this second fire was being extinguished, the match was applied in the garret, and the house was soon one grand mass of flames.

It seems sad to burn such beautiful residences, but our boys reason in this wise, and reason correctly, too, I think. The wealthy people of the South were the very ones to plunge the country into secession—*now let them suffer—let South Carolina aristocracy have its fill of secession.*

Feb. 4th.—Broke camp at 7 A. M.—marched some 10 miles—saw several splendid plantations to-day—boys found plenty of forage—corn, beans, chickens, turkeys, geese, ducks, hogs, sorghum, flour, hams, bacon, &c. Reached camp about sunset, being some 12 miles from the river. The 15th corps had some of a skirmish with the enemy yesterday, but they were routed, a portion of their forces retreating over the road we are now on. The inhabitants complain bitterly of Wheeler's men, saying they are quite as bad as the Yankees. One woman, with whom I talked, thought this war never ought to have been commenced, and never would had it not been for the "highflies," as she called them. Said the poor people couldn't do anything, as the "highflies" had it all their own way.

The country looks richer through here than most we have yet passed over. But ruin and desolation are everywhere seen.

Sometimes as the crackling, roaring flames are seen, and the huge, dense columns of black smoke go up, the boys simply say, "Go it South Carolina," or "South Carolina, the traitor's doom," or "How do you do, South Carolina?"

Sunday, Feb. 5th.—Many people expressed surprise to-day that Sherman's army should make such rapid progress—they seemed to have no idea that we had got so far along.

Found the road barricaded in several places. Saw many buildings in flames. Could frequently see the huge black columns of smoke far away over the tops of the tall pines in several directions.

We have been making towards Augusta, but to-day turned to the north east, toward Branchville. If we keep on in the present direction, we shall strike the railroad about 15 miles from our present camp. We camp near Buford's Bridge, on the Salkahatchie. Had bad roads to-day—barricades again, and many indications of rebel camps all along.

The rebels are evidently at a great loss what course Sherman intends to take. Some negroes informed me that there is now a most terrible excitement among the whites. A few hundred of Wheeler's men keep ahead of us, telling the people all along that they are going to make a stand soon—that they intend to stop the Yankees—that we can never get to Augusta—that they will fix us if we presume to go to Branchville, and all that sort of thing.

Saw quite an oldish looking man to-day, nearly white, who said he was a slave.

The blacks seem highly pleased to see their masters' property taken or destroyed. They seem really delighted to see the gin houses go off in flames, thinking they will not have quite so much picking cotton to do, for a time, at least.

A few days since, as Charley I—— was out foraging, he called at a house and inquired of some of the black girls where they kept their sweet potatoes?

"Right there, massa," they replied, pointing to an old house near by.

He went in the direction indicated, when several of the girls came running in, inquiring if he didn't want some help. Told them "yes," when about half a dozen took hold, with a hearty good will, evidently being perfectly satisfied with the foraging arrangement.

While they were thus at work, their mistress came to the door, telling them they must not pick out all the large ones.

"Well, missus, we just have to, for the Yankees make us," they replied, hardly able to keep from laughing.

Large numbers are falling into our lines every day. They all come inspired with that magic word—*freedom*.

Many of our soldiers treat them roughly, still they look upon Sherman's army as their great deliverers, and they wish the Yankees success in whipping the rebels.

At one place to-day, some of the people were complaining about the army's taking everything, when one of the boys remarked, "You are unfortunate living in this State, for South Carolina is bound to suffer."

"That is just the way Wheeler's men talk. They accuse South Carolina of being the cause of the trouble. They come to our homes saying 'Shell out your stuff here, since you commenced this muss.'"

So between Wheeler's men and the Yankees, the country will soon find out the *meaning* of secession.

Feb. 6, '65.—The rebels had strong works near Buford's Bridge, but were driven out by the 15th corps— the men wading a deep swamp.

There was considerable skirmishing to-day in our front, but the enemy continually fell back.

They burn all the bridges in their rear. We were hardly out of sight of burning houses to-day. The black columns of smoke could be seen in all directions. Has been a cold, raw day—cloudy, with rain last night and through the evening.

Our boys are living on the very fat of the land.

This morning a miserable slave-holder whipped some of his slaves for a very trifling thing, and when our boys applied the torch to the gin-house, the blacks seemed fairly overjoyed.

This afternoon a young man by the name of Jenkins of the 105 Illinois, Colonel Dustin's regiment, with another soldier of the 1st division, went out on a scouting expedition to the left some five miles. While riding along, they discovered a couple of horsemen ahead of them, but at so great a distance they were not certain whether they were our men or not. The other man said to Jenkins, "I believe they are Johnnies, and as we are two and two, suppose we try our luck."

At first they rode along rather leisurely, but discovering by and by that they were rebels, they put spurs to their horses and dashed in upon them, calling upon them to surrender. The rebs proved to be a Lieutenant and a Sergeant. The Lieut. wheeled his horse, drew his revolver, and seemed determined not to be easily taken.

Jenkins armed with a Henry rifle, 16 shooter, cocked it and leveled it at him, saying as he did so, "put that revolver in your sheath, or I will blow you through."

Not caring to compete with a Henry, he put up his revolver, and the two were soon led into our camp. Each of them was armed with two revolvers, and had a very good horse, saddle, &c.

Jenkins was one of the party who captured and burnt the rebel boat Ida, on the Savannah river, about the time we arrived near the city. He is an excellent scout and loves the business very much. He has had some very narrow escapes, and much experience of a very exciting character.

Thus, we have men for all kinds of work and business.

Feb. 7th, being in the rear to-day, we did not get started from camp till about 11 A. M. The morning opened with a hard, cold rain. Rained more or less all day.

Found the roads very bad—swampy and muddy so that the trains moved very slowly indeed. Travelled but about 7 miles, and at this rate did not get into camp till 10 o'clock at night. The night was very chilly and raw, thus rendering soldiering anything but pleasant.

The fences along the road made us plenty of fire-wood. Burning houses, fences and cotton-gins, somewhat relieved the night of its dreariness. Lay down to rest about midnight.

This P. M. the Quartermaster of the 19th Michigan, captured one of General Anderson's orderlies with his horse, and delivered him to Colonel Dustin. This orderly was sent out by the General to tell their pickets to fall back slowly, skirmishing with the enemy, and delaying him as much as possible.

By mistake, he ran into the Quartermaster's squad, and so fell into our hands.

Had some conversation with him as we rode along. Says Wheeler has about 8,000 men, but they are very much scattered.

Feb. 8th, a bright, clear, cool morning. The sun comes up gloriously after such a day of gloom as we had yesterday.

Camped last night within about half a mile of the railroad, and some sixteen miles from Branchville, west. So this important line of railway is severed, and Charleston and Augusta are parted. I would like to see the morning papers of either city this morning.

Wonder if they think Sherman will take Branchville now?

At about 9:30 A. M., we broke camp—moved across the burning railroad, and turned west to Graham's Station, some two miles. Here we found all the railroad buildings on fire, together with several hundred bales of cotton—the negros say 400.

Feb. 9th, a very cold night—froze quite hard. Broke camp at 7 A. M., passing along the railroad east—left smoking ruins behind us.

While at Graham's Station, General Wheeler addressed a note to General Howard, proposing that our troops refrain from house-burning, and he, (General Wheeler) would discontinue cotton burning. He said in earnest of his good faith, that he had spared from the flames at that place 300 bales of cotton, worth in their money one and a half millions.

This letter was submitted to General Sherman, who replied to him thus:

HEADQUARTERS MILITARY DIVISION OF THE
MISSISSIPPI, IN THE FIELD, Feb. 8th, 1865.

GENERAL:—Yours, addressed to General Howard, is received by me. I hope you will burn all the cotton, and save us the trouble. We dont want it, and it has proved a curse to our country. All you don't burn, I will.

As to private houses, occupied by peaceful families, my orders are not to molest or disturb them, and I think my orders are obeyed.

Vacant houses, being of no use to anybody, I care but little about, as the owners have thought them of no use to themselves. I don't want them destroyed, but do not take much care to preserve them.

I am, with respect, yours truly,

W. T. SHERMAN.
Major-General Commanding.

Major-General J. Wheeler, Commanding Cavalry Corps,
Confederate Army.

The following story is one among many that happen from day to day in our grand tramp through the confederacy:

TWO REBEL SOLDIERS SURROUNDED BY A FEDERAL OFFICER.—On the night of the 30th a Captain of the 16th Michigan infantry, while riding out, came upon two rebel soldiers in the woods near the pike. The officer, seeing it would not do to attempt an escape, in a very authoritative tone demanded what regiment they belonged to. They replied to a Mississippi regiment. "What are you doing off from your command at a time like this? You have no business here." The soldiers replied that they were only looking around a little. "Very well," replied the officer, " come right along with me, and I will take you to your regiments." The soldiers followed, and in a few minutes they found, to their dismay, that the witty officer was in the Federal service, and had led them into a Yankee camp.

Probably the rebels can also tell some pretty sharp things about their exploits. Each side has its daring, cunning, and fearless men.

LETTER XV.

FAYETTEVILLE, N. C., March 12, 1865.

As there is a chance to communicate with the outside world, I will embrace the opportunity of telling you that we are all safe and sound. Arrived here last night, and camped just a little out of the city. From my journal which I send home, you will be able to gather a tolerably clear idea of our march through South Carolina. Each day was alike for the most part, varied perhaps by incidents more or less exciting, according to circumstances.

Striking the railroad near Branchville, each corps had its share of work laid off, and most faithfully was it performed, and I think they will not soon have their roads in running order that way again. Sherman has been swinging his big scythe right and left, and South Carolina has tasted some of the legitimate fruits of nullification and secession. I think her people are perfectly satisfied with their experiment.

Striking off into the interior of the State, destroying the entire network of railroads in every direction, burning and laying waste the country generally, we at last reached Columbia, the capital of the State—a beautiful city. In order to prevent the large amount of cotton stored there from falling into our hands, Wade Hampton ordered it to be set on fire. It was done, and a heavy wind arising, the burning cotton was blown over into the city, and soon a large portion of the town was a mass of smoking ruins.

Probably there will not be many tears shed at the North over the destruction of Columbia.

At Cheraw, we captured 17 guns, 3,000 small arms, and a large amount of ammunition.

At this place is an old church, said to have been built in Revolutionary times. General Marion was buried here. On a tombstone in this ancient burying ground, is a quaint epitaph, written as follows without name or date:

> My name--my country--what are they to thee?
> What--whether high or low my pedigree?
> Perhaps--I far surpassed all other men!
> Perhaps--I fell below them all--what then?
> Suffice it, stranger, that thou see'st a tomb,
> Thou knowest its use--it hides no matter whom.

A rebel surgeon at Cheraw, in answer to my question, "What do the people through here think of the war?" remarked, "They are generally despondent, thinking something must be wrong somewhere, as your army seems to be marching where it pleases—but the *army* is hopeful."

A rebel clergyman in Cheraw remarked that the people along the track of our army, were becoming very bitter toward us on account of the destruction of their property.

Well, let them rage. We have their hatred already, and they have sworn eternal separation, so that any little increase of hate will not materially affect matters. They have the alternative before them in plain English—*submission*, or *coercion* and *subjugation*.

As I was riding along through the place one morning, I met an old negro, and accosted him thus:

"Do you live in this place?"

"Yes, sir," politely lifting his hat and bowing.

"How many inhabitants does Cheraw contain?"

"Don't know sir."

"When did the rebels leave?"

"The morning you came in."

"Was there any fighting before they left?"

"No sir—they all ran as fast as they could across the bridge."

"Who was in command?"

"General Hardee. *I see him.*

"Why didn't they fight?"

"Why didn't they fight you before you got here?"

"Where do they propose to fight us next?"

"The Lord only knows. Probably when you get them into a corner somewhere, but they run now," at the same time extending his coat tail out straight behind and stepping forward a few steps.

"You know," said he, "that a rooster after being badly whipped will sometimes fight a little when cornered."

I was quite amused with him, as he seemed to be a warm Union man, and also quite intelligent.

Speaking of intelligence, suggests a remark made by a woman to one of our boys, who inquired how far it was to Fayetteville.

"I don't know," said she, "as I haven't any *edification.*"

It is really sad to see the lamentable ignorance of the masses of the South.

They are dirty and ignorant, the women, and even *lit-*

tle girls, chewing tobacco and dipping snuff! I have seen some of these Southern women squirting tobacco juice till I was completely disgusted, and prayed that my destiny might never be linked with any of them.

The people of the South have lately been learning two very important facts:

1. That cotton is not King.
2. That slavery does not always pay.

How nicely everything seems to work with Sherman. Just about the time his army reaches this city, up comes a vessel, thus opening communications with the outside world once more.

We are now 120 miles from the mouth of Cape Fear River.

The city contains 5,000 inhabitants, and is quite a pretty place. There is a large arsenal here, commenced in 1837, by the U. S. Government, but not much was done to it till the breaking out of the war, when the rebels erected some extensive and beautiful buildings. As we shall not need them ourselves, Sherman has ordered them to be battered down, and this work is being done as I write.

A touching little incident occurred this morning, which I will relate. A couple of gray headed old men came to the picket line early this morning, pleading to be let through, that they might once more look upon the Stars and Stripes.

They were granted the privilege, and came within our lines. They then wanted to go to the city so as to see the old flag floating over the place. And as they once more saw the glorious emblem of our nationality waving so proudly in the morning breeze, they could not repress their deep emotion.

As a contrast to the above, let me give you the following, which I copy from the original: Mr. Greenwood was taken a prisoner by the rebels, and while in Savannah, he addressed a note to an uncle, asking for some little favor. The following was the reply of the uncle:

Savannah, August 4th, 1864.

M. L. GREENWOOD, ESQ.

Sir :—Your note came to hand this morning, and I only say that I am surprised that you have had the presumption to write to me at all.

I am a loyal subject to the Confederate Government, and can hold no correspondence with the enemies of my country. I pity you for having suffered yourself to be led so far astray as to try to oppress a people, that have never injured you or the Government, in whose service you are. I must decline seeing, or having any correspondence with you, unless of a strictly business character.

I am sir,

W. H. BORDLY.

We shall probably remain here only a day or two, and we shall then start once more across the country. We have now been seventy days on the road from Savannah. Many a weary day's march has been made, and we have seen the desolations of war on every hand. South Carolina has suffered most terribly.

The general impression now is that we shall strike for Goldsboro, as that is considered the most important point in that direction.

But we do not expect to reach that place without some severe fighting. Charleston, Wilmington, and several other places have fallen, and now we shall have to meet the combined forces probably not many days hence. Thus far we have seen but little fighting, but we expect more in the future.

Let the friends at home keep up good courage. The war is rapidly drawing to a close. Sherman is severing the arteries of the rebellion.

Yours truly,
G. S. BRADLEY.

P. S. Be sure to write a good long letter that I may hear from you at Goldsboro—you see I am confident about getting through.

Johnston cannot stop us.   G. S. B.

LETTER XVI.

Arrival at Goldsboro—Battle of Averysboro—Battle of Bentonville—The Panic—20th Corps save the day—The Grand Army rests.

GOLDSBORO, N. C. 3D DIVISION
HOSPITAL, March 25, 1865.

The smoke of battle has cleared away somewhat and we are able to realize the magnitude of the contest, though not fully able to gather the amount of loss. It has been severe, however.

In the battle of the 16th, our division lost about 160; the 2d brigade losing 50.

During the terrific fighting on the 19th 20th and 21st, our brigade was not engaged at all, though we expected every moment to go into the thickest of the fight. Had not the 20th corps come up when it did, the 14th would have been annihilated, losing hospital, trains and everything. The rebels had them in a trap, and it was only by the timely arrival of our corps that the wavering fortunes of the day were restored.

Soon the 15th and 17th came up, then the 23d and parts of the 24th and 25th, so that the rebels thought it best to get out of the thing as soon as possible.

They have probably gone toward Raleigh. Sherman will not attempt any further offensive work at present, I think, but will concentrate his army near Goldsboro and let it rest awhile. We have had a long campaign, and many of our soldiers are barefoot and destitute of clothes, and need rest.

Our brigade is now camped out of the city some three miles. Goldsboro has been quite a flourishing place of 2,000 inhabitants. The 23d corps is now garrisoning the city. Our Hospital is located in a pleasant part of the city. We have not far from 300 in the 3d Division Hospital. Probably many of them will soon be sent to Newbern or Wilmington.

I heard the whistle of cars this morning, with the welcome intelligence of "mail from the North." The boys in the hospital fairly cheered the engine as the whistle sounded.

The weather is quite warm—peach and apple trees are in bloom. G. S. BRADLEY.

HD. QRS. 2D BRIG. 3D DIV. 20TH A. C.
NEAR GOLDSBORO, N. C. March 27, 1865.

Since I wrote you at Fayetteville we have marched nearly 100 miles and fought two battles. We hardly expected the rebels to permit us to go on unchecked to our base. They had hovered about our column (the left wing) for over two weeks, capturing our foragers, and at times making dashes upon the pickets and cavalry. Several prisoners captured by us, also their deserters, gave us information which proved to be nearly correct.

On the 15th, Kilpatrick was checked by a rebel force stationed at Smith's Plantation, near Averysborough, reported to be strong. This caused the main column to halt and go into camp; while the 2d brigade, 1st division moved up to support the cavalry. A short time had elapsed when cannonading was heard but five miles distant; it continued to a late hour of the night. At 4 P. M. the rain commenced to fall, and the prospect looked gloomy.

THE ADVANCE.

We were ordered forward at daylight on the 16th; two divisions of the 20th corps (1st and 3d) were ordered forward unincumbered; pack mules, wagons, etc., were to follow. The 4th corps came up behind us. Here let me state that the 2d division of the 20th corps, and the 3d division of the 14th corps were detailed to go with the principal part of the train on another road (to our right) since leaving Fayetteville. The column moved on at a rapid rate through mud and mire, as the roads were made miserable by the heavy rain during the past twelve hours. Soon we heard the booming of the cannon and the sharp crack of the skirmishers' guns. Kilpatrick had worked all night, and as morning dawned we were advised of their position.

POSITION OF THE ENEMY.

The enemy were reported on a hill, or rise of ground, across the road running direct to Raleigh. Their works were quite strong, but in plain view, as part of their line extended to our left, across an open level field; this, however, was an outerwork, and the right flank of their main line. The rebels opened fire from two guns in their field work upon our skirmishers, but were soon silenced by our sharp fire.

THE FORMATION AND CHARGE.

The 3d division, 20th corps formed upon the left of the road, while the 1st division formed upon the right; three batteries (Winnegar's, Geary's and Knapp's Pennsylvania battery) were planted in our line and opened a furious fire to cover the formation and advance. The 1st brigade, 3d division, 20th corps, commanded by Col. Case of the 125th Illinois regiment, was sent around to the left to turn the right flank of the rebels. The cavalry were formed for the rout in case there should be one.

Time had been given for the first brigade to move around; all was ready on the right of the road, the skirmishers were busy, and the order came to advance. Col. Dustin's brigade (the 2d of the 3d division, 20th corps,) covered the open field, and the line was single, and as it moved up toward the works of the enemy, they opened a sharp fire upon us. The whole line charged, and the cannon poured a covering fire for us upon the "Johnnies." Just then came in upon their right flank the 1st brigade— and such commotion! The rebs ran this way and that way, and finally were routed, leaving their cannon and dead and wounded in their works. Our lines halted to gather breath and eat dinner, when we advanced and took position in front of their second line, a mile distant. Their wounded were left all along the road, and a great many dead were found in the works we had driven them from. This is a little surprising to us, as it was ascertained that their force outnumbered our own as far as the engagement was concerned; but our artillery excelled everything in its effect, and the flank movement was a complete stunner upon them.

Our corps went into camp or bivouac for the night, and the 14th corps took position on our left.

OUR LOSS.

In the 3d division, our loss did not exceed 300, killed and wounded; the enemy's loss was far greater judging from the wounded in our hands. Our division captured 165 prisoners, among them several captains and lesser officers; three officers were killed upon the works, and several wounded fell into our hands. Our loss in officers was heavy in proportion. The 19th Michigan lost two officers killed; the 22d Wisconsin lost only eight wounded, they being protected by a rise of ground in front of the works. Our total loss during the day was 50—10 killed and 40 wounded.

THE ENEMY FALL BACK.

During the night the enemy retired, and we were ordered out at an early hour. The two divisions of the 14th corps took the advance, and the 1st division of the 20th corps followed, while the 3d division moved on a road to the left leading to Averysboro, eight miles distant, where we were to cover some roads leading into the flank of the main column. At this place we found 32 wounded rebels, whom we paroled. Remained here that day, and at 6 A. M. of the 17th, we took the back track for the main column.

Nothing but very bad roads and the ponderous train interfered with our progress until the 19th, when it was reported the enemy had a strong force in our immediate front, and, as we could hear the dull roar of cannon in the distance, we believed it. Our division guarded the trains, while the 14th corps took the advance; the 1st division of the 20th corps brought up the rear. At 4 P. M. an order came back to us to leave the train and push on at a double quick. The division arrived just in time, for the left of the 14th corps had been driven back, and our position looked "mixed." The order had been issued to abandon the hospitals, and details of men were made to remain with them in case they were. But when the old "Star Corps" came up, a shout rent the air. The 14th corps, beaten back and whipped by superior forces, rallied and took position; battery after battery wheeled into position; our corps filed into line on the left.

It was soon ascertained from prisoners and deserters that the whole rebel army of North Carolina was ready to fight us. These conclusions were confirmed by a charge on our center. Charge upon charge, and the din of the cannon and musketry told us plainly that the enemy were massing to break our center. The 3d brigades of the 1st and 2d divisions were moved down to support the center, and all had a taste of war; wagon load after wagon load of ammunition being hurried across the vast open field to the edge of the wood that marked our lines. The rebels were repulsed in five distinct charges, but they came on until the seventh charge had been repulsed. There has never been fiercer fighting on the part of the rebels. Night was coming in thick with the smoke of battle, but the roar of our "death-tide" still flowed. Our line was as yet undisturbed. Our men had thrown up strong works, and were standing "at arms." There was a lull in the storm, and our weary soldiers lay down to rest.

The morning brought no change in our position. The enemy had given up his project and we were content. We learned on this day that our right wing had wound round and covered Kingston, and that Schofield was at Goldsboro; that our base was reached, and Sherman was himself. Do you wonder we were so content. After a lapse of seventy days, we were again to hear from the United States, and could again procure clothing, coffee, sugar and hardtack. Sherman had told us at Fayetteville that we must march again before our true destination was reached. We have made the march, whipped the enemy twice, and here we are at our *true destination*, busy preparing for another glorious campaign.

Yesterday, Sunday, we received a large mail, with letters dated as late as March 1st. We have promise of another to-day.

But I must close without telling you half—how our boys have marched without shoes or hats—how we have been without soap for three weeks, and obliged to cook over pitch pine fires—how, with "giant great hearts," they have waded through sloughs of despondency, and have finally secured rest, food and raiment. But I must tell you a little about a class in our army (and no inconsiderable portion of General Sherman's army do they compose) called "Bummers." Imagine a fellow with a gun and accoutrements, with a plug hat, a captured militia plume in it, a citizen's saddle, with a bed quilt or table cloth, upon an animal whose ears are the larger part of the whole. Let us take an inventory of his stock as he rides into camp at night. Poor fellow! he has rode upon that knock-kneed, shaved tail, rail fence mule over 30 miles, has fought the brush and mud, and passed through untold dangers, and all for his load, which consists of, first, a bundle of fodder for his mule; second, three hams, a sack of meal, a peck of potatoes; third, a fresh bed quilt, the old mother's coffee pot, a jug of vinegar and a bed cord. You call him an old, steady bummer. I'll give you one more picture. Here comes a squad of eighteen or nineteen, no two alike. Look at the chickens, geese, beehives; see that little fellow with a huge hog strapped upon his nag's back. There rides the commander, a Lieutenant, completely happy, for the day has been a good one, and his detail has got enough for a day's good supply for his regiment.

These "Bummers" were detailed for foragers, and upon them the army depended for subsistence; for be it known that we started with a very small stock of supplies, and our campaign was lengthened after starting from our base (Savannah), consequently the "Bummers" were the life of the army. About 5,000 strong, not a field or house or barn, but was searched by them; not a town or hamlet but the "infernal bummers" (as Kilpatrick said) managed to plunder before his cavalry came up. They met the enemy at Fayetteville, and drove him across Cape Fear river; they entered Columbia as skirmishers, not only for "Johnnies," but for meat and bread and goodies. Many outrages were committed by them. To enter a house and find the feather bed ripped open, the wardrobes ransacked, chests stripped of contents, looking glasses taken from the walls, cooking utensils gone, and all the corn meal and bacon missing, bed quilts stripped from the beds, the last jar of pickles gone, was no uncommon sight, and one to make a soldier blush with indignation. Every effort that could be made was made to check the demoralization of the foragers; but the occupation tended to demoralization, and "the army must be fed, and the Bummers must feed us." Thus we reasoned, but deprecated the means used to bring about the result. Some would discriminate, others would not, and thus the few have caused a great deal of unnecessary suffering.

I must close with the "Bummers," saying that they exist no more as an organization; but the spirit will live throughout the lives of at least one-half of those who served in the capacity.

OUR SITUATION.

Orders—congratulatory orders, regulation orders—have been issued. We are to remain in our present position to fit up for another campaign. We face north. Significant, is it not?

The army under General Schofield occupies the center, in and about the city; the 15th and 17th corps rest on the right, covering the railroad and Neuse river, and the 20th and 14th corps are on the left. We are to have two railroads in working order in two or three days—one from Wilmington, the other from Newbern; some bridges are to be built, &c. Our wagon trains will go to Kingston for supplies. Everybody is busy, and we are all feeling well; but we look rough after our campaign of 70 days, from our base.

CHAS. A. BOOTH,
Lt. and Pro. Mar. 2d Brig., 3d Div., 20th A. C.

LETTER XVII.

News of Lee's Surrender—Rebellion about played out—Johnston in a tight place.

RALEIGH, N. C., April 14, 1865.

As I have a chance to send you a few lines through

private hands, I will embrace the opportunity. We left Goldsboro last Monday, the 10th, the troops pushing on unencumbered by trains. The 22d were detached from the Brigade and detailed as train guard; and for several days we were almost the only troops guarding the whole train. The day we started quite a heavy rain set in, and in a short time the roads were *awful*. People at home can form no idea of pulling such trains as we have, through the mud. For four nights in succession we were out till midnight, and after. The first night I lay down in the rain, with a single rubber blanket under me and one over me, and at one time was awakened by the rubber's allowing the drops to fall upon my face. *This is soldiering;* but still we are healthy and strong. Yesterday we marched some twenty miles and camped for the night, about nine miles from Raleigh; to-day we entered the city, joining our command. Our forces entered the place about nine A. M. yesterday, with but little opposition. There has been more or less skirmishing all the way from Goldsboro, but has not amounted to much.

Johnston has fallen back to Hillsboro, and citizens inform me that the programme was, to join Lee somewhere west of this and push for the Mississippi; but the Lee part of the performance proves to be a little shaky.

To-day Gen. Sherman has been reviewing several of the corps, in front of the State House. We march to-morrow, and the 20th corps will be reviewed by him as we pass through the city.

We shall probably push on after Johnston, wherever he goes. The general impression among the citizens is, that it is a very foolish thing for him to longer continue the contest.

Our army is highly elated over recent victories near Richmond, and the subsequent capture of Lee and his army.

There is an impression that we may follow Johnston into Tennessee, but no one can tell what a few weeks may bring forth.

Raleigh is a very pretty city of some 6,000 inhabitants. It contains a Deaf and Dumb Asylum—a splendid building; also an Insane Asylum, a very large building, 700 feet or more in length; both of the above buildings being brick and stuccoed. There are many very fine residences in the city, and everything bears the impress of taste and enterprise. The city is finely shaded by trees on all the streets. The rebels, on leaving, set fire to a large railroad warehouse, containing a large amount of grain.

Citizens say that Davis recently telegraphed to Johnston, that "a terrible calamity had befallen Lee and his army, but you must hold out to the bitter end."

Some think we shall go to Augusta. A portion of the 23d corps will remain to guard Raleigh, while the rest of us push on. It is evidently the intention to keep open communication for the present.

We are well, generally. Let all be hopeful; a few weeks longer and we shall see a winding up of the whole affair. "The end draweth nigh."

Yours truly, in haste,

G. S. BRADLEY, Chaplain 22d Wis.

LETTER XVIII.

Johnston Surrenders—The War Closed—Going Home.

HD. QRS. 22D WIS., 2D BRIG. 3D DIV. 20TH }
A. C., RALEIGH, N. C. April 28th, 1865. }

I need not tell you that the war has closed; that the rebellion has been crushed; that the Union army has triumphed; that slavery is dead, and that the Stars and

Stripes float over almost every portion of our broad land, for you have heard it and seen it flashing along every wire, of late; you have heard it from every pulpit, seen it in every paper, talked about it on the streets, in the counting room, around the fireside, in your sanctum, printed in large letters, in your papers, till you are fairly intoxicated with the pleasing news. And it is all a *fact.*

But amid all this joy of a nation's overflowing heart, comes the terrible news that our noble LINCOLN has fallen by the assassin's hand. As you felt then and feel still, so with our army. The night following the intelligence, they had to double their guard around the city, or it would have been laid in ashes; in fact, several attempts were actually made to fire the buildings, and soldiers were overheard planning their mad schemes. There was a most intense feeling; and when our soldiers get home, woe to the man who dares to express any sympathy for the assassins.

As you are perhaps aware, negotiations have been going on with Johnston for several days, but he was unwilling to surrender unless his men could have the privilege of taking their arms home and depositing them in their own State arsenals. Of course, our Government would accord no such condition.

On Tuesday last, the 20th Army Corps (the 14th had moved several days before, stretching from Holly Springs to Cape Fear River—some fifteen miles,) was ordered to move out in a southwest direction, to Jones' Cross Roads, some fourteen miles, thus cutting off Johnston's retreat, should he attempt it that way. Here we lay for two days anxiously waiting for the thing to close.

Last evening news came that hostilities had ceased;

that Johnston had surrendered North and South Carolina, Georgia as far North as the Chattahoochie, and the larger portion of Alabama.

This morning orders came for us to return to Raleigh. We arrived here about noon.

To-morrow morning the right wing of our army, Gen. Howard, 15th and 17th corps, will start for home, and on Monday morning, May 1st, the 14th and 20th corps will go. It is reported that we shall go to Alexandria, via Richmond. We expect to march the entire distance, but this the boys will do with pleasure, for we are going *home*.

It is thought we shall be mustered out of the United States service at Alexandria, and then sent to Wisconsin to be mustered out of the State service.

We expect to spend the next 4th of July at home, and won't the boys have a big time!

We are all in the best of spirits, and trust in the course of a few weeks to see you face to face.

     Yours truly. G. S. BRADLEY.

LETTER XIX.

Homeward Bound—Libby Prison—Jeff. Davis' House.

    NEAR RICHMOND, MAY 10TH, 1865.

Our friends at home will be glad to learn that we have arrived near Richmond. We camped here yesterday about noon, after a weary march of some ten days from Raleigh. The weather was good, though very warm a portion of the time, and the roads excellent. We traveled about 170 miles.

There was quite a strife between the 20th and 14th corps which should get to Richmond first; the result was, that our march was a forced one, the comfort of the men being almost totally disregarded.

General Sherman ordered that we average fifteen miles a day, but this was not followed. Several men are said to have died on the way—exhausted and sun struck.

In company with several officers, I have been to the city to visit Libby Prison, Jeff. Davis' house, &c. We went all over Libby. Saw Castle Thunder and various places of interest.

Dick Turner—the wretch who used to abuse our prisoners so—is confined in a small cell in the basement of Libby. They are feeding him on bread and water. This is right, and I wish old Jeff. was there himself.

We expect to be reviewed by General Halleck in Richmond to-morrow, and then we shall start for Washington. It will probably take us some ten days to get there, and then after another grand review, we shall go *home*. All feel glad with the prospect.

G. S. BRADLEY,
Chaplain 22d Wisconsin.

HOME AT LAST.

During the latter part of June, the several regiments of our brigade, excepting the 33d Indiana, were sent home and discharged. The 33d was sent to Louisville—kept there till about the middle of July, and then discharged.

Yes, home at last!

The following is an approximate statement of the distance marched by our brigade:

By railroad,..........................2,700 miles.
By steamboat,........................1,400 "
On foot,.............................2,400 "

Total,..............................6,500 "

GENERAL SLOCUM'S FAREWELL.

Head Quarters Army of Georgia,
Washington, D. C. June 6th, 1865.

General Orders,
No. 15.

With the separation of the troops composing this Army in compliance with recent orders, the organization known as "the Army of Georgia," will virtually cease to exist. Many of you will at once return to your homes. No one now serving as a volunteer will probably be retained in service against his will but a short time longer. All will soon be permitted to return and receive the rewards due them as the gallant defenders of their country.

While I cannot repress a feeling of sadness at parting with you, I congratulate you upon the grand results achieved by your valor, fidelity and patriotism.

No generation has done more for the permanent establishment of a just and liberal form of Government,—more for the honor of their Nation,—than has been done during the past four years by the Armies of the United States, and the patriotic people at home, who have poured out their wealth in support of these Armies, with a liberality never before witnessed in any country.

Do not forget the parting advice of that great Chieftain who led you through your recent brilliant campaigns.

"As in war you have been good soldiers, so in peace be good citizens."

Should you ever desire to resume the honorable profession you are now about to leave, do not forget that this profession is honorable only when followed in obedience to the orders of the constituted authority of your Government.

With feelings of deep gratitude to each and all of you for your uniform soldierly conduct,— for the patience and fortitude with which you have borne all the hardships it has been necessary to impose upon you,—and for the unflinching resolution with which you have sustained the holy cause in which we have been engaged, I bid you farewell.   H. W. SLOCUM,
                Major General Comd'g.

IN MEMORIAM.

Inscribed to Mrs. A. H. LATHROP, whose son, WM. R., died in hospital at Washington D. C. of Typhoid Fever Sept. 26, 1862.

BY MRS. G. S. BRADLEY.

Calm be the spot where our Willie is lying—
Sweet be the murmur of winds o'er his head,
Never a tempest to rouse him from slumber—
Never a storm-cloud to shadow his bed.
Far from the scenes of the blood-red Potomac,—
Sweeter the music than bugle or drum ;
Saved from the camp and its thousand tempta'ions,
Saved from the horrors of battles to come.

Gone, ere thy youth's sunny morning had vanished,
Gone, ere thy manhood was bowed with dull care,

Ere thou hadst known how the sick soul may languish,
Waiting and praying in heaven to share.
Gone, ere the contest for Freedom was ended,
Gone, but thy life was not given in vain,—
Each drop of blood from the veins of the Northmen,
Serves but to loosen the African's chain.

Heart, be thou silent; cease ever thy pining;
Call him not back to the conflicts of life;
What if a dark rolling tide is between us,
Seeming to mortals with tears so rife!
Saw I not seraphs approaching to guide him?
Heard I not rustle of wings as they came?
Saw I not joy lighting up his pale features,
As angels low whispered my loved Willie's name?

Heard'st thou, my darling, thy sister among them?
Tell us, pray tell us, the sweet words she said;
Sang she the strains of the heavenly choir,
As o'er the dark tide thy freed spirit she led?
Wore she a crown in which diamonds were flashing?
Gave thee one also like that of her own?
Shines it amid thy locks witchingly gleaming,
Emblem of heirship to yonder bright throne?

Spake she of lands where the glorious sunshine,
Will in its splendor forever beam on,—
Flowers in the freshness and spring-time of beauty.
Blooming profusely, will never be gone,—
Ravishing music to charm all the senses,
Dreamily floating the summer day through,—
Beautiful beyond which the fancy can picture,
Ever affording us pleasures anew?

Heart, be thou silent! our Willie is joining
Angel Louise, in the hymn of the spheres,
Tuning his harp-strings to sing the glad chorus,
"*Freedom to all when the new year appears.*"
Join, O my soul, in the glorious anthem;
Check the warm tear, and repress the deep sigh,

Patiently waiting, perform every duty,
Knowing in weakness, on whom to rely.

Mourn not, my heart, for the loved and the absent ;
Trust, though cloud-shadows envelope the way ;
Clearer and brighter the visions of heaven,
Come to our scenes as friends pass away.
Labor and pray on my remnant of loved ones,
Time will soon carry us over the tide ;
Then with the loved who have passed on before us,
We may find rest by the dear Savior's side.

PARSONAGE, Mt. Pleasant, Wis.

RELIGION IN THE ARMY.

That there is a good deal of wickedness connected with the army no one doubts. There the restraints of home are thrown off, and men are left comparatively free to act as they please. Without doubt many soldiers hav been greatly surprised at their own want of steadfastness in the right. They have fallen into many temptations when they thought they could stand firm. In the army, home influences, and home props are all taken away, and the man must stand alone if he stand at all. Before thus stepping out into the world, no one knows how much all these home associations have to do in keeping him in the path of virtue.

Still men can live christians in the Army! Men can live moral in the Army! Many have done it, and have died in full hope of a blessed immortality. We have seen them die upon the battle-field and in camp, and have listened to the enraptured thought expressed, that they would soon be beyond the storm and roar of battle, "safe on the evergreen shore."

But there are many drawbacks in the army.

1st. Most of the officers are irreligious men, and make light of religion.

2d. There is no Sabbath in the army. Many of our most terrible battles have been fought on this day, and it would seem frequently as though officers took especial pains to fill up the day with marching, camp duties, reviews or fighting.

3d. Many professed christians left home with the idea that they could not live christians in the army, so laid aside their religious life and became like other men.

Alas! alas!

But we may remark here that with all these drawbacks, a great many were faithful christians, whether on the march, in camp or on the battle-field,—their trust was in God. Then, too, a large number have been converted in the army. Many who left home swearing men, are now returning praying men. They go home to bless their families, the church, and the world.

Chaplains, who have been the men for the positions, have found the most ready access to the hearts of soldiers, and no more respectful or attentive congregations could they anywhere find.

How many pleasant memories gather around the history of those long, weary marches. Many who look over these pages will do so with tearful eyes, as they think of those sweet, refreshing seasons around the camp fire in the dark pine forests of the South. The memory of such will serve to nerve us for the future, and lead us to be faithful wherever we may go, knowing that whether in soldier or civil life, the faithful man will receive a reward for his labor.

The following will be read with deep interest:

INCIDENTS.

A christian brother of the 19th Michigan related to me the following:

During one of our terrible battles in Georgia, he felt a very strong and strange impulse to go upon the battle-field, although he carried no gun, being a cook. At first, he resisted the feeling, thinking he could do no good there, but as he heard the roar of artillery and rattle of musketry, he could not resist longer, so turning over the mule he was leading to some other one, he followed his company in the deadly charge. He saw a man fall—felt that it was a dear friend of his, although he was not near enough to tell. Seeing a man stooping over him to search his pockets, he rushed up—found it was indeed his best friend—saved his pocket book, containing over one hundred dollars, and bore him from the field, bleeding and fainting.

The strange impulse to go upon the field that day was now clear to his mind. It was to save his dear friend. Thus the providences of God lead us in a way we know not.

A soldier of the 85th Indiana lay in the hospital dying, but he thought of the loved ones far away at home, and he wanted to have some of his little treasures sent to them, together with a letter.

"Are you a christian?" he was asked.

"Oh, yes; I was before I joined the army. Tell mother that God is with me; all is well."

Then taking out the rings he said: "That is for mother, that is for sister, and sister will know to whom to give the other."

"There is one thing more," he added, after a pause. A little package was taken from his knapsack and brought to him. In it were three photographs. He took up the first, looked at it intently, and said: "Oh, thank God for a pious mother! Through her prayers and instrumentality I was brought to Christ. Good-bye, mother, we shall meet in Heaven." He kissed it and laid it down on the cot. He took up the second, and said: "Thank God for a pious sister! We have held sweet communion on earth, and will hold sweeter communion in Heaven. Good-bye, sister," and he kissed it and laid it down with the other. He took up the third, the nameless one, and as he looked fondly at it, his eyes filled with tears. "Oh," said he, "I did hope that you and I would have many precious seasons on earth, but God has ordered otherwise. My country demanded my services. I gave them cheerfully, yet, thank God! ere long we'll both be where there'll be no wars, but where all will be peace throughout eternity. Yes, thank God! we'll meet again." And he put the precious picture to his lips and kissed it, and breathed his last with the photograph lying on his lips.

Blessed trust! Glorious hope! How precious in such an hour to feel that all was well! It was at the midnight hour that the above affecting incident occurred, but though darkness gathered around, yet he looked beyond this world, and all was light, and glory, and immortality.

BEAUTIFUL PEACE AT LAST.

BY MRS. C. E. WEAVER.

Brightly lay a sunny vineland, purpling in a summer clime ;
Lovingly the soft winds lingered 'mid the orange groves and lime,
Blossomed there the rich magnolia, and the tall palmetto waved ;
Rippling rivers, on their bosoms bearing shivered sunbeams, laved
Bloom and beauty ladened landscapes ; surely never scene more
    fair.
Vision gladdened, earthland burdened, fragrance breathed thro'
    summer air.

On her blessed errand, Mercy paused, this goodly land to see,
What the fruitage and the promise of the vintage there might be ;
While she looked, behold already, had the wine press just been
    trod,
And the new wine from the vintage, crimsoned all the fresh green
    sod.
And the crushed fruit, heaped and purple, clustered thick upon
    the plain,
As the reaper, in the harvest, leaves behind the ripened grain.

Oh the wine that stained the greensward, was the rich red wine of
    life,
For the vine-ground, darkly crimsoned, lay a field of mortal strife ;
And the fruit there, heaped and mangled, dead and dying heroes
    lay,—
Precious off'rings, freely given, that the right might win its way—
Loving hearts with anguish bleeding, mother—souls, shall know
    the price
Of the Nation's purifying, what the costly sacrifice.

Mercy, kindly, pitying angel, saw the mourning in the land,
Vacant places at the fireside—saw each stricken household band—
Sadder grew; then thus besought she, Justice stern, the scourge to
    stay ;

"In the blood already poured out, be the dark stain washed away;
Has there not e'en now been given, agony for agony?
Vengeance—hath it not already, blood for blood, and cry for cry?"

To the earnest, tearful, pleading, Justice bent relenting ear,—
Stayed his hand, and softly beckoned Peace, white winged and
    hovering near,—
Bade her stretch her silver scepter, o'er each fierce contending
    horde,
Bid them turn the spear to pruning, and to plowshares beat the
    sword;
Let the "forward march" be "homeward," henceforth learning
    war no more!
"Right hath triumphed," be the glad song chorused to the farthest
    shore.

Now upon the crested mountain, now o'er all the valleys *free*,
From Superior to the Gulfland—from Missouri to the Sea,
Peace hath spread her beauteous pinions,—Peace hath set her foot-
    prints bright,—
Peace hath bathed our own loved country, once more in her per-
    fect light;
But above our *hero martyrs*, tears, to-day, proud tears shall fall,
For their dying gives the harvest—*Freedom's birthright unto all.*

COTTAGE HOME, Hudson, Mich.

[NOTE.—The above beautiful lines were written expressly for this work, by one whose poetic effusions will surely find way to public favor more and more.—AUTHOR.]

THE MONTH OF APRIL.

The month of April, 1865, has been replete with great events—the greatest, perhaps, in the history of our country. Four years ago this April, our great civil contest commenced, which has resulted in the loss of half a million of lives, and many millions of money. What an eventful four years!

April 1. General Sheridan routs the rebel forces at Five Forks, Va., capturing three brigades.

2. Assault along the whole line in front of Petersburg, and a brilliant victory achieved. Twelve thousand prisoners taken.

—News received of the burning of the steamer General Lyon, between Wilmington and Fortress Monroe, March 31st; 400 or 500 soldiers perished.

3. The Union forces under Weitzel occupy Richmond.

—Great rejoicings all through the loyal States on account of the fall of Richmond.

4. Fire in Brooklyn, N. Y. Several firemen killed.

6. General Sheridan attacks and routs the forces of General Lee, and drives them across Sailor creek.

9. Surrender of General Lee and his whole army to General Grant.

10. Extraordinary rejoicings throughout the loyal States on account of the surrender of Lee and the end of the rebellion.

12. Mobile occupied by the Union forces.

—General Stoneman occupies Salsbury, N. C., after a series of victories, he having advanced upon that State from the west. Vast amount of military property captured with the town.

14. Assassination of President Lincoln by J. Wilkes Booth, an actor, and attempted murder of Mr. Seward, Secretary of State. Mr. Frederick Seward badly injured.

15. Death of President Lincoln.

—The whole country in mourning. A very solemn day.

—Andrew Johnson, Vice-President, takes the oath prescribed by the Constitution and becomes President of the United States.

—The flag removed by General Anderson from Fort Sumter, in 1861, hoisted by him on the same fort, with appropriate ceremonies.

16. Great fire in New York. Loss $2,000,000.

18. Second great fire in New York. Loss $1,000,000.

—Arrest of Payne, the supposed author of the attempt upon the life of Secretary Seward.

—General Sherman concludes a treaty with General Johnston, which is not ratified. He is ordered to resume hostilities at once.

19. The funeral of President Lincoln at Washington.

21. The reward now offered for the arrest of J. Wilkes Booth, the murderer of the President, is $150,100.

—The remains of the late President are taken from Washington, on their way to Springfield, Ill., where they are to be finally deposited.

26. J. Wilkes Booth, the assassin of the President, is shot and killed by a party of cavalry sent out to arrest him. Harold, an accomplice, is taken.

—General Johnston surrenders to the Union forces with all the troops in his department.

27. The boiler of the steamer Sultana exploded on the Mississippi, setting the boat on fire. One thousand five hundred Union soldiers, just released from rebel prisons, were lost.

29. President Johnson appoints Thursday, June 1st, as a day of humiliation and prayer.

30. Plot discovered to burn the city of Philadelphia.

—Great fire in Boston. Loss estimated at $150,000.

CONCLUSION.

During many hundred miles of weary tramping, we were with you. Sometimes we bent over you in the hospital, and tried to add a little comfort in your hours of pain. It was pleasant to be able to assist you, and as some of the dear boys were laid away in soldier graves, an earnest prayer went up that their fall might not be in vain.

Once again together here, we have lived over the past. We have fought over our battles, and thought over many incidents, but now we come once more where our paths diverge. Let each of us act well our part on life's stage. May God bless you all!

In closing, I cannot do so better than by quoting the following beautiful lines:

MUSTERED OUT.

Let me lie down,
Just here in the shade of the cannon-torn tree,
Here, low in the trampled grass, where I may see
The surge of the combat, and where I may hear
The glad cry of victory, cheer upon cheer:
Let me lie down.

Oh, it was grand!
Like the tempest we charged, in the triumph to share;
The tempest—its fury and thunder were there;
On, on, o'er the entrenchments, over living and dead,
With the foe underfoot and our flag overhead;
Oh, it was grand!

Weary and faint.
Prone on the soldier's couch, ah, how can I rest,
With this shot-shattered head, and sabre-pierced breast?
Comrades, at roll-call, when I shall be sought,
Say I fought till I fell, and fell where I fought,
Wounded and faint.

Oh, that last charge!
Right through the dread lead storm of shrapnell and shell,
Through without faltering---clear through with a yell,
Right in their midst, in the turmoil and gloom;
Like heroes we dashed at the mandate of Doom!
Oh, that last charge!

It was a duty!
Some things are worthless, and some others so good,
The nations who buy them pay only in blood:
For Freedom and Union each man owes his part,
And here I pay my share, all warm from my heart.
It is a duty!

Dying at last!
My mother, dear mother, with meek, tearful eye,
Farewell! and God bless you, forever and aye!
Oh, that I now lay on your pillowing breast,
To breathe my last sigh on the bosom first pressed:
Dying at last!

I am no saint,
But, boys, say a prayer. There's one that begins
"Our Father," and then says, " Forgive us our sins;"
Don't forget that part; say that strongly, and then
I'll try and repeat it, and you'll say Amen!
Ah, I'm no saint!

Hark! there's a shout!
Raise me up, comrades! We have conquered, I know!
Up, up on my feet, with my face to the foe!
Ah, there flies the flag with the star spangled bright;
The promise of glory, the symbol of right.
Well they may shout!

I am mustered out!
O, God of our fathers, our freedom prolong,
And tread down rebellion, oppression and wrong!
O, land of earth's hope, on thy blood-reddened sod,
I die for the Nation, the Union, and God!
I'm mustered out.

APPENDIX.

COL. COBURN'S REPORT OF THE BATTLE OF THOMPSON'S STATION.

HEAD-QUARTERS 3D BRIGADE, 1st DIV. RESERVE CORPS,
MURFREESBORO, TENN., Aug. 1st, 1863.

CAPT. BURR H. POLK, A. A. G. 1ST DIVISION:

Captain:—I have the honor to report that on the 2d day of March A. D. 1863, my brigade, composed of the 33d Indiana, the 22d Wisconsin, the 85th Indiana and 19th Michigan Volunteer Infantry, and the 18th Ohio Battery, being encamped at Brentwood, Tenn., I received an order from Brig. Gen. C. C. Gilbert, then in command at Franklin, Tenn., to march to that place, then threatened by a rebel force; an attack having been made on his southern line of outposts on that day.

The brigade was at once moved, and arrived at Franklin that night at ten o'clock, and there remained during the next day. At 11 o'clock at night of the 3d, an order was received to march the brigade, together with the 124th Ohio Infantry, and six hundred cavalry, composed of parts of the 9th Pennsylvania, 2d Michigan and the 4th Kentucky regiments, on the next morning at an early hour.

A foraging train of eighty wagons was to be taken, and the men were to be supplied with four days' rations.

The expedition was to proceed to Spring Hill the first day and encamp; on the second day the force was to be divided, a part to go to Raleigh Hill, and there await till night to meet an armed force coming from Murfreesboro. If the force did not come by nightfall, to return to Spring Hill without delay.

The other part of the force was at the same time to march in the direction of Columbia, and returning to Spring Hill, there meet the force that had been to Raleigh Hill.

I was not informed as to what force was coming from the direction of Murfreesboro, nor anything about it.

On the morning of the 4th of March, the entire command, consisting of 2837 men and officers of all arms, moved out from Franklin, the weather being cool and favorable. The road is a turnpike, and the men marched with facility. Having advanced to the south about four miles, a considerable force of cavalry was discovered in front of us. It proved to be about a thousand mounted men, with a section of artillery. I had the forces brought up at once. The cavalry deployed to the right of the road and advanced. The 33d Indiana and 22d

Wisconsin were posted on the right, with a section of the battery; the 19th Michigan and 124th Ohio, with a section of the battery, were placed on the left. The 85th Indiana remained in the rear with the train, about half a mile.

The face of the country here is much broken, presenting to the eye long swells and ridges, from fifty to two hundred feet in height, and in many places quite steep and precipitous. A view greater in extent than a quarter of a mile could not be had, except in the direction of the road to the south.

Our guns, posted on a slight elevation, had a range of nearly a mile, uninterrupted by the hills, directly down the road.

The enemy opened fire from his artillery, and was replied to from ours. For about an hour, a brisk cannonade was kept up by both parties, resulting in no loss on our part, but, according to the report of the enemy, on theirs, of 15 men and several horses killed and wounded. While this was progressing, three regiments of infantry and a portion of the cavalry were advanced, the 33d Indiana under Lieut. Col. Henderson, the 22d Wisconsin under Col. Utley, and the 19th Michigan under Col. Gilbert. As they advanced, the enemy fell back and totally disappeared in front for a time.

Quite a number soon after appeared on the hills to our left, and it being reported that a force of some twelve or fifteen hundred were on the Louisburg road, a mile to our left, and attempting to gain our rear, I ordered the advanced forces to fall back to our first position, which was done. Here they remained about three hours, and having reported the previous occurrences, I awaited orders from Gen. Gilbert. In the meantime, the cavalry had been directed to examine thoroughly the country on our left, and drive back any force that might attack us in that direction. No attack was made by either party, and the result of the skirmishing in that direction was two slightly wounded on our side. At length, orders came to send back the foraging train. This was done at once, half of it having been already loaded. An advance of some two miles was made, with slight skirmishing in front, when the force went into camp for the night.

The loss in this days engagement on our part was three (3) men slightly wounded, one of the 19th Michigan, and two of the 9th Pennsylvania, and one piece of artillery disabled.

Apprehending an attack that night, the command was put upon the alert, and a considerable force slept under arms. An occasional picket firing during the night was all that occurred. A new supply of artillery ammunition was sent for, and arrived before daylight.

The 9th Pennsylvania, was also newly armed with the Spencer rifles during the night. Soon after daylight, two negro boys, about twelve years of age, were brought into camp, who said they had come from Van Dorn's army, and that it was out on the road this side of Spring Hill, and was coming on to take Franklin. I sent them, at once, with a messenger and some mounted men, to General Gilbert at Franklin. I heard nothing from my messenger or the General.

Patrols were sent out on the flank, right and left; scouts were dispatched in all directions, with orders to scour the country, and I awaited reports from them.

At about eight o'clock, no force having been discovered as yet, we moved on. The cavalry in advance, with a line of skirmishers extending about half a mile on each side of the road. One piece of artillery was placed with the advanced guard some three-fourths of a mile to the front of the main force. Advancing slowly, with frequent halts, the skirmishers of the enemy alone could be seen in the road, or in the woods, fields and hills, on either flank, retiring as we advanced.

After an hour's march, I was informed that a small party of the enemy, apparently an outpost, were seen on the Louisburg turnpike. I directed a small force of cavalry at once to drive them and thoroughly test the strength of the enemy there. Time was given to the cavalry to inspect the country thoroughly, which continued broken and was in many places covered with woods; the farms being very irregular in shape, and not very extensive on account of the hills and ravines.

Quite a large outpost of the enemy was driven in about a mile from Thompson's Station, and some two miles from our camp. They retired, skirmishing with our dismounted cavalry, who pushed them handsomely across the fields and over the hills, to the Station.

Before reaching Thompson's Station, on the north, the road passes a wooded hill on the left, with a field in the valley on the right and still beyond it—this field being bounded by a range of hills.

This field extends south on both sides of the road to the range of hills just north of Thompson's Station—being narrow on the east side of the road, and extending to the south east, ending there in a gap through the ridge.

This ridge, or range of hills, traverses the road at nearly right angles, running east and west, and is broken into knolls, some of which are covered with a thick growth of cedar. This ridge is also intersected by other gaps right and left. The turnpike and railroad pass through it by a gap together. Beyond the ridge, is an open farm about a fourth of a mile wide, on each side of the road.

On passing through the gap, the railroad turns from the general direction of the turnpike to the right and west. The Station is situated about the middle of the clearing, and nearly three hundred yards west of the turnpike.

Here the ground is somewhat depressed, and a small stream flows by it to the west. Beyond the Station and field, is an extensive wood on each side of the road. The ground ascends as it is approached from the north, and continues to ascend toward the south, and is broken into irregular knolls. Here the enemy lay.

As our force approached the gap, the head of the advance guard being in it, the enemy began with a fire of artillery raking the road, his battery being stationed in the wood on the west side. This fire failed of effect.

The skirmishers of the enemy who had occupied the ridge on either hand had already been dislodged and driven to the Station, where they took refuge and rallied for a time, but retired before the skirmishers of the 33d Indiana, and under a fire from our battery, which had been brought up and stationed—two paces on the right of the road, and three on the left on the ridge, at that place about fifty feet above the valley, and the field in front.

In this position, they commanded the front from a half to a full mile.

The 33d and 85th Indiana, were stationed on the right of the road, and 22d Wisconsin and 19th Michigan on the left of the road, out upon the ridge, supporting the positions held by the battery.

Some companies of dismounted cavalry were placed upon a cedar crowned knoll to the left of the 19th Michigan, with directions to hold it. In their rear the main part of the cavalry were stationed.

To the rear, a third of a mile, was the 124th Ohio, whose duty it was to guard the ammuniton train. Such being the disposition of the forces, a demonstration was made by our cavalry on the extreme left, and the 33d and 85th Indiana were advanced to the Station with directions to charge the battery on the right of the road, if practicable. The 22d Wisconain and 19th Michigan, and a portion of the cavalry were held in reserve.

The battery, in the meantime, kept up a continuous fire, and was answered by guns stationed at two points. The firing was kept up with great vigor during the advance to the depot, our column moving forward under a constant fire of shell and cannister, as well as musketry from a brigade posted behind a bank and stone fence beyond.

The loss was slight, and the troops moved forward in separate columns by divisions, regularly and steadily to the depot buildings. As this force advanced, a large number of the enemy arose from their cover on the extreme left, and rallied to the battery beyond the depot. At this moment, I was informed that a force of a thousand or more cavalry had been discovered advancing beyond our left, a mile or more distant, in the neighborhood of the Lewisburg road.

I immediately ordered the regiments to withdraw from the depot, intending at once to retreat, being convinced that we were in the neighborhood of an overwhelming force. Lieutenant Bochman, my Quartermaster, bore the order.

The two regiments began to retire, and the enemy with loud cheers followed. Colonel Jordan of the 9th Pennsylvania was directed to bring two companies of his cavalry to support the regiments as they retired. He went off. I saw him no more. I saw his cavalry no more, although I sent for them. He thus in a cowardly, unsoldierly and dishonorable manner left the field.

The firing of musketry and artillery on our retiring men was heavy and galling, but they rallied on arriving at the ridge in good order, and repulsed Whitfield's, Cosby's and one regiment of Armstrong's brigades, driving them back beyond the depot.

They sustained and repelled here three successive charges. To prevent an approach on our right, Captain Laton with two companies of the 33d Indiana was posted upon an eminence about an eighth of a mile in that direction, keeping back all approaches there.

During the advance to the depot, the battery did good firing, but on being ordered to fire more slowly and carefully, it ceased firing altogether, and as our men were falling back from the depot, began to leave its position.

I directed the battery to resume firing and keep its position. On being told that their ammunition might be exhausted, I directed Lieut. Adams, Acting Assistant Adjutant General, and Lieut. Bochman, Acting Assistant Quartermaster, to examine all the ammunition chests and report the quantity on hand.

They informed me that they then had about seventy rounds to the gun, of shell, grape and cannister. Deeming this ample for our retreat, I directed very careful use of it. Lt Bochman was directed to turn the wagon train preparatory to retreat, which he did expeditiously.

In the mean time, while the enemy were pressing with great vigor our right, they bore down with Forrest's division and Armstrong's brigade on our left. The dismounted cavalry on the hills to our left fell back, and the rebels planted two pieces of artillery in their position. This fire enfiladed the 19th Michigan, and it changed its front toward the left. This was followed by a furious assault by infantry on our whole left. They were repulsed, and the attack was repeated, the 19th Michigan falling back to the rear of the 22d Wisconsin. The enemy were again repulsed. They charged up the road to gain the space between the 33d Indiana and 22d Wisconsin.

The two companies on the extreme right of the 33d were brought over to its left; the 19th Michigan was ordered by me to move across the road and placed on the left; the 85th Indiana had already been brought from its position on the right of the 33d Indiana, and placed to the left of the position occupied by the 19th Michigan, and near to a school house. The 22d Wisconsin now severely pressed, fell back across the road to a position on the left of the 85th Indiana, and retired a short distance to the rear. * * * *

The enemy now charging across to the west side of the road, made several successive assaults upon the front of the 19th and 85th, but were repulsed and driven off, and several prisoners taken.

The battle flag of Armstrong's brigade was captured by the 19th Michigan. At this point the enemy were completely routed. * *

During the attack on the left, Whitfield and Stearns renewed the attack on our right—the 33d Indiana—but were again repulsed.

As our right was being attacked, and before any serious assault had been made on our left, the cavalry disappeared, the artillery under Captain Aleshire followed hastily, without the loss of a horse or a man. and when it was still a position of personal safety to the men, although Lieuts. Adams and Bochman of my staff attempted to rally them, put them in position, and thus assist in covering our retreat.

The battery was partially put in position in our rear, by Lieutenant Adams, but by the directions of Colonel Jordan and Captain Aleshire, was ordered to move off without firing a gun upon the forces which were closing around our left flank.

The force thus falling back, took with it the 124th Ohio, the ambulance train, and with them, all hope of an orderly retreat or a continued successful resistance.

As they disappeared, our whole front was pressed with the greatest vigor, requiring a firm resistance, or resulting in a confused flight and the utter rout of the entire command.

To the firmness with which our position was held. is due the safety of those who retreated to Franklin, holding the enemy as we did, at least two hours after they had gone—*on the very ground they had left.*

Had all thus have stood firmly, the chances of escape and an orderly retreat were in our favor, even with the immense preponderance of force against us, but the task would then have been most difficult, accompaied by severe loss and the constant exercise of caution, courage and the highest activity.

The enemy at length having been driven from our front at all points and silenced, our ammunition running low, and our train having gone, the brigade was moved to the woods upon our right and rear. Here they met and attacked Forrest's division, which had gained our rear by the left, having come through the gaps in that direction, and being posted behind fences, trees, and other favorable positions, from the left across the road to our right Martin's brigade had also gained the rear of our right. These forces occupied the entire opposite slope of a deep ravine which lay directly in front of our new position, and whose precipitous side it would have been difficult to ascend. The brigade was formed in line, bayonets fixed, and all things made ready for a charge under a galling fire, which cost us some of our best men.

The men would willingly have made the desperate venture without a shot in their cartridge boxes—nothing remained but to give the word.

I was now convinced that a massacre would ensue to little purpose, that a few might escape, but the many would fall or be captured in a vain struggle for life with unequal weapons. I ordered a surrender. I believe it was justified by the circumstances. It was then found that we had been opposing General Van Dorn's entire army—six brigades, under Generals Forrest, Martin, Cosby, Stearns, Jackson, Armstrong, and Colonel Whitfield—that the greater part of this force had advanced on us that morning from Spring Hill, three miles off—where they had been encamped a week, having ferried the river at Columbia some two weeks before.

The whole force amounted to about fifteen thousand men, with twelve (12) pieces of artillery—six and twelve pound guns; while the force under my command at the time of the surrender amounted to about one thousand and fifty men—over one hundred and sixty being taken at other places. The whole rebel force fought as infantry, and were armed with good carbines, Mississippi and Enfield rifles. The distance to Franklin was nine miles—the contest had raged nearly five hours—no reinforcements were in sight—none had been heard from—the enemy held the road far in our rear—our cavalry and artillery had already been gone two hours—we had no ammunition—the enemy was mounted—his batteries raked the road, and his men by thousands hung upon every advantageous post in our rear—we had exhausted all means of destruction except our bayonets, beyond the reach of which we were powerless.

That a Colonel of cavalry, and a Captain of artillery, should, without orders, and against orders, leave the field with their entire commands in haste, and without notice to me, at the very moment they should have put forth their greatest exertions to repel the enemy rushing upon us—and in addition, carry also with them an infantry regiment on duty as a reserve with the teams, and with it all of our ammunition, was a contingency, against which, human foresight could not provide, and left the surrounded and unflinching men who withstood the storm, no alternative but a disgraceful and fatal flight, or to do, as they *did*, fight till further resistance was vain. Had it been even possible to retire from the immediate presence of so large a force, it was only so by the united action of every man. But with a thousand men suddenly withdrawn—with our two most formidable arms in retreat—cavalry and artillery—with the way thus opened for the flanking forces, the contest was reduced to a mere question of endurance.

Perhaps had all stood firmly, the result would have been the same. I think it would not. If reinforcements had come, even amounting to a single regiment and a battery, I am confident our withdrawal could have been handsomely effected.

To the commanding officers of the regiments, Colonel Utley, 22d Wisconsin, Colonel Baird, 85th Indiana, Colonel Gilbert, 19th Michigan, and Lieutenant-Colonel Henderson, 33d Indiana, I am compelled by their conspicuous daring and gallantry to return my thanks. They did all that officers in their position could do.

The other field officers, Lieutenant-Colonel Crane, 85th Indiana, Major Craig, 85th Indiana, Major Shafter, 19th Michigan, Major Miller, 33d Indiana, and Major Smith, 22d Wisconsin, were at their posts bravely doing their duty. The Adjutants of the regiments, Crawford, Tompkins, Bones, and Pickering, did nobly.

To the line officers and the men, who so faithfully and fearlessly drove back the foe, is due whatever can be said of heroic daring and self sacrifice. Their firm, persistent, triumphant repulse of assault after assault by overwhelming numbers, gave proof that on a fairer field victory would have been an easy prize.

My staff officers present, Lieutenants Adams and Bochman, and Captain Foll, rendered me most valuable assistance, and were cut off in the retreating column, vainly endeavoring to rally the scattering forces, and place the artillery in such positions, as would have prevented the flanking force under Forrest from effecting his purpose.

The officers of the 124th Ohio, so far as they came under my eye, did well. One of my orderlies, Mr. Brown, 19th Michigan, did bravely and faithfully all that was required.

I append a list of killed, wounded and missing in battle, showing the number of each. I refer to the reports of regimental commanders herewith forwarded, for their names. I also append a list of the number of those who died by exposure and cruel treatment during captivity:

REGIMENTS.	KILLED.	WOUNDED.	DIED OF EXPOSURE, ETC.	TOTAL.
Thirty-Third Indiana	31	69	9	109
Twenty-Second Wisconsin	7	19	16	42
Nineteenth Michigan	33	79	30	142
Eighty-Fifth Indiana	13	21	30	64
Ninth Pennsylvania Cav.	2	5		7
Second Michigan Cav.	2	11		13
Fourth Kentucky Cav.				
One Hundred and Twenty-Fourth Ohio Infantry				
Eighteenth Ohio Battery				
Aggregate	88	204	85	377

The whole number captured, including all who died as above, and many of the wounded, was 1,206 men.

The losses of the enemy were much greater, I believe, than ours, as they by repeated charges in open ground, were much more exposed. We saw many of their killed and wounded, among them Colonel Earl, of the 3d Arkansas, and Captain Watson, Adjutant-General of General Armstrong.

Among the many noble men we lost, I will name Captain Floyd, of the 85th Indiana, shot dead at the head of his company, and Lieutenant Holmes, Quartermaster of the 22d Wisconsin, who died from cruelties of the enemy while prisoner. *   *   *

I am sir, very respectfully, your most obedient servant.

JOHN COBURN.

COLONEL BLOODGOOD'S REPORT OF THE CAPTURE AT BRENTWOOD.

HD. QUAR. OF THE 22D REGIMENT, WIS. VOL. INF.
BENTON BARRACKS, St Louis, May 23, 1863.

To Brigadier-General Baird,

Sir :—I have the honor to make the following report:

On the 25th day of March, 1863, the situation of my command at Brentwood, Tennessee, was as follows: According to orders, I had placed my command as near the Pikes as would command those roads, the railroad and store-house. Pickets were placed at proper distances upon the Franklin Pike, south of the camp.

The same on the Wilson Pike—south, at the railroad and storehouse, and through the woods west, and also on the Franklin Pike, about 100 yards north of the bridge, where the Franklin Pike crosses the railroad   I had felled trees on three sides close to my camp, as a defense against a dash of cavalry by night. A detachment of the 19th Michigan was stationed at the Stockade near the railroad bridge about one and a half miles south of Brentwood.

On the morning of the above date, a messenger from the stockade rode into camp with the information that the enemy were upon them, and destroying the railroad. My command, comprising but about four hundred (400) effective men, was soon in line. Three companies were immediately directed to move forward to the assistance of those at the bridge, but after advancing a short distance from camp, the enemy in superior force were discovered deploying from the pike into line of battle on both sides of the road, and moving upon us. I immediately deployed those three companies and placed them under the charge of Major Smith of our regiment, and rode back to place the remaining three in position.

I then endeavored to telegraph to Franklin, but found the wires cut both in front and rear. I then ordered two couriers to Nashville to take news of my attack, and ask for reinforcements. Only one succeeded in getting out—whether he got through the enemy's lines I never knew. At this time, a flag of truce was sent by the enemy, announcing that General Forrest had surrounded us with his entire com--

mand, demanding our unconditional surrender, and threatening to cut us inpieces if we attempted resistance.

Word was sent back to General Forrest, "come and take us."

Previous to this, I had given orders to have the wagons loaded and move toward Nashville, as I feared from the superior force of the enemy, thus far developed, I might be compelled to fall back in that direction. The last wagon had not left the camp, when those in front were stopt by the enemy. In the meantime the advance companies had opened fire upon the enemy.

I had barely time to post the other companies, when I discovered we were completely surrounded by the enemy in overwhelming force. I disposed of my men so as to keep them at bay as long as posssible, but they advanced rapidly, pressing me closely, and soon brought two pieces of artillery close up to my lines. I had no artillery to keep them at bay. My position was without defence natural or artificial, for the protection of my men. I had no hope of aid from any quarter. The force that surrounded me was evidently five to ten times my number, and I was satisfied that in fifteen or twenty minutes we must be overbalanced after great sacrifice of life, without—in consequence of our inferiority in numbers and equipments—inflicting adequate injury on the enemy.

I therefore deemed it for the interest of the service, and but justice to my men, to surrender, which I accordingly did.

The contest, from the opening of our fire up to the time the enemy had succeeded in surrounding me, and was about bringing his artillery to bear, was from twenty-five to thirty minutes.

After my capture, I learned that the enemy had not attacked the force at the railroad bridge before coming upon me, but had rode by it. They surrounded and took this force after my surrender.

I then found the enemy's force to be three or four brigades of mounted infantry, numbering from five to eight thousand men, under the command of Brigadier-General Forrest, and including an independent Arkansas regiment under the command of Major Sanders, all of which officers were on the field with their commands.

Also, at that time, I learned that the enemy had sent a force to Nashville and Franklin to drive in our pickets. A body of our cavalry came up and made an ineffectual dash at the enemy some two hours after we were captured.

Four of my command were wounded, and left upon the ground with two of the regimental Surgeons. The loss of the enemy so far as I learned was 3 killed, including a Lieutenant, and 5 wounded.

The enemy while in action, with the exception of a sufficient number acting as cavalry, were dismounted and fought on foot. They had made a forced march during the night, and came in through the country to the west of our camp, and about a mile beyond our pickets. I was informed by General Forrest that he had captured a courier sent to me by General Baird that morning, with orders to fall back immediately with my command to Nashville, but I did not see the courier among the captured.

My command after being taken were marched to Tullahoma, Tennessee, and there sent by rail to Richmond.

The men were paroled there and sent to Annapolis, Maryland. After being exchanged with other officers. I had to go to the hospital at Annapolis, and from there was ordered to report to my regiment at Benton Barracks at St Louis, Missouri.

All of which I respectfully submit.

I am, Sir, very respectfully,
E. BLOODGOOD.
Lt. Col, 22d Regt. Wis. Vol. Inft.

(NOTE—We intended to insert in this work several tables of statistics, rosters of regiments, &c., but most of those we have are very imperfect—many officers failing to forward us what we wanted. We have many other items of interest on hand, but our limits are full, and we must consequently omit them.—AUTHOR.

GENERAL DUSTIN'S FAREWELL.

HEAD QRS. 2D BRIGADE, 3D DIVISION, 20TH A. C., }
NEAR WASHINGTON, June 6th, 1865. }

Officers and men of the 2d Brigade :

My own regiment, the 105th Illinois Volunteers, having been mustered out of the service, my connection with this brigade is necessarily dissolved.

My grateful acknowledgements are due you, for the uniform kindness and respect that have been extended to me, during the time that I have had the honor to be your commanding officer.

All honor to the Second Brigade, for the gallant and noble manner in which it has sustained its position in that magnificent line of battle, that has ultimately closed in, surrounded, fought, conquered and destroyed the Great Rebellion.

As you have in an especial manner, so bravely withstood the hardships and dangers of a long and bloody war, so will you be the sharers, in an eminent degree, of the glorious results consequent upon the brilliant and sublime combination of victories, with which the terrible conflict has been brought to a close.

It is with proud satisfaction that you may exclaim, "Now lettest thou thy servants depart in peace, for our eyes have seen the salvation of our country."

With expressions of profound sorrow for the fate of your brave comrades, who have fallen, my kindest feelings of respect and esteem will go with those of you who are about to return to your homes, and will also linger with those who may remain in the service.

God bless you all, and crown your future with that full measure of peace, prosperity, and happiness, which you so richly deserve.

DANIEL DUSTIN,
Brevet Brigadier-General.

www.ingramcontent.com/pod-product-compliance
Lightning Source LLC
Chambersburg PA
CBHW022111230426
43672CB00008B/1345